Bracelets	Earrings	Rings

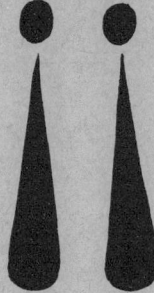

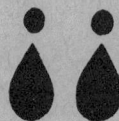

Nineteenth Century Jewellery

FABER COLLECTORS LIBRARY
edited by Kate Foster

Antique Paste Jewellery by M. D. S. Lewis
British Profile Miniaturists by Arthur Mayne
Staffordshire Pot Lids and Their Potters by Cyril Williams-Wood
English Delftware Tiles by Anthony Ray
Ikons by John Stuart

Nineteenth Century Jewellery

PETER HINKS

Faber and Faber · London

First published in 1975
by Faber and Faber Limited
3 Queen Square London WC1
Printed in Great Britain by
W & J Mackay Limited, Chatham
All rights reserved

ISBN 0 571 10650 1

The manufacturers of jewellery are entitled to creditable consideration in any remuneration of the influences at work to increase the morality of the nation by increasing its culture in the only way in which this can be effectually done—by enlarging the enjoyment and the happiness which comes naturally from the gratification of our tastes and attractions

Great Industries of the U.S., 1872

TO ELSA, CHARLOTTE AND LEAH

Contents

ILLUSTRATIONS   *page* 11

INTRODUCTION   15

1. THE REVOLUTION AND NAPOLEON   17

2. THE POST-WAR YEARS   28

3. THE MID-CENTURY 1840 TO 1860   38

4. SECOND EMPIRE AND HIGH VICTORIAN   52

5. FIN DE SIÈCLE   66

6. ARTS AND CRAFTS AND ART NOUVEAU   75

7. MOURNING JEWELLERY   84

8. JEWELLERY IN EARLIER STYLES   88

9. PEASANT JEWELLERY   98

10. COLLECTING   103

APPENDIX: GOLD AND SILVER MARKS   110

BIBLIOGRAPHY   113

INDEX   114

Illustrations

(All pieces illustrated are reproduced life-size unless otherwise indicated)

COLOUR PLATES

A. Lapis lazuli, enamel and pearl PARURE of the Napoleonic period   *facing page* 16

B. Gold, emerald and diamond PARURE. *Circa* 1830   17

C. Gold NECKLACE set with Roman mosaics. *Circa* 1835   32

D. (a) Gold BRACELET decorated with champlevé enamels   33

    (b) Gold BROOCH set with a Geneva enamel copy of a painting by Caracci   33

E. (a) Sardonyx CAMEO. 1860–70   *preceding page* 65

    (b) Labradorite CAMEO. Late nineteenth century   65

    (c) Art nouveau opal CAMEO   65

    (d) CAMEO HABILLÉ. Italian, nineteenth century   65

F. (a) PENDANT by Civilotti in Renaissance taste   *facing page* 65

    (b) PENDANT in late Renaissance style. French, *circa* 1880   65

    (c) 'Holbeinesque' PENDANT. English, *circa* 1870   65

G. (a) Enamelled PENDANT in Renaissance style   80

    (b) 'Holbeinesque' PENDANT set with sapphire, rubies and rose diamonds   80

H. Diamond, sapphire and emerald BROOCHES. French, late nineteenth century   81

MONOCHROME PLATES
after page 64

1. (a) Diamond PADLOCK (b) Spiral EARRINGS (c) Emerald and rose diamond cluster RING (d) Revolutionary RING (e) Cornelian RING

2. A pair of cameo BRACELETS

3. A NECKLACE of malachite cameos

4. NECKLACE of enamelled amatory motifs

5. Berlin iron NECKLACE

6. Paste DEMI-PARURE

7. Ruby and diamond TIARA

8. Diamond chain NECKLACE

9. Diamond COMB and two BROOCHES

10 & 11. Amethyst cannetille SUITE

12. Five SEALS, QUIZZING GLASS and chalcedony EARRINGS

13. STOCK PINS and embossed gold EARRINGS and BROOCH

14. Three MALTESE CROSSES; spinel and diamond PENDANT
15. Topaz NECKLACE and CROSS
16. Bird BROOCH; guitar BROOCH; CROIX-À-LA-JEANETTE bouquet: BROOCH; half-pearl cluster RING
17. BRACELET with miniature at centre; Swiss enamel BRACELET
18. Portraits of MRS HOGG and LORD BEACONSFIELD
19. Four LONGCHAINS
20. BRACELET design and list
21. Snake NECKLACE
22. Two mid-nineteenth-century BROOCHES
23. Four BROOCHES: malachite ivy leaf; diamond linked-ring brooch; shell cameo brooch; jet brooch
24. SUITE of diamond jewels
25. Seed-pearl NECKLACE and BROOCH
26. Three flexible BRACELETS
27. Three BRACELETS
28. EARRINGS of the 1860s
29. NECKLACE and EARRINGS of amphora motifs
30. Tortoise-shell DEMI-PARURE; gold-fringed PENDANT; calibré-cut turquoise EARRINGS; BRACELET set with a cameo of a Moor
31. Circular jewel designs: white cloisonné and carbuncle BROOCH; turquoise BROOCH; turquoise enamel and half-pearl basket-weave PENDANT; Florentine mosaic BROOCH; Scotch pebble BROOCH; crystal intaglio cat BROOCH
32. Silver horseshoe BANGLE; coral COMB
33. Silver LEONTINE; half-pearl and coloured gold BRACELET
34. Coral SUITE
35. Lava DEMI-PARURE
36. Diamond ribbon bow BROOCH; diamond rose-spray BROOCH
37. Two heavy BANGLES
38. Bohemian garnet COLLAR and BROOCH
39. Madras silver NECKLACE
40. Four late Victorian BROOCHES: dragonfly; star; clover leaf; crescent
41. Half-pearl NECKLACE
42. Diamond NECKLACE and sunburst PENDANT
43. Imperial Russian TIARA
44. Enamelled CROWN; peridot and diamond PENDANT; stag beetle and butterfly BROOCHES; heart PENDANT; jubilee BROOCH
45. Two half-hoop BRACELETS and a curb link BRACELET
46. Late Victorian TIE-PINS
47. Two bar BROOCHES; diamond RINGS; half-pearl and miniature BROOCH; opal and diamond rosette BROOCH; four-leaf clover BROOCH
48. Three Fabergé JEWELS

49. Two Wilson JEWELS and an Ashbee BUCKLE

50. Three Liberty JEWELS and a NECKLACE by Marcus

51. Early Lalique bow BROOCH; fern TIARA in horn and rose diamonds

52. 'Bubbles' PENDANT by Lalique; leaf helmet PENDANT by Lalique; poppies BROOCH by Lalique; wisteria BROOCH by Fouquet

53. 'Swan lake' PENDANT by Gautrait and gold BUCKLE by Boucheron

54. MEMORIAL JEWELS: two small brooches; rosette pendant; woven hair serpent brooch; cherub brooch; three rings

55. MEMORIAL JEWELS: enamelled cartouche brooch; circular brooch; onyx and half-pearl pendant and reverse; hair bracelet

56. Giuliano NECKLACE

57. Giuliano NECKLACE

58. Amphitrite DEMI-PARURE

59. Two Renaissance reproduction JEWELS; NECKLACE of dolphins

60. Hellenistic style NECKLACE by Giuliano

61. BULLA and seashell NECKLACE by Giuliano

62. Gold swivelled BANGLE set with scarabs by Castellani; mosaic BROOCH by Castellani; Medusa head BROOCH by Melillo; two FIBULAE by Castellani

63. Gold NECKLACE with female heads as pendants

64. Cloisonné enamel PENDANT set with cameo by Castellani; BRACELET with rosette centre by John Brogden; BROOCH by Childs and Childs; LOCKET in Japanese style by Falize

65. Mosaic PENDANT in Egyptian taste; Scotch pebble PENANNULAR BROOCH; pharoah's head PENDANT; Egyptian style die-stamped DEMI-PARURE

66. Frisian gold HEAD-DRESS

67. Frisian girl and two diamond 'NEEDLES'

68. Coral CHOKER

69. Norwegian SØLJE

70. Italian gold EARRINGS

71. Woman wearing EARRINGS

72. Portuguese MARRIAGE JEWEL

FIGURES

1. The cameo cutter's tools (Archibald Billing, *The Science of Gems, Jewels, Coins and Medals*, 1875)   *page* 22

2. The jeweller at work (*The Book of English Trades and Library of the Useful Arts*, 1821)   41

3. Jewels made by Lemonnier for the Queen of Spain (*Catalogue of the 1851 Great Exhibition*)   49

4. Jewels by Fontenay in the Paris Exhibition of 1867   59

5. A selection of late nineteenth-century lockets from Pringle's catalogue, 1878   62

6. Rings from Pringle's catalogue, 1896   72
7. A gold châtelaine by Boucheron shown at the 1867 Paris Exhibition   93
8. Three Irish ring brooches by Waterhouse of Dublin shown in the London
       Exhibition of 1851   96
9. Two brooches and a bracelet in Viking style by Christesen of Copenhagen
       shown in the Paris Exhibition of 1867   97

ACKNOWLEDGEMENTS FOR PLATES

I. M. Angyalfi   Graus Antiques   Mrs. Anita Rhodes
Armytage Clarke   Mrs. Mary Keays   B. Rossi
Bentley and Co.   A. Lewis   Sotheby & Co.
N. Bloom   S. Lubliner   Contessa Cao di San Marco
Cameo Corner   John Grey Murray (by the   L. S. Scott
Mrs. R. A. Cox   gracious permission of   Manfred Seymour
E. Malachy Doris   Her Majesty the Queen)   Gerald Smookler
David Drager   Miss M. Popper   J. Tom
Fisher Antiques   Martin Rayner

Introduction

We feel attracted to antiques not simply because they are old—not even because they are necessarily beautiful. Their appeal comes from the glimpses they give us into the lives people lived long before we were born. For an antique should not be an object simply to possess and invest in, but a chink in the door of the past, a whisper from a bygone age that thrills the collector like a signal from a distant planet. A Victorian moustache cup and a Roman alabastron both have something to tell us about their first owners, about their habits and attitudes and the half-forgotten trivia of their daily lives. Historians may unroll for us the panorama of great events without wringing out a single tear; a battered Victorian doll can fill us with tender amazement. It is often precisely because these objects are so trivial and so everyday that the insights they give us have such poignancy.

Jewels have no practical function at all. They exist to make people more beautiful: nothing can be more intimate or more intensely personal and for this reason no other object can speak to us more clearly of the tastes, pretensions and obsessions of the society that produced it. Many of the jewels examined in this book are not 'antique' according to the legal definition of an object more than a hundred years old—some could even have been made for people who are alive today. This in no way dilutes their interest, quite the reverse, for the Victorians are more remote from us in their customs, thoughts and morals than the inhabitants of some earlier periods.

Most of the ideas that flavoured nineteenth-century life can be seen in the jewels of the period. This was the century of romanticism, and, like the painter and the novelist, the jeweller looked back to the past for ideas. At first his inspiration came from the Renaissance and the Middle Ages, but as the century progressed and archaeology developed from mere tomb-robbing into something like a science, the craftsman discovered to his amazement that the ancient Greeks and Etruscans had been able to do things with gold that he had never dreamed possible. Excavations for canals and railways led to other accidental finds which were widely reported in the press and eagerly copied by jewellers.

The people of the nineteenth century were intensely curious about the world in which they lived. Current political and military events were read about in sensational detail in the newspapers and illustrated magazines, and had a profound influence on fashion in both dress and jewellery. The theatre at this time played a role in people's leisure lives that is shared today by television, radio, and the cinema, and it too exerted an influence. The invention of the steam-engine permitted cheaper and more comfortable travel, gratifying the romantic tourist's formidable appetite for ancient ruins and creating a healthy demand for souvenirs which the local jeweller gladly played his part in satisfying. Scientists and explorers discovered marvel upon marvel to astound the public: it was an age of miracles inhabited by people avid for novelty and sensation. Fashion followed fashion with increased momentum, some lasting a decade, others no more than a single season. Jewel designs had to be full-flavoured and well spiced with colour and rich decoration in order to be noticed at all.

For the collector, one of the most attractive things about nineteenth-century jewellery is that there is so much of it, both in quantity and in variety. More jewellery was made during these years than at any time previously or since. Victorian love of display created the demand; mechanical production methods and new discoveries of precious stones and metals fulfilled it.

But jewels were not only made from gold, silver and gems. There were also jewels of tortoise-shell, horsehair, ivory, porcelain, bog oak and papier mâché—indeed anything which could be shaped, woven, or set and fastened upon the human body. No matter where the collector operates, in the most illustrious shops in town or at the jumble sale at the parish hall, there will be something to delight and perplex him, and when he comes to specialize there will always be delectable temptations to seduce him from his purpose.

A A PARURE of the Napoleonic period, the lapis lazuli cabochons mounted within open borders of enamel and small pearls. Note the manner in which the small pearls are set and also the liberal use of milled gold wire

See pages 21, 23

B (*over page*) A gold, emerald and diamond PARURE of the post-war period in cannetille style. Note the cruciform pendant, the triple chains of piqué links forming the back and the peapod and tendril scroll decoration. Fine quality emeralds are unusual in jewels of this kind

Circa 1830 *See page* 29

1. The Revolution and Napoleon

For good or ill, the French Revolution had a deep effect on the life of every Frenchman in all three estates. The clergy and the nobility gave up their lands and often their lives; the milliners, jewellers, perfumiers and couturiers, the actual creators of the material luxury from which most Frenchmen were excluded, gave up their livelihoods. The government, the calendar, even the state religion might change, but society still needed bakers, harness-makers and gunsmiths. Unfortunately it had little use for jewellers. Jewellery was quite out of style (it might almost be said that style was out of style) for jewellery is personal and idiosyncratic and out of step with the self-sacrificial republican ideal. Deputies of the assembly were even asked to set an example by surrendering their shoe-buckles of silver to aid the national economy, and woe betide anyone caught wearing a pair after that.

Legislation, too, struck hard at the jewellery trade in France. On 17th March 1791 the Constituent Assembly finally abolished the masterships. Before he was allowed to practise his craft under the ancien régime, the goldsmith had to serve a long apprenticeship and then submit to his guild a *chef d'oeuvre* to demonstrate his skill. This custom is still observed in Britain today. It was the cornerstone of the trade in France and its passing meant that the guilds no longer had any control over standards of workmanship. The result was a decline in standards too awful to be tolerated when life in France began to return to normal, and the state took over where the guilds had been obliged to leave off, supervising the training and examination of apprentices, assaying and hallmarking precious metals: work best done by men who had grown up with it rather than by civil servants.

But it was the reign of terror, for reasons that are crudely obvious, which dealt the most telling blow. We read in Vever, 'the guillotine struck off heads which had formerly worn aigrettes and diadems, to say nothing of crowns'.* Those who did not perish on the guillotine fled, taking with them gold coin and anything portable which could be sold to sustain life. Enormous quantities of precious stones and metals must have left France at this time. One of the characteristics of the jeweller's materials is that they are virtually imperishable so that they can be remoulded, reset, and restyled time and time again. A small fraction of the gold in circulation today has undoubtedly been in use for thousands of years! The craftsman of the time not only had very few customers to make jewellery for—he had very little to make it with. Gifted sons of families who had worked in precious metals for centuries now began to ask themselves seriously why they should continue to make cheap jewellery in debased metal that was paid for, if the

* Henri Vever, *La Bijouterie Française au XIXe Siècle*, 1908, Vol. I, p. 13.

customer had not lost his head in the meantime, in money that was not worth the paper it was printed on. Other trades beckoned, more prestigious and better paid, and there was the promise of glory and danger in the revolutionary armies. It was such itching ambitious souls who now left the trade, the very ones who had contributed inventions and new ideas to the workshop, people who could not only think up the most original designs but sit down at the bench and translate them into gold and precious stones. Design was a natural organic growth that grew up within the workshop walls and designer and craftsman were usually one and the same person. Now few people could work out designs which were not only original but also wearable and practicable to manufacture. Aware of their own shortcomings the jewellery houses now sought out painters, architects, and sculptors to design for them, with lamentable results. The designs proved to be difficult to make and unsuited to their medium. A tragic schism developed between designer and craftsman which never quite healed.

Even jewel fashion succumbed to the tidal wave of revolutionary propaganda. Jewels took the sterile forms of the lictor's fasces, or the Phrygian cap which was to become the symbol of the Revolution. Rings bore the stamped portraits of revolutionary heroes (see plate 1d). These were made in gold or silver that was debased almost beyond recognition. Others were made from the stones and iron of the vanquished Bastille, but most typical of the obsession which had Paris in its foetid grip during the terror were those jewels made in silver gilt to represent the engine of death itself—the guillotine. Some wore these jewels because they wanted to, others because it was politically smart to do so. The latter were probably the same people who, when the Bourbon monarchy was eventually restored, wore a mother-of-pearl ring carved with fleur-de-lis and the inscription 'Dieu nous le rend'.

The rule of the Directorate brought a slow return to normality. Classical nakedness was all the rage and women tried to look like Greek statues: as Talleyrand remarked of the fabulous Madame Tallien, 'it is not possible to expose oneself more sumptuously'. The lightest of muslins and tulles revealed the essential woman not only to the appreciative eye, but also to the brisk Paris air, and as if this were not enough they were often damped so as to cling more revealingly to the form. Bangles, worn on wrist, forearm or upper arm were used to accent a well-rounded limb, and a sautoir, or long chain of large links was slung obliquely over the shoulder or criss-crossed over the breasts. These sautoirs were often decorated with the classical key-fret. Small pendants took the form of shield or heart-shaped padlocks, very flat, like all the jewellery of the period, with borders of half-pearls or diamonds. Versions of this jewel may have a crystal compartment at the centre to contain a lock of hair and a key and a ruby heart hanging as pendants below (plate 1a). (In London, Moll Raffles, mistress of the Marquis of Wellesley, bought a diamond padlock from Rundell and Bridge for 800 guineas.) The elaborately casual coiffure was sometimes gathered into a loose knot which was transfixed by a large pin. At the neck might be a simple string of coral beads or a chain of garnets.

Jewels then in the final years of the eighteenth century were being worn again, but still sparingly. Their purpose seems to have been to emphasize the contours of the female form rather than to accent and enrich the costume. For this reason designs were kept simple and two-dimensional with clean outlines and flat surfaces and were usually based on flat geometric forms like lozenges, octagons or shields. The decoration embossed on the surface depended for effect not upon the highlights and shadows of deep relief, but on the contrast between lightly embossed bright and matt surfaces, and between a background of densely massed dots or hatching and the mirror-like design of acanthus scrolls, key-fret or anthemion occasionally relieved by a thread of opaque ultramarine enamel. Most if not all of this work was produced on a machine, a kind of stamp called the *marteau pilon*, the mechanics of which are said to have been based on the guillotine. The flatness of many jewels at the time may have been partly because the machines and alloys available could not produce a really deep stamping. In these early days the machine was used not so much to produce a jewel in its entirety but to provide components which could be assembled together with hand-made elements.

The coiffures of the time—à la Grec, à la Titus, à la Hollandaise—with the hair piled on the head encouraged the wearing of earrings. These were often of the interesting *poissarde*, or fishwife, design of three geometrical motifs arranged one below the other and trimmed with coarse filigree. The fitting at the back of the jewel extended right from top to bottom in a sweeping loop. Creole earrings were also worn, perhaps in honour of the beautiful West Indian lady whose brief stellar progress was to illumine European society for a decade, Josephine Beauharnais. When she married Napoleon in 1796 the jeweller's tribulations were finally at an end. Josephine's prodigality was astounding, her appetite for clothes, hats, and above all, jewellery, insatiable. With the typical prudishness of the despot, Napoleon was against the public nudity that was incidentally ruining the Paris fashion trade, and furthermore the impoverished and desiccated jewellery designs of the period did not accord with his own personal vision of glory. In 1803 the French crown-jewels were taken out of pawn for Josephine to wear when she accompanied Napoleon on his state visit to Belgium as first consul. It was the first time they had been worn since Marie Antoinette had surrendered them to the National Convention. Napoleon had them remounted for his coronation as Emperor by the jewellers Foncier and Nitot, the superb Regent diamond being set in the hilt of the conqueror's sword by Nitot. David's painting of the coronation shows the ladies of the now Imperial family wearing tiaras low upon the brow with locks of hair escaping from them at forehead and temples. Some take the form of a diamond wreath of leaves, others a bandeau with large clusters centred by coloured stones. The Empress herself wears a magnificent tiara, a comb on top of her head and a cameo bracelet on her wrist.

The craze for cameos dates from the Italian campaign of 1796. By the Treaty of Tolentino the Pope was obliged to pay for the upkeep of the invading armies and he plundered the Vatican treasury and the churches under his direct control to do it. Many fine cameos must have been sent to France. Napoleon was fascinated by engraved gems: his will specifically mentions 'the antique cameo which Pius VI gave me'. He founded a school for gem engraving under the direction of Jeuffroy* the medallist, and in 1805 a

---

* Romain Vincent Jeuffroy, 1749–1826.

Prix de Rome which placed the glyptic art in the same rank as painting, sculpture and architecture. There were cameos in every kind of jewel, cameos of agate, emerald, malachite, jasper and humble shell (plates 2 and 3).

Louis XV owned a cabinet of eighty-two cameos which became the property of the state in 1790. Napoleon had twenty-four of them set in a pearl collar and a parure of diadem, comb, bracelets, earrings, ceinture and medallion. At the restoration the parure became the property of Louis XVII and the remaining cameos were placed in the Bibliothèque Nationale.

Elisa Bacciochi, Napoleon's sister, shared his passion for cameos and was for a time the patroness of Benedetto Pistrucci,* probably the finest cameo cutter of the century. Pistrucci cut many fine gems for the Princess and enchanted her by the gift of an onyx cameo portrait of her 'no bigger than a fly' which she eventually had mounted with brilliants into a bracelet and presented to Marie Louise. He emigrated to London where the English paid as much as fifty or one hundred guineas for a cameo. Eventually he became chief engraver at the royal mint and cut the dies for the George and Dragon on the new coinage. Not only did Pistrucci carve hardstone with almost miraculous skill, but he seems to have had an uncanny knack for making jealous and bitter enemies of most of his associates. In his first job a fellow apprentice stabbed him in the belly with an engraving tool and his work at the mint seems to have been carried on in the teeth of a storm of contention. Precocious in all things, he was a fully fledged master of his craft at sixteen, and married with two children at twenty: one of his daughters was eventually to become a gifted gem engraver herself. Pistrucci always signed his work, but when he found that in his early days in Rome dealers were erasing the signature and passing off his gems as antique he hit upon the trick of hiding a secret mark amid locks of hair or folds of drapery. The faking and doctoring of gems had long been a kind of local industry in Italy since Renaissance times and the dealers had it down to a fine art. After the gem had been engraved in suitable style it was crammed into the crop of a living fowl. In a short time the abrasive contents of the bird's gizzard convincingly reproduced the network of fine scratches normally imparted by two thousand years of wear. The stone was then painted with a solution of iron filings and animal dung in aqua-fortis to discolour it. Sometimes the faker would go so far as to break the stone in two as a finishing touch. When these fragments were set the missing part was usually replaced with a plate of gold. The Italian Bonelli was notorious for dealing in faked stones and made the rounds of all the European capitals in search of his victims, and as gem collecting was a fashionable preoccupation for the rich man with pretensions to taste they cannot have been difficult to find. Payne Knight, the great doyen of gem collecting, possessed a fragment for which he had paid five hundred pounds to Angelo Bonelli. The stone was a 'Flora' on sardonyx and in Payne Knight's opinion 'the finest Greek cameo in existence'. Pistrucci laughingly told him that on the contrary it was his work, and that his secret mark, a Greek Λ, was there on top of the head to prove it. The punch-line of the joke was that he had originally done the work for twenty Roman crowns. The humour of the situation seems to have

* Benedetto Pistrucci, 1784–1855.

been lost on Payne Knight, however, and the incident perhaps sheds some light on the causes of Pistrucci's unpopularity. The carving of gems and the engraving of dies for coins and medals pose similar problems of design and technique so that some of the finest craftsmen were employed at some time or another by state mints. The intaglio cutter, Marchant (1755–1812), a German by birth, but taught, like Pistrucci, in Rome, was also employed by the Royal Mint. Girometti* was another engraver of great skill who worked in the Papal mint in Rome.

The equipment used for carving hardstone was simple, almost primitive. The *ordegna* was a kind of treadle-operated horizontal drill which rotated an iron bit or *rotine* (fig. 1). The bits were interchangeable, the heads being of various shapes and sizes according to the needs of the job. The engraver drew the subject to be cut with a brass point on the matt unpolished surface of the stone which was cut by pressing it against the spinning iron tool. It was not of course the iron which did the cutting as this is softer than the majority of stones used for cameos, but the diamond dust with which it was impregnated. Olive oil was the lubricant. The gem was finally polished with rottenstone and water.

Imitation cameos were made in glass and porcelain but the doublet was the most difficult to detect. In a doublet the design or relief was cast in opaque white glass and cemented to a background of real stone, usually cornelian or onyx. However, the absence of tool marks on the relief and the unnatural flatness of the background are usually enough to give a doublet away.

The finest way to show off an engraved stone is in a Roman setting in which the gem is surrounded by a channelled flange of gold. This plain style of mounting is the perfect foil for the intricacies of a finely cut cameo or intaglio, but it takes a good man to accomplish it cleanly and well without chipping the stone. The Roman setting is not suitable for fragile materials like shell which are usually secured in light gold mounts often surrounded by a single course of milled gold wire resembling the bass string of a guitar. That simple but effective device was used on every kind of jewel in the years between 1800 and 1820 (colour plate A). Sometimes the wire was rolled flat on the sides leaving the top like the milled edge of a coin. In this form, too, it was bent into a scrollwork decoration for the combs and hair ornaments which were so fashionable.

A favourite necklace design was formed of several cameos linked by skeins of very light gold chain (plate 3). So-called 'Roman mosaics', made up of innumerable minute shards of glass fitted together within a border of black or coloured glass or mother-of-pearl, often took the place of cameos in this kind of necklace. Usually the mosaic plaques represented the more celebrated architectural landmarks of Rome like the hippodrome, but birds were also a popular subject (see colour plate C) and a whole suite in this style was called 'une volière de Clarisse'. Roman mosaics continued to be made right through the century and are still set in tourist jewellery to this day.

The idea of a skein of delicate gold chains was carried into bracelet designs with a single topaz, cameo or diamond as both centre and clasp. Unfortunately these bracelets

* Giuseppe Girometti, 1780–1851.

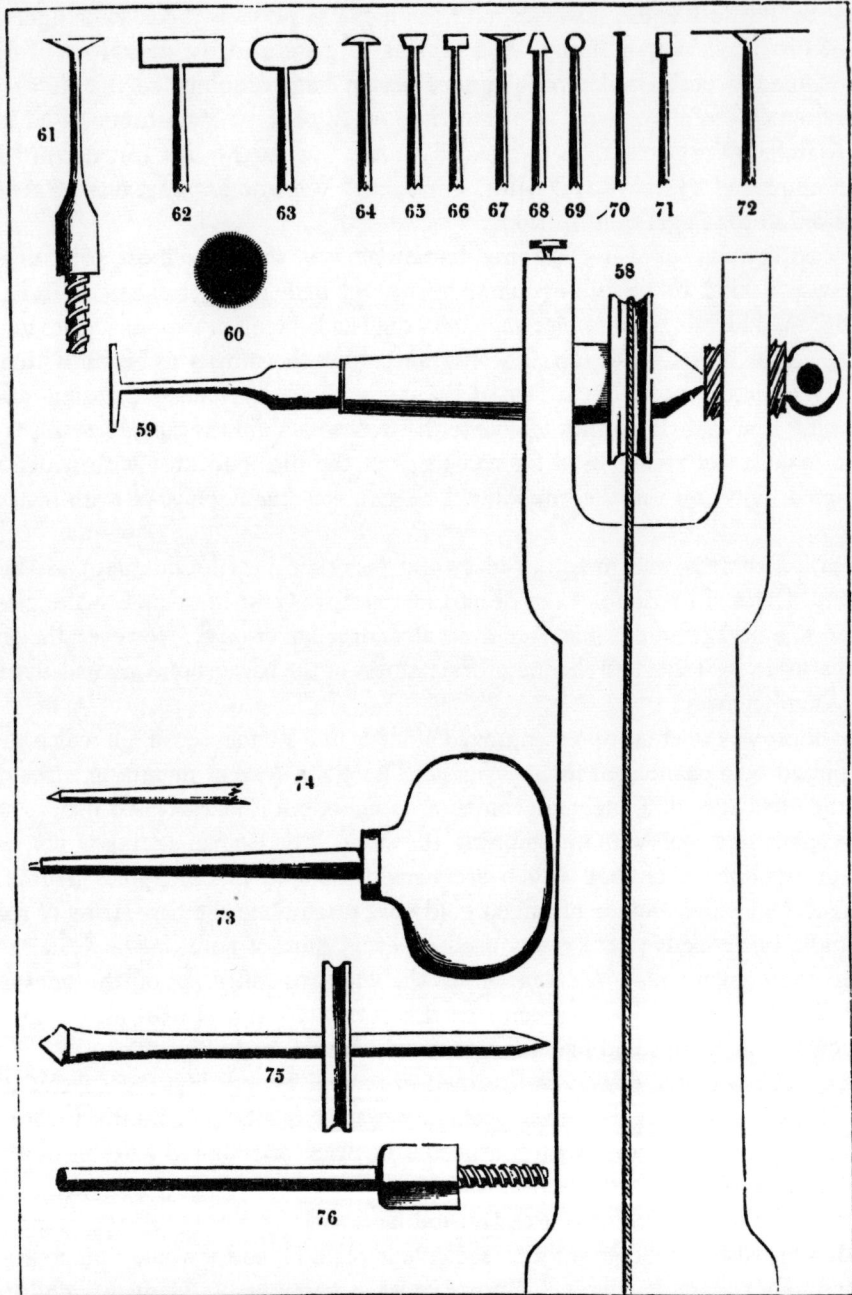

Fig. 1 THE CAMEO CUTTER'S TOOLS
(Archibald Billing, M.D., A.M., F.R.S., *The Science of Gems, Jewels, Coins and Medals*, London, Daldy, Isbister and Co. (Ludgate Hill), and J. Mitchell (Bond Street), 1875)

have an exasperating tendency to tie themselves in knots. A kind of medallion suspended as a pendant from several strands of gold chain was an adaptation of the same idea. In its most typical form a cameo was set in an oval or hexagonal border decorated with milled gold wire, or perhaps a low relief of repeated husk motifs on a matt gold ground.

Stones of the agate family were often linked in single rows as rivières or bracelets. Curiously marked 'eyed agates' with a target-like spot on a pinkish ground are not unusual in these and many other kinds of Napoleonic jewel. Bloodstones, red jasper, mocha-stone (a cream-coloured jasper with tree-like markings), lapis lazuli, malachite and blue-patterned Venetian paste are all to be found, in settings of red or yellow gold. Small pearls frequently formed a border to these stones, each secured individually in a tiny ring of milled gold wire by a twist of fine wire passing through the drill-hole (colour plate A). Small pearls were also mounted up to represent bunches of grapes or currants.

Spanish combs were popular with prongs of tortoise-shell or metal, the heads of gold scrollwork set with three stones, often cameos (colour plate A). At the end of the Empire period a gallery of gold filigree was finished with a row of gold or amber knobs, or most often coral beads engraved with criss-cross hatching. A parure of jewellery was not complete without a comb.

The typically French motifs of hearts, doves, hymeneal torches, quivers and cupids were only temporarily eclipsed by the Revolution and soon reappeared under the Directorate. Many were pure eighteenth-century designs which triumphantly re-emerged practically unchanged (see plate 4).

Rings seldom conform closely to the mainstream of jewel design, probably because the manner of their wearing imposes its own special limitations on the designer. A brooch or pendant can be of almost any size or shape; the form of a ring is largely predetermined. It is probably this which accounts for the recurrence of a few basic designs right through the centuries. The half-hoop ring has its stones set in a band across the finger. At this period five cabochon corals were often mounted in such a way in the plainest of settings. In these, as in many other rings in the first years of the century, the shank was formed of two or more wires soldered side by side and splayed out to form the shoulders (plate 1c). A variant has at the shoulders a slender, grooved leaf-like motif between the two wires. Another half-hoop design was set with a double row of diamonds. The cluster ring has for a bezel a cluster of stones arranged like the petals of a flower around a centre stone. The cluster was used not only on its own but with a circular background of blue enamel edged with white. The shank of this kind of ring was often worked from plain gold sheet, quite undecorated and tapering from the shoulders. Such a ring had its origins in the previous century and was much worn by men.

The most typical bracelet design took the form of a band of light knitted chain with a filigree clasp enriched with granules of gold or tiny sequin-like discs. Bracelets were worn in pairs and would be for the next thirty years or so. The custom was well established: for at Dieppe during a consular tour of Normandy, when a little girl presented Josephine with the official bunch of flowers and Josephine gave her a bracelet in return, to the embarrassment of the assembled dignitaries the child presented her other wrist. Without a thought Josephine took off her own bracelet and gave it to her. From that moment on Josephine always wore on her own person the jewellery she was to give to others: it was typical of her joyous, flamboyant style. Napoleon may have protested at her extravagance —on one splenetic occasion he even ordered the arrest of her milliner—but he would never have to write to her as he wrote to Marie Louise in 1812 on the subject of presents for ladies in waiting:* 'you must not give gold snuff boxes, that is in bad taste, you must have rings with your monogram worth 1200, 2000, 3000 and 6000 livres. . . .' And elsewhere:† 'you must be generous when couriers bring you good news; you must give them money, when they are officers, diamonds.' At the wedding of Marie Louise the ladies of the Imperial family seem to have favoured tiaras in the Hellenistic Greek style, that is to say rising in a gabled point above the centre of the brow and diminishing towards the sides. The style was to reappear at the beginning of our own century.

Another style of head ornament which emerged during the Napoleonic period to be copied time and time again up to the present was the coronal of laurel leaves, its foliage pavé-set with diamonds to contrast with ruby berries. Superb tiaras were made in a loose diamond openwork design so that large pearls or briolettes could be freely suspended in it. The fashion returned during the second Empire. Josephine herself possessed a tiara like this in emeralds, pearls and diamonds.

Both directly and indirectly Napoleon's influence was everywhere in European fashions and social life. When he went to fight in Egypt, obelisks and sphinxes appeared in the design of all manner of objects, including jewels, and in 1813 when the Prussians rebelled against his rule, this inspired the cast-iron jewellery which is so prized by collectors today. The need for money to equip and pay the Prussian troops was so urgent that patriotic ladies were asked to sacrifice their gold jewellery and were presented with jewels of cast-iron in its place, suitably inscribed 'gold gab ich fur Eisen'. Men wore watch-chains and seals set with medallions of allied victories. Jewels in this style were still made after the war and set with an iron profile-cameo of the Duke of Wellington (plate 5). Even gold wedding rings were exchanged for iron rings cast in the royal foundry by Rudolph Verkmeister and inscribed 'Eingetauscht zum wohl des Vaterlands'. Cast-iron jewellery was also made at Frankfurt-am-Main. In fact jewels in this unlikely material had been in use long before the Battle of Leipzig had invested them with any political significance: in 1810 at the funeral of Queen Louise of Prussia, Countess Doenhof wore a collar of leaves and flowers forty centimetres long.

The early iron jewellery has a captivating delicacy and sureness of touch: a necklace in the Victoria and Albert Museum is composed of *fonte de Berlin* classical scenes which have the wistful charm of silhouette pictures enclosed in simple settings of reeded gold. Such early work is rare. Later the foliate designs which were so fashionable in other jewels began to appear in *fonte de Berlin*—vine and currant motifs in particular—their forms traced in a kind of skeletal black openwork that resembles fine black lace. Gothic designs appeared after the war with fine rosettes centred by discs of bright steel. Berlin

* Letter from Marienburg, 12th June.
† Letter from Champaubert, 11th February 1814.

iron was not long to remain a German monopoly for Richard was making cast iron jewellery in Paris not long after the war. Although in such an unorthodox material, Richard's jewels conform to prevailing taste: bracelets composed of a wide ribbon of gauzy mesh clasped with a cameo, a necklace with three such cameos connected by festoons of knitted chain.

Napoleon confirmed for Paris an ascendancy in the world of fashion which has only recently been challenged, and the pronouncements of the *Journal des Modes* would sooner or later be discussed over the coffee-cups in Vienna, Stockholm or even London, blockade or no blockade. The fashion for cut steel originated in London, however. Developed in Birmingham by Matthew Boulton in the eighteenth century, cut steel was taken across the Channel by 'Anglomanie'. Highly reflecting steel was lapped and polished like a precious stone and then set into jewels and accessories of every kind. The fashion declined during the Revolution but revived under the Consulate, and at that time a courtier's sword-hilt, cockade and watch chain would all be of cut steel. By then, cut steel was being made in France, principally by Frichot, Provent, Mme. Schey, Blanchet, Cordier and Boquet.

Around the turn of the century—exactly when it is difficult to say—there was a considerable advance in the setting of diamonds. Until this point it was customary for the back of the jewel to be entirely enclosed so that none of the stone would be visible from the reverse. This meant that no light was admitted around the pavilion of the stone which naturally subdued its brilliance; it was also possible, if the setting edge was not squeezed absolutely airtight around the stone, for dirt to work its way in and for the inside of the setting to tarnish. Once this happened nothing could be done except to remove the stone from the setting, clean it and remount it, which was seldom practicable. The closed setting did give the setter one considerable advantage, however, especially with coloured stones: it enabled him to lay a piece of metal foil at the back of the stone so that light was reflected back at the observer. If the emerald or topaz was perhaps a little too pale the setter could even help nature by tinting the foil to a suitable shade. It is fair to say that the foiling of precious stones was more the rule than the exception in the eighteenth century. Around 1800, or perhaps a little before, it was discovered that diamonds showed to their best advantage if the back of the setting was left open to the light. Brilliant-cut diamonds were almost invariably set *à jour* in this way: but coloured stones continued to be foiled.

The type of setting favoured at the time and throughout most of the century was the cut-down collet. The stone sat in a short tube which was chamfered away from the top leaving little buttresses or claws to do the work of holding the stone in place. A rivière was a chain of diamonds set in this fashion and worn as a collar. Collet-setting was used for single stones or clusters; where a surface was to be encrusted, or *pavé* with stones, another method was resorted to. Holes were cut in the metal into which the stones just fitted. An engraving tool was then dug into the metal next to the stone to raise a little upstanding burr. The hollow point of a special tool was rocked over it to form a little bead of silver which could be worked over the edge of the stone to hold it in place. This is the method still in use today, and when the job is done properly very little metal is visible. Diamond jewels were always set in a laminate of two metals, gold and silver: silver at the front to accentuate the brilliant whiteness of the diamond, gold at the back which would not mark the skin or the clothing. These settings were used right up to the end of the century, by which time they were superseded by mounts made entirely of platinum or white gold. The expert invariably turns an antique diamond jewel over to examine it, to see whether it is gold-backed, open or closed, and also perhaps because the honeycombed intricacy of a fine setting is very satisfying to the eye.

Most diamonds of the period came from India. Sometimes these Indian stones are of a fine whiteness when they are called 'Golcondas' after the region in which they were found. Such stones were often cut very shallow, probably because they had been recut from diamonds already worked into the thin gems favoured by Indian lapidaries.

When the Brazilian mines were first discovered in the eighteenth century the rumour was put about by those with an interest in the Indian trade that these stones were false. To circumvent this the Brazilian dealers sent their diamonds to Goa and marketed them from there. They even went so far as to have the rough stones cut into traditional Indian forms in Venice, regardless of the loss of material that it entailed. The fact that a diamond is cut very shallow therefore does not mean that it is a Golconda.

Diamonds of more than four grains weight were sorted out and invoiced separately. The rest were graded according to size and carefully packed into a 'bulse', a sort of parcel, or poke of cotton material, the neck being tightly bound with tape and fastened with a seal bearing the shipper's name and a detailed description of the weight and quality of the stones. The merchant would purchase entirely on the strength of this invoice without examining the contents of the bulse. A bulse might pass through the hands of many middlemen before reaching Europe, each of whom would append his seal. The invoices were always scrupulously accurate and invariably tallied exactly when the bulse was opened.

In England during the first twenty years of the nineteenth century diamond jewellery was often on a very lavish scale. Formal scroll arrangements were fashionable and compositions of clusters and chains of diamonds. Collars were made in the form of a chain of oval or oblong links, very plain, set with both rose and brilliant-cut diamonds. Small circular lockets, pavé-set and with a hair compartment mounted off centre, were quite common in diamonds as well as pearls. The Maltese cross seems to have been a particularly English design for a brooch, or above all a pendant. The earliest occur in a kind of transitional style in which the small stones forming the borders are in closed settings and the larger collets are *à jour*. They probably date from the turn of the century although the design was popular during the thirties and forties, and the style was revived in late Victorian and Edwardian times.

In spite of the war, Paris still gave London fashions the lead and most of the trends to be noticed on the other side of the channel were eagerly picked up by English society. The increased rents consequent on rising grain prices made the landowning aristocracy of Britain very rich indeed and they spent their money as though anxious to be rid of it. The years before 1815 were fat ones for the London jeweller, and for one jeweller in particular—George Rundell of Rundell and Bridge. Everything Rundell did seemed to fly in the teeth of both convention and providence. At a time when the London market was glutted with the jewels of the French emigré nobility, Rundell bought—and went on buying, long after everyone else had stopped. He was unfailingly rude to aristocratic customers—the bluer the blood, the more pointed the insult, and the Marchioness of Sligo remarked that he was the most impudent shopman she had ever met. To the great courtesans who came to his shop, however, he was said to have been polite—even ingratiating.

One of Rundell's employees, George Fox, summed the man up in a vigorous, if somewhat caricatured thumbnail sketch:* 'Mr. Rundell was naturally of a violent disposition, very sly and cunning, and suspicious in the extreme, and avarice, covetousness and meanness were so deeply rooted in him that it affected every feature of his face and entered into every action of his life.' Violent, he undoubtedly was: once when exasperated by an officious employee he aimed a wild blow at the man which struck out a front tooth—and then, overcome with remorse he pulled out his purse and gave the man a guinea. The payment was repeated annually and for life. Rundell seems to have had a great capacity for living life across the grain, but his partner Bridge was his exact opposite and made up for all his shortcomings in tact and prudence. 'His back was exceedingly flexible and no man could bow lower and oftener than Mr. Bridge. He used to say that the nearest way to my lady's boudoir was down the area steps through the servants' hall and from there to the housekeeper's rooms and so upstairs to my lady.'

Rundell died in 1827 leaving one and a quarter million pounds. In his firm's heyday, they had employed over a thousand hands, and he was always the first to be offered any important jewel that came on the market, or any new technical process that might be discovered. Some of the diamonds that passed through his hands were legends in their own right—the Nassuck, the Arcots, the Piggot—and the firm's ramifications extended to St. Petersburg, Constantinople, Calcutta, Alexandria, Smyrna and Manila. On his deathbed Rundell gave orders that the shop should be closed for one day only at his funeral and that his partner Bridge should follow the coffin. He then declared 'you know well that I have astonished you in your lifetime, and by God if you fail me I will come back and astonish you again'.

---

* Unpublished account of the firm of Rundell, Bridge and Rundell, London, jewellers, written between 1843, the year the firm was finally dissolved, and 1846, the year of the death of the author George Fox.

2. The Post-War Years

With the restoration of the Bourbon monarchy in France the surviving aristocrats of the ancien régime returned to court: some from impecunious exile abroad, others from refuges in the more distant provinces that had not glimpsed the fitful light of fashion for half a century. Such jewels as were left to them by the needs of everyday existence were, of course, in the style of Marie Antoinette, and this, together with a certain nostalgia for the old days, led to a revival of eighteenth-century styles in diamond jewellery. Distinguishing these later jewels is rarely difficult, however, as the diamonds are nearly always in open settings. Another link with the old days was the reinstatement of Bapst* as crown jeweller: he was commissioned to remount the crown-jewels for the new King (see plate 7).

Naturalism had been making a gradual return to diamond jewellery. Leaves and flowers did appear in the diamond jewellery of the Napoleonic era but in a stylized form and ruthlessly subordinated to a formal design. Now from the best workshops came diamond nosegays of meadowy freshness—campions, cockle, cornflowers and ears of wheat. And there were even more luscious horticultural creations of fuchsias, morning glories and roses. The style flourished on both sides of the Channel, and Rundell and Bridge were commissioned to set a magnificent coronal of hydrangea blooms for George Watson Taylor. Jewels in this style continued to be made right through the century, reaching a climax in the sixties (see plates 8, 9a and 9c).

In direct contrast, formal designs were also very fashionable. Necklaces of diamond chain were made, the links either plain rectangular, oval or enriched with scrollwork (see plate 8). Wide Brooches were pierced with dense scrollwork (see plate 9b) and occasionally hung with three drops in chatelaine style. In necklaces and also in rings, diamonds and sometimes emeralds were grouped in open clusters of five with fine silver scrolls that recall some eighteenth-century work. But above all in diamond jewellery trumpet scrolls and stylized rose-buds abounded in designs that contrived to be both formal and casual at the same time (see plate 7).

But in post-war Europe there was little money to be spent on diamonds and most of the jewellers' patrons had to be content with semi-precious stones. Now that the ocean routes were safe from privateers these began to arrive in quantity, mostly from Brazil: topazes, amethysts, chrysoberyls and aquamarines, although the beautiful deep-green tourmalines are never to be seen in the jewellery of this period. These semi-precious stones were mainly mounted in a kind of filigree work known as cannetille after a type of embroidery which it resembled. Usually the stones were in simple quincunx groupings

* The firm of Bapst was founded in 1725 and appointed crown jewellers in 1788.

among tendril scrolls of tightly coiled wire, and peascod motifs of gold granules aligned within a pod-like border of wire (see colour plate B). A little later this filigree base was garnished with leaves, flowers and seashell motifs stamped out of variously coloured gold (plates 10 and 11). Settings are invariably closed and foiled. Foiling was used by the setter in many cases where there were a large number of stones of the same species in a jewel to bring the colour to a good match. Necklaces of Brazilian topaz, for example, often contain as many as fifty stones or more and to match as many stones as this by selection alone would clearly be very difficult. Topazes were used in their natural sherry colour, or 'burnt' to a pretty pink. The lapidary used to heat the stone in a pipe bowl of ash to bring about this change. Many stones change colour on heating like this: amethyst turns brown or yellow, and zircon loses its colour altogether.

Some dealers, either through ignorance or intent, do not make the distinction between topaz and citrine. There is a small difference in the colour: topaz is warmer, redder; and a big difference in the price as topaz is about twenty times the cost of citrine at current values. A refractometer will distinguish the two stones immediately, but few people own a refractometer. A good rough and ready test is to rub the surface of the stone with the thumb: being a good deal harder than citrine, topaz takes a higher polish and is therefore slippery to the touch. The surface of a topaz is more lustrous for the same reason. In time one comes to recognise the soapy feel of a true topaz and it is a knack well worth acquiring.

Always examine the tongue pieces of necklace and bracelet clasps on delicate cannetille work, and the small rings that link the parts together. An assay mark is most likely to be found here as these are the only places substantial enough to be stamped. A powerful lens will be needed as the marks are minute. A ram's head means that the piece was made in France between 1819 and 1838, an eagle's head signifies that it was made in that country after 1838. The hook fittings of earrings are often so marked, although these may well have been replaced. There seems to have been a preference for amethysts and large pale-green chrysoprases among French jewellers working in this style, and for decorations of red enamelled flower-heads and coloured gold work, but it would be an error to pick up these points and use them as a proof of provenance as they occur in English work too; only the assay mark is proof positive.

The Portuguese have always had a preference for pale yellow chrysoberyls in all kinds of jewellery and early nineteenth-century filigree is no exception. Light in colour and relatively brilliant, these stones were often used in the nineteenth century to do the work of a diamond in relieving the heaviness of richer coloured stones like turquoises and carbuncles. The Portuguese, however, were accustomed to using them by themselves and in large numbers.

The cannetille fashion seemed to appear from nowhere in the immediate post-war years, often, as in England, in countries where there was no indigenous tradition of making filigree. Other countries, especially Portugal, had been making filigree jewels for centuries, and it may have been that souvenirs brought home by Peninsular veterans were imitated by the jewellers of London and Paris. Filigree work in Europe was to a large degree a peasant art and a new species of man, the tourist, was beginning to 'discover' the countryside and its inhabitants. More than one peasant jewel was copied in the towns and filigree may have been transplanted in the same way.

An interesting possibility is suggested by the likeness between European filigree and some Indian work, notably that of Delhi and Madras. This could be a classic chicken-and-the-egg situation as Indian jewellers in the nineteenth century were great copyists and borrowed many European ideas themselves. What indicates at least some movement from east to west is that cannetille flourished in those countries whose links with India were strongest—Britain, France and Portugal. Also, some French jewels of the immediate post-war years often have hemispherical motifs encrusted with granulation which resemble strongly the babul work of Delhi which can be traced back to Dravidian times.

All we know for certain, however, about the beginnings of cannetille are the hard economic facts—that money was short and that an ounce or so of gold can be turned into a great deal of filigree jewellery.

Hand-made cannetille is not known in silver or base metals, but a kind of cheap imitation was stamped out of brass and roughly gilded. Combs, tiaras and hair ornaments set with red or green pastes or imitation pearls were manufactured in large quantities (plate 6), and oblong clasps of this quality often formed the centres of bracelets of glass or coral beads.

English filigree work was of a very high standard and sometimes set with quite valuable stones, especially emeralds and little rubies and diamonds: sapphires on the other hand are unusual. Peace brought its own special problems for the English jeweller. The incomes of the great land magnates fell smartly with the price of grain and the jewellers' takings diminished in consequence. Gold fell back from £5. 10s. per ounce to its pre-war price of £3. 7s. 10½d. and jewellers who were carrying heavy stocks suffered losses. But in spite of this, English jewellery could be very sumptuous (plate 18a). The ubiquitous Mr. Creevey's observation on the soi-disant Princess Olivia of Cumberland are worth repeating, if only for their almost sublime cattiness:' . . . her person is on the model of the Princess Elizabeth, only at least three times her size . . . diamonds in profusion hung from every part of her head but her nose and the whole was covered with feathers that would do credit to a hearse.' Elsewhere we read 'Lady Londonderry is the great show of the balls here in her jewels which are out of all question the finest I ever beheld—such immense amethysts and emeralds, etc. Poor Mrs. Carnac who had a regular haystack of diamonds last night was really nothing by the side of the other.' These were purely nocturnal displays, for by this time the idea of a special toilette for the evening was well established and little jewellery was worn during the day.

Many rings were made in designs which were closely related to the cannetille technique. The stones, garnets, pearls, rubies, emeralds or diamonds, and usually five in number, were either mounted in a quincunx or in a single row in the classical half-hoop style. The settings of these rings were enriched with granulation and the shoulders finished with a little garnish of filigree. The cannetille fashion lasted until it was replaced by repoussé work of plump scrolls. Shallow and ineffectual-looking stampings were made in both yellow and pinkish gold in the early thirties. These designs were improved and had supplanted cannetille completely by 1840 (see plate 13f).

Gold is too soft to be used in jewellery in its pure state and it is always alloyed with some other metal to make it more durable. As one might expect, the kind of metal mixed with the gold influences the colour of the resulting alloy: a proportion of copper results in a reddish shade and silver gives metal with a strange greenish cast. Even blue gold can be obtained by adding a small percentage of iron—this is rarely seen in jewellery however. Jewellers exploited these effects in exquisite harmonies and contrasts. The shine of the metal was always muted with a matt surface highlighted with the occasional chisel-cut where the design of flowers and scrolls required it and, when set with the turquoises which were so fashionable around 1830, the effect is most warm and charming. The most pleasing use of coloured gold is perhaps in the little English brooches which represent a sprig of flowers (plate 16d), often the rose, thistle and shamrock, the blooms in coloured stones, the leaves and stalks in red and yellow golds engraved and matted. A little later, large and elaborate brooches were made in the form of a bouquet of flowers, the leaves, stems and petals in gold repoussé and with coloured stones in the flower centres. The gentlemen's fob seals which were so *de rigueur* at this time were often exquisitely garnished with coloured golds. They were frequently worn in bunches: Gogol's collegiate assessor Kovalev 'always had on him a quantity of seals, both of seals engraved with coats of arms and of seals inscribed "Wednesday," "Thursday", "Monday," and the rest'. Actually miniature seals on large gold split rings in bunches of seven and set with cornelian intaglios bearing the days of the week do come up for sale from time to time. The most typical kind of seal, however, was set with an intaglio of the owner's crest or coat of arms engraved in an amethyst, citrine, smoky quartz, crystal or cornelian of rounded rectangular form. The hemispherical setting would be surmounted by a lyre, a stirrup or a baluster motif by which it was fastened to the watch-chain (plates 12a and c). Rarely, seals were set with sapphire or topaz intaglios. Some seals were very large and of fanciful design, especially of some sporting subject (plate 12d)—a stag's head, or a gundog sniffing out a brace of birds.

Hubert Obry,* a Frenchman, excelled at this kind of work. His father was employed as a huntsman by the duc de Berry, and Hubert himself was retained by more than one celebrated *équipage*, so that the first part of his life was spent among men and beasts dedicated to the pursuit of the stag, the fox, the hare and the boar—his father had even christened him after the patron saint of hunters. In this absorbing and exciting milieu it is a wonder that Obry's talent for carving precious metal should ever have come to light, and it is hardly surprising that when it did he should have employed it on carving seals, signet rings and other masculine trinkets with forest creatures perfect in every tine and bristle. Eventually Obry set up as a ciseleur in the Place Dauphine, Paris. His apprentices were devoted to him, but Obry would tolerate none who could not give a good account of himself on the hunting horn. He had a passion for the hunting horn—he even composed music for it—and when the days began to shorten and game started to stir in the forests he and

* Hubert Obry, 1808–1853.

his companions would forsake the workshop and take to the road. They would stop at a château and play outside until the owner invited them in out of curiosity. A good musician, a fine talker and a delightful man, Obry and his companions were invited to many excellent tables. They would explain that they were working jewellers on holiday—and indeed they would be delighted to show their host some samples of their work if that was his wish. In this eccentric fashion the little band would pay its way until the time came to return to the Place Dauphine and the servitude of the bench. Hubert Obry never managed to hold on to any money for very long, however. He died a poor man, but his house was a refuge for the starving artists of the Latin quarter right until the end.

Seals varied enormously both in materials and in workmanship. The best were superbly worked in massive 22 carat gold and set with precious topaz or even sapphire. At the other end of the scale were those in roughly cast and gilded metal, the stone a bright mauve or yellow paste crudely claw-set and often with a comical or sentimental inscription of almost painful archness, for those who did not run to a crest and motto.

The vast majority of early nineteenth-century seals fall between these two extremes in being neither gilded nor solid gold, but formed of a sort of casing of light gold sheet filled with base metal. The usual way of testing for gold is to scrape the surface in some inconspicuous place to remove any gilding and then to apply a drop of acid. If the metal is not gold it will fizz and change colour. With a good quality gold-cased seal it is not possible to expose the base metal core without defacement. Generally the hole in the top of the seal by which it is suspended from the watch-chain is worn around its lip by the chafing of the split ring which passes through it, and here the core is often exposed. Other salient parts of the decoration may also be worn through. In another interesting type of seal the stone takes the form of a three-sided bead, usually amethyst, crystal or citrine engraved with three different devices and pinned horizontally to swivel in a richly-chased stirrup-shaped mount (plate 12b). Swivel seals of this kind can be very handsome especially when the unengraved parts are covered with glittering facets, as indeed they usually are. Another version had as many as six seals arranged like the spokes of a wheel around the pivoted centre. These were often gilt metal and paste. Jewellers seem to have lavished more ingenuity on these little toys than upon almost anything else, and there are seals with horses, dogs, flowers, anchors, snakes, knights in armour and many other motifs.

Pins for neckwear also took bizarre forms (see plate 13). They were usually longer than those worn during the previous century or later on in the nineties. Eighteenth-century pins were formed in a zigzag to prevent them coming out of the tie. Those of the nineteenth century were given a few twists about two thirds of the way up with the same object. Occasionally they were made in pairs connected by a fine chain—one of the most successful designs of this type has pear-shaped heads of blue or white enamel caged in gold scrollwork.

Cut steel stayed in fashion after the war and held a noteworthy place in the Paris exhibitions of 1819 and 1832. Until the latter date it was in use for all sorts of jewels and accessories, but by now mechanical production methods had gained a foothold and the

C A gold NECKLACE set with Roman mosaics
 Circa 1835   *See page* 21

D   (*a*) A gold BRACELET richly decorated with champlevé enamels
     See page 35

    (*b*) A gold BROOCH set with a Geneva enamel copy of Annibale Caracci's painting
     See page 34

little steel studs were not always lapped and polished separately but stamped out of sheet metal in strips.

After Waterloo, European fashions still conformed to the high-waisted Directoire model, but the mood was turning against the free and easy ways of wartime and this was reflected in women's fashion. Life became more elaborate, pretentious, prescribed and as society began to settle into the nineteenth-century pattern so the flounces and trimmings multiplied. In 1820 the waistline dropped to a more modest position just above the hips. The year 1820 marks a kind of watershed in jewel fashions too, for it is 1820 rather than 1815 that sees the end of Napoleonic classicism. In 1829 the leg of mutton sleeve appeared in France and for the next eight to ten years one outrage succeeded another. The leg-of-mutton sleeve was inflated to great size above the elbow with structures of whalebone but tapered rapidly towards the wrist so that several bracelets could be worn on the forearm.

Above the waist a woman now became a sort of equilateral triangle, sloping from the shoulders to a huge wingspan at the elbows. At the apex was a coiffure in which diamond ears of corn, artificial songbirds, combs and pins waged a kind of jungle warfare in a terrain of false locks and feathers. It was a style so grotesque as to defy parody, but it did at least bring with it the ferronnière. This interesting jewel is named after *La Belle Ferronnière*, a painting by Leonardo of the blacksmith's wife who was the mistress of Francis I and who is seen wearing a jewel in the middle of her forehead, a fashionable ornament during the the first years of the Italian Renaissance. The ferronnière really came into its own in 1836 when hair styles became simpler and were worn well away from the forehead. It took the form of a light chain of decorative motifs which encircled the crown and from which a small pendant dangled in the middle of the forehead. A style so eccentric and so dependent on hair fashions could never last for long, so most ferronnières finished up as necklaces or bracelets. Bracelets of this origin can usually be detected because they were originally tailored to fit the head and not the wrist, so that the sides spring out of the centre at a slight angle (foot of plate 24). The ring or hook from which the pendant hung may also be present, or at least the scar where it has been removed. Ferronnières are always of dainty proportions: obviously massive jewels would not be suitable for wear in this way.

Evening gowns in the early thirties were worn very décolleté, and for emphasis a big jewelled collar was worn not so much on the neck as around the shoulders. This could be a very elaborate affair of clustered diamonds and coloured stones, linked by festoons of diamonds and hung with pearl drops. Some superb emerald and diamond necklaces were made in Russia. The emerald deposits of Siberia were already discovered by this time although the emeralds in Russian jewellery are not always of Russian origin. Apart from emeralds, the jewellers of Moscow and St. Petersburg used gems rarely seen in western precious jewellery like cinnamon-brown hessonite garnets and bright red spinels, often of unusual size (plate 14d). The Russian jeweller usually placed the coloured stone within a border of largish brilliants in the usual manner, but the actual work of holding the stone was accomplished cleverly by a row of pavé-set rose diamonds which crowded over the edge of the stone. This kind of setting is very strong evidence of Russian workmanship.

The very best amethysts come from Siberia, stones of deep imperial purple which glowed wine-red by candle-light. Stones as fine as this need no elaborate setting to show them off: a light cut-down collet is enough and this is how they were set in necklaces all over Europe graduating from walnut to pistachio sizes. Fine cairngorms received the same treatment. Topazes, both pink and yellow, were also set in rivières, but in foiled, cup-shaped settings (plate 15). Jewels of this kind were often accompanied by a cross-shaped pendant and a pair of earrings composed of a pear-shaped stone suspended from a smaller round one. Oval garnets, rather thin and heavily foiled, were also cheaply set in necklaces, either in clusters or a single row. These probably originated in central Europe where the stones were found. The prettiest took the form of a chain of flowers, the petals of pear-shaped stones. An interesting collar of the 1830s was designed as a garland of pansies, almost life size, the bi-coloured petals represented by two different gems—perhaps topaz and aquamarine or citrine and amethyst. The stones are inevitably foiled in this type of necklace.

At this time a belt of material, quite wide, was worn at the waist and the buckle which fastened it could be quite elaborate. Of upright oblong shape it was generally cast or stamped in base metal and decorated with champlevé enamels. Enamels were widely used in jewellery around 1830, a fashion which seems to have originated in Switzerland where enamelling had reached a high degree of technical perfection. Geneva was the principal centre of this craft where 215 enamellers were working in the early nineteenth century. The finest Swiss enamels take the form of a miniature painting. The subjects chosen were lake and mountain landscapes, St. Bernard dogs, and girls in peasant costume (plate 17) although excellent portraits also occur.

Sometimes a well-known work of art was copied (colour plate Db) and Raphael's *Madonna de la Sedia* was a favourite. The painting can be very fine, in a delicate if over-sweet palette of pastel tints with lavenders and pinks predominating. The landscapes in particular are often of really excellent quality; the surface of liquid smoothness without a bubble or a blemish. These enamels are always fired on thin copper sheet, and their settings are always open so that the 'counter-enamelling' is visible from the back: this is usually blue speckled with white, although its function is not decorative as might be supposed. To make a painted enamel the craftsman would prepare a copper plate of suitable size, stiffen it by hammering to a slightly domed form and roughen the surface so as to give the enamel a purchase. The enamel, a cake of hard glass coloured with a metal oxide is powdered very finely and washed with scrupulous care. The background enamel is spread over the surface of the copper plate which is then heated in a furnace to melt it. When the work has cooled, layers of colour, ground to dust-like fineness with a glass mull and mixed with an oil vehicle, are painted on and the work fired between each application. If the enamel is applied to one side only it will buckle the copper plate by contracting when it cools: the counter-enamelling on the back of the plate counteracts this by pulling in the opposite direction. In the enamels of peasant girls the counter enamel often bears the name of the canton from which the elaborately costumed girl hails, and, rarely, its coat of arms. The little miniatures were often mounted up into quite elaborate parures, the mounts in gold stamped in an openwork design of flowers, scrolls and scallop shells.

Usually the mounts were champlevé enamelled with black predominating. In Switzerland was also developed the technique of applying tiny decorative motifs stamped out of gold foil to a background of coloured enamel, usually blue, and then protecting them with a layer of clear enamel.

In champlevé enamelling the design is engraved or chased in the gold. Powdered enamel is laid in these small hollows and fired, with the result that the surface of the enamel finishes flush with the surrounding gold (see colour plate Da). In the 1830s this type of work was usually set with a mixture of small coloured stones: black and white were the dominant colours, enlivened with opaque pea-green, celandine yellow, lavender and translucent red.

Although of Swiss origin, this type of champlevé enamel was made all over Europe: in France, where black dominates the palette to the exclusion of most other colours, and in Italy where the craftsman inclined to the more brilliant end of the spectrum. Sometimes the more sombre enamels were relieved by a riot of assorted coloured stones. Necklaces were made of a succession of thick panels of scalloped outline looking as though they had been formed with a pastry cutter, and with a different coloured stone at the centre of each: topazes, sapphires, spinels and quartzes of every possible colour.

Gold was a far rarer and relatively more costly metal at that time than it is now. It was undoubtedly this which held back the advance of machine production in the jewellery trade. There was little use in paring down production costs when such a high proportion of the finished price lay in the materials. In the 1830s some machine-made jewellery was made in gold of an uninteresting pinkish colour, shallow lightweight stampings for the most part. Most multiple production, however, was of what we should now call costume jewellery in the base metals. Many jewels had a slim decorative border stamped with shells, flowers and feather scrolls. This was rolled or punched out in lengths and is seen in all kinds of jewels—rings, seals, brooches and pendants. The tiny rectangular brooches which fastened ribbons and bonnet strings were often trimmed with it, and a particular kind of locket, round and engine-turned like a little watch, invariably had such a border. It is as well to test this kind of decorative border with some care as it is all too often of gilt brass!

Some of the prettiest brooches of the era were designed as birds (plate 16a), and there is more than a passing resemblance between these dove-like, earthward-swooping birds and the St. Esprit of northern French peasant jewellery. It could be that they were taken up by the city jeweller in the same way as the *croix-à-la-jeannette* would be a little later. Usually a heart hangs from the bird's beak, and if it does not a small ring remains to show that one did at some time or other. Sometimes the stiffly outstretched wings are mounted tremblant on springs so as to quiver like a living bird. Sometimes these jewels are of gold filigree and set with a variety of coloured stones, others are thickly encrusted with turquoises or else richly carved and chased in coloured golds. Occasionally, instead of a heart the bird has an olive branch or a sprig of forget-me-not in its beak. These pretty toys are eagerly sought out by the collector and they command quite high prices.

Maltese crosses were very popular in England during the thirties (plates 14a, b and c).

The richest were pavé-set with diamonds, although a less costly version had the broad triangular arms cut from slices of white chalcedony, or more rarely cornelian, and springing from a dainty foliate centre set with small turquoises, rubies and emeralds. Sometimes a pendant cross like this formed a demi-parure with a large pair of earrings, the torpedo-shaped chalcedony drops decorated with sprigs of gold and precious stones (plate 12g).

Such long pendants were the most typical earrings of the thirties. Most of them were attenuated hollow drops of gold, sometimes plain, sometimes pressed all over in a piqué or herringbone pattern, but always decorated with little frills of filigree and small coloured stones. They are fragile jewels and have usually suffered some damage over the years.

Portraits of the thirties and forties often show a lady wearing a very long chain in a variety of ways. Sometimes it was tucked into the girdle, sometimes pinned at the bosom so as to hang in two wide festoons. This versatile jewel could be used to carry a muff, or a watch, or just worn for its own sake. A portrait of Queen Adelaide in the London National Portrait Gallery shows the chain thrown loosely about her shoulders and ending in what appears to be a watch to one side of her belt. 'Longchains' as these are usually called in the auctioneer's catalogue were made in a variety of patterns (plate 19). Many are of orthodox form, the links round and plump and quite massive looking, but in reality of very light weight. On this type the gold is always stamped with a figured pattern of one kind or another, usually stars, spots, or chevrons on a matt ground. Another type is of slighter links joined in a thick cord. Both types can have bobbin or barrel-shaped clasps garnished with filigree and set with turquoises. Another fastening takes the disquieting form of a lady's hand emerging from a lace cuff, and complete even to the ring upon her finger. This mysterious, even vaguely sinister motif is typical of the romantic age, and is related to those miniatures of a young girl's eye, clear and candid, the rest of the face as absent as the Cheshire cat, which had already been mounted in jewellery for some time. The following advertisement from the 7th October 1843 issue of the *Illustrated London News* gives some idea of how longchains were graded and priced:

'LADIES' GOLD CHAIN, London-made,—for facility of reference the weight is given by comparison of sovereigns; the quality of the gold is warranted equal to any that is worked into articles of this description.

	Length, inches	weight	simple chains	with stars on links	Fancy patterns
A Neckchain	45	3	£4. 4s. 0d.	£5. 5s. 0d.	£5. 15s. 6d.
"	45	4	£5. 5s. 0d.	£6. 6s. 0d.	£6. 16s. 6d.
"	45	5	£6. 6s. 0d.	£7. 7s. 0d.	£7. 17s. 6d.
"	45	6	£7. 7s. 0d.	£8. 8s. 0d.	£8. 18s. 6d.

Drawings of the various patterns kept for the purpose of sending by post to any part of the country. T. Cox Savory, Goldsmith etc. 47 Cornhill (seven doors down from Gracechurch Street) London—N.B. goods for Madras, Bombay, Calcutta, Hobart

Town or Quebec, also for the West Indies can be paid for on their arrival to the agents of the firm'.

This type of jewel could be quite elaborate and costly, however. Sometimes each link was a little cage of scrollwork, sometimes a slim cartouche of champlevé enamel flowers edged with scrollwork and linked by rosettes. Rarely and enchantingly it can be a procession of little enamelled snakes, gleaming black as liquorice and with orange spots. Men sometimes wore a similar type of chain, and a drawing after Daniel Maclise shows the young Disraeli wearing one around his neck, with the watch it supported tucked into his waistcoat pocket (plate 18b).

There begins to appear in jewels at the time a literary, symbolic element. In the same way that paintings were made to tell a story, jewels often had some kind of a message too, a secret meaning. At its simplest this was just an inscription. Some English jewels are inscribed in French, partly because French was thought to be smart, partly because a foreign language made the most homely sentiment mysterious and incomprehensible except to the initiate. Sometimes the message was a lover's conceit that had a meaning for only two people, sometimes it was a rebus on a name, or some uplifting motto. Later jewels would be designed around the cross, anchor and heart which represent faith, hope, and charity. Some jewels were in a code—the regard ring is a good example. It is in the traditional half-hoop form of a row of stones running across the finger, but the stones are of different kinds so that the initial letters of each gem's name spell out a word—like this: R(ruby) E(emerald) G(garnet) A(amethyst) R(ruby) D(diamond). 'Dearest' was treated in the same way, and so were various female christian names. If the jewel is not of English origin, deciphering will be doubly difficult because the names of the stones will be different as well as the word which they are intended to spell. In France rings of this kind were introduced at the time of Napoleon and were called *bagues hieroglyphiques*. Sometimes they represented the days of the week in which case they were called *semaines*; these last made their appearance in the late 1820s.

Brooches, too, were made with puzzle motifs, often as a long cartouche with a row of stones at the centre. Occasionally they were more elaborately conceived: as a miniature guitar (plate 16b), for example, in coloured golds with the stones mounted in an arc below the sound-hole which was covered with a disc of glass or crystal so that it could contain a lock of hair. Hair compartments are to be seen on every kind of jewel from this time on.

Jewels of this description are a typical product of the romantic age when writers and painters sought out the mysterious and the bizarre as subjects for their works and when the line between sentiment and sentimentality was thinly drawn and often transgressed.

3. The Mid-Century 1840 to 1860

Until the middle of the century, gold was a very scarce metal indeed, and stocks were so limited that the demand could only be met by melting down existing jewels that had gone out of fashion. It was the age of the explorer, however, and where he went the prospector followed. The California gold rush in 1848 and that in Australia three years later altered jewellery fashions just as the discovery of diamonds in the Cape was to do in later years. One fortunate result for the collector was that an easier supply of metal relieved the pressure on existing jewels. Now it was no longer necessary to have old jewellery melted down to make new so that a great many really fine jewels of the Regency and Restoration periods still remain to us. By the same token jewels and *objets de vertu* of the Napoleonic period are a lot rarer. Freer supplies of metal allowed more gold jewellery to be made, but this plentiful supply would have been of little use to the jeweller without a greatly increased demand. Fortunately the demand was growing lustily. The prime reason for that lay in the role of the Victorian woman who had become a kind of shop-window for the display of her husband's wealth and success. Since the days of Beau Brummell men had worn sober garments of black, brown, or dark blue and it was now difficult to tell a mill owner from his well turned out clerk. In order to affirm his place in the social order a man had, like Dickens's Mr. Merdle, to obtain a bosom. 'It was not', the author explains, 'a bosom to repose upon, but it was a capital bosom to hang jewels upon. Mr. Merdle wanted something to hang jewels upon, and he had bought it for the purpose. Storr and Mortimer* might have married on the same speculation.'

The young Queen, too, set a glittering example in the matter of personal decoration. Her toilette on the royal visit to Scotland in 1842 was described in detail in a London press report:† 'Her arms were covered with long lace gloves. Each arm was encircled about two inches above the wrist with a broad diamond bracelet. The clasp of the bracelet of the right arm contained an oval-shaped miniature. On her right shoulder glistened a small but beautiful diamond thistle. On her left she wore the Order of the Garter, and the blue scarf of that order was thrown across her breast, and fastened to the right side of her belt with a magnificent diamond ornament. A small square-shaped brooch was fixed in the upper part of her stomacher. Her Majesty wore a slender necklace with a locket depending from it. Her neck in other respects was bare, and her elegant bust displayed to full advantage. The head of Her Majesty was dressed so plainly as to contrast with the ornamental coiffure of those around her. Her hair was braided low upon each cheek in the

* Storr and Mortimer were one of the most important London jewellers of the time.
† *Illustrated London News*, 3rd September 1842.

simple mode displayed in most of her portraits. It was bound by a slender hairband in which a small diamond was set at the front. The bow behind was placed very low and surrounded by a narrow diamond circlet which was scarcely visible except on a profile view.' By inference a good deal of information can be sifted from this sort of account. The Queen seems to have been wearing a simple ferronnière of some kind. It also seems that although she was wearing a bracelet on each wrist they were not a pair, and that the custom of wearing bracelets in matched pairs was already defunct. The fashion for bracelets with miniatures at their centres was to remain for some ten years or so.

This was a time when royal patronage really mattered to the jeweller. The court looked to the Queen for what it should wear, and the rest of the nation looked to the court. Royal influence was so strong throughout the century that the death of the Duke of Clarence was later to precipitate a depression in the trade. For the jeweller the highest recognition he could receive was the cachet of royal approval. For Dixon and Sons of Hatton Garden who patented a 'Ladies Watch Protector', a kind of brooch designed to secure a lady's watch to her waist, an order from the queen for one bearing the Star and Garter and the Imperial Crown was of inestimable importance. Quite a number of these must have been made and must still be in circulation although probably modified from their original purpose.

In 1845 a deputation from the Birmingham fancy trades presented some examples of Birmingham jewellery to His Royal Highness Prince Albert, and the Queen was asked to take into gracious consideration 'the present depressed condition of the operative jewellers of Birmingham by wearing British jewels'. The presentation was of a bracelet, the centre with a sprig of diamonds on blue enamel bordered by nine pearls in oak leaf settings, the tapered band enamelled with olive branches, cornucopia and linked circles (symbolizing 'peace and plenty for ever') with roses, thistles and shamrocks in between and with diamonds and rubies in the buckle clasp; there was also a seal representing the Warwick vase supported by Ceres and Mercury and over-flowing with grapes, and a watch-chain of vine and oak motifs: at this time almost as much attention was lavished upon a watch key as upon its companion seal. The last item was a buckle for the Queen's belt, itself of strap and buckle design. These strap and buckle motifs became popular after Her Majesty as Sovereign became invested as the head of the Order of the Garter.

All of these jewels are typical of the period, and especially the elaborate symbolism with which they are overloaded. Their total value was put at £400. It is particularly interesting that the delegation emphasized that making the jewels had engaged the skills of twenty-two different trades. This complex specialization was and is a peculiarity of the jewellery trade. In Birmingham there were makers of gold chains, silver chains, gold jewellery, gilt jewellery, cases, studs and links and wedding rings.

Birmingham had been growing in importance as a centre of jewellery manufacture since the end of the previous century. The demise of the shoebuckle trade left a pool of suitably skilled and intelligent labour that the infant jewellery industry could draw upon. The fact that coal gas was laid on early is also significant because a reliable source of heat is one of the working jeweller's first needs. In spite of the depression Birmingham's leadership in the manufacture of cheap and medium-priced jewellery really began in the forties. Not only were people wearing more jewellery, but the invention of electrogilding allowed it to be produced more cheaply. Good diamond jewellery could only be made by hand, and that is still the case today, but the medium class of semi-precious jewellery, of gold ornaments set with garnets, amethysts, aquamarines and so on, and cheap costume jewellery of gilt-metal and paste could be made satisfactorily by mechanical methods. There was nothing new about this: the ancient Minoans, Greeks and even the Vikings used dies or punches to produce repeats of a design that pleased them. At the close of the eighteenth century stampings from sheet metal were widely used in jewellery mainly as components to be assembled together with hand-made elements—ornamental chain links, for example, were mainly punched from sheet gold. In Birmingham two machines were in use, the deadweight kick stamp which used the power of a falling twenty pound weight to punch the metal into the contours of the die, and the hand press which worked on the principal of the old printing or linen press in which power was transmitted by a vertical screw. Most jewellery was made on the hand press. In the first half of the century machines were worked by muscle power only: it was not until the sixties that steam or gas engines were harnessed to the jewellery workshops.

The key operative was the die sinker. The die was a block of hard steel into which was sunk a recess corresponding exactly to the shape of the projected jewel or part of a jewel. A punch was made which fitted this exactly with an allowance for the thickness of the metal, of course. This work requires great skill and concentration and a good man could earn as much as 70s. a week, a lot of money in those days. The die was fixed in the bed of the machine with the punch accurately aligned above it. A sheet of metal, previously annealed, or softened by heat, was laid on top of the die. The punch was driven home by the machine, squashing the metal into every nook and cranny of the die. Sometimes only one stamping was used and the back of the jewel left hollow. But obviously if the back of the piece is enclosed with another sheet of metal the result will be not only much stronger, but also neater in appearance, and this was usually done. The prudent workman never enclosed this space altogether: he always left a hole somewhere, even if it were no bigger than a pin. It may take some finding, but it is almost invariably there. It was not just a quaint custom. The hole is a gas vent: if the space is enclosed altogether the air and gases inside would expand when the workman heated the piece and even explode in his face; many a man has lost his sight like this. In the manufacture of the cheaper types of gilt jewellery the stampings were often turned out in one workshop and assembled in another. It was the factor who co-ordinated these operations and often supplied the raw materials— he too who pocketed most of the profit. Many of the simpler operations were done by 'garret masters' who worked in cheaply rented attics and employed their own children making wedding rings, for example. In most towns jewellers tended to gather together in one district, partly for mutual security against thieves, partly for the convenience of buyers and factors. In Birmingham it was around St. Paul's churchyard and until quite recently, in the Hockley district. In London, where the best quality work was produced, it used to be in Clerkenwell. Some workshops employed perhaps a dozen men, but conditions

Fig. 2 THE JEWELLER AT WORK
(*The Book of English Trades and Library of the Useful Arts*, London, F. C. and J. Rivington, 1821)

were ideal for the skilled and enterprising man who wanted to set up for himself (fig. 2). All he needed was a week's rent for a small room, a jeweller's bench, a leather apron, the tools he already possessed and the down-payment on a gas blowlamp which was easily obtained on credit from the gas company. Working conditions were nearly always bad as these premises had invariably been built as dwelling houses. Such fine work obviously took a heavy toll on the eyesight and to reduce glare the workman stood a glass vessel of copper sulphate solution against the light. The workshop was, and still is, organized so that not a scrap of the precious raw material was wasted. The bench had a deep bay cut out of its thick beechwood top so that a sheepskin could be suspended beneath it to catch the filings, or lemel. The surface of the bench was lovingly swept with a rabbit's foot* to which the filings will not stick. A wooden grid covered the floor; it was lifted at the end of the day so that the floor could be swept and the sweepings sent to the refiners together with any old files or aprons. The washing water was carefully filtered, and it was even said that the jeweller would comb his hair and beard over a basin before knocking off for the day. Gold coins provided the jeweller with metal, melted down into bars and then rolled down or drawn into sheets or wires as required. It was also possible, by the process of 'sweating', for the jeweller to get his gold and spend the money too. The workshop apprentice was given a bag containing a hundred gold sovereigns and told to shake it till his arms ached. At the end of this alchemical process the money, battered but still negotiable, was removed, leaving a few precious pennyweights of gold dust in the corners of the bag. The jeweller got his materials wherever he could. Mr. Gerald Smooklers' father recalled buying a teaspoon from a maidservant for threepence and making from it three pairs of earrings which he sold for six shillings.

Much of Birmingham's cheaper output was destined to be hawked in the street-markets and on the doorsteps. The pedlar's wholesaler was the 'swag shop'. As Henry Mayhew described it 'the window of a swag shop presented, in the like crowding and in greater confusion, an array of brooches (some in coloured glass to imitate rubies, topazes &c., some containing portraits, deeply coloured, in purple attire, and red cheeks, and some being very large cameos), time pieces with and without glasses'† and so on. Those who go to jewellery auctions will recognize many brooches like this among the job lots in nearly every sale, also perhaps, a plump gilt finger ring. These 'belcher rings' were the stock in trade of the 'fawney dropper' and they used to cost sevenpence a dozen at the swag shop. 'Fawney' was the current argot for a ring, and through this simple medium the artist could earn a living in many ways. 'A woman' as Mayhew's informant explained 'is made up so as to appear in the family way—pretty far gone—and generally with a face as long as a boy's kite'. She would then find a sympathetic female audience and tell them how her husband had run off and left her, and how she was obliged to sell her gold wedding ring to provide a mouthful of food for her starving children. It rarely failed. But the real aristocrat of fawney dropping was the man who worked the racetracks. Costumed like a

* This rabbit's or hare's foot was a kind of emblem of the jeweller's calling in France. When a lad finished his apprenticeship in France it was ceremonially suspended around his neck with a ribbon. He was then expected to stand his mates a meal.
† *London Labour and the London Poor*, London, 1861.

contemporary swell in white gloves, choker, quizzing glass on a ribbon and all the rest of it, he would explain in suitable accents how a friend had wagered that he could not sell gold rings for a penny each. In fact a wager like this had once taken place and the fame of it had spread far and wide. The rings would be displayed on a pot-lid lined with tinfoil. This species of fawney dropper was of necessity a bird of passage whose stay on any one pitch was limited to the length of time it took his first genuine customer to get to the nearest pawnshop and back. Travelling tinkers also made sham rings out of worn out brass buttons.

Crimes of stealth and deception were increasing. Not only was there a variety of fawney droppers and confidence men of that kind, there were pickpockets, 'prop-nailers' who stole pins and brooches, and 'thimble screwers' who plucked watches from their guards. But these crimes did not inspire the same terror as the bloody robberies with violence which had formerly made townspeople too frightened to wear their jewels or watches in public, and this was another reason for the popularity of personal ornaments in the middle of the century.

Criminals, whose lives depended so much upon chance, were given to the carrying of charms and talismans especially 'Newgate tokens'. These were made from copper or silver coins and crudely punched with hearts, initials or a motto like 'once these hearts in love was joined, now one is free the other confined'. Sometimes the sentiments expressed were obscene or seditious. Not all can have been made in prison and some from their design and workmanship look as though they may have been made by sailors.

It is interesting to note that in the great shops at this time jewellery was sold by women as well as men. Shopwomen were mentioned as working for Rundell and Bridge in the early years of the century. When Mr. Dorrit visited a Parisian jewellers he was attended by a sprightly little woman who came out of a green velvet bower to attend him.

In 1844 the Queen presented a 'richly jewelled turquoise serpent bracelet, value £25 as a prize in the lady's archery contest at Prado'. The serpent design, one of the most successful of Victorian fashions, was already in style both for collars and bracelets (plate 21). The bodies of the serpents were of a supple gold linking that suggests very strongly the dry scaly touch of a reptile. Sometimes the head was pavé-set all over with turquoises, with perhaps a small cabochon ruby to suggest the eye. With this type the body might also be sprinkled all over with turquoises, one collet-set on each scale. In a bracelet the reptile would simply coil once about the wrist with its head as the clasp so that it appeared to be biting its tail like a cookery-book whiting. The collars were usually designed so that the tip of the tail clicked into the side of the head which enabled the jeweller to hang a heart-shaped locket from the creature's jaws. The most sumptuous bracelets in this style were enamelled in translucent royal blue with bursts of diamond flame on the crown of the head and the snout. This kind of bracelet took one and a quarter turns about the wrist and was made of hinged enamelled segments, the joints masked with diamonds and sprung so that the whole thing could be wound around the wrist and would remain there without a clasp. Sometimes the enamel of the body is sprinkled with rose diamonds in teardrop settings and occasionally a white Hungarian opal is set in the head. These are very satisfactory jewels, delightful to wear and feel and see, and beautifully engineered. Unfortunately enamel is a brittle substance and if the bracelets are roughly flexed it tends to fly off in chips, and it is a rarity and a great pleasure to find one whole and unblemished. These serpents have a mythological, heraldic quality which charms away the repugnance which some people have for reptiles without weakening their ancient potency and mystery. Somehow they contrive to be serpents without being snakes.

Very rarely the snake idea was taken more literally in large collars that are as close to nature as the goldsmith's and enameller's very considerable skill could make them. Every scale was decorated with champlevé enamels and so prefectly fitted and jointed that realism comes a little too close for comfort. These jewels are of Swiss origin and very uncommon.

Contemporary with the serpent in jewels was the *croix-à-la-jeanette* (Plate 16c), and sometimes the two designs overlap! Originally this was a French peasant jewel but although in its original form it differed from region to region the jewel worn by the ladies of London and Paris showed little variation. Although the materials of which it was made might differ, the design always took the form of a heart with a cross hanging beneath it. The cross could be of royal blue or turquoise enamel, sometimes of carbuncles skilfully cut to shape and fitted in the arms. The cross was usually 'fleury' with diamond foliage sprouting from the tips, and was sometimes entwined with a diamond serpent. The heart would always be of the same kind of work as the cross, sometimes forming a *couloir* or slide, through which the sinewy chain ran in a loop which served to support the cross.

Eyeglasses for men, introduced in the thirties, reached a climax of absurdity in 1844 (plate 12f). Either circular or in the form of a rounded oblong they were framed with a narrow edging of the seashell and feather scroll decoration already mentioned and a short handle projected from one side in the manner of a frying pan. A ribbon attached to a wide ring at the end of this was fastened to a waistcoat button. The effortless retention of an eyeglass in the eye was a necessary accomplishment of the man-about-town. A journalist of the time wrote:* 'I have seen this passion carried so far as to decorate the riding whip with an eyeglass as if the poor equestrian could not distinguish between the horse's head and tail.'

Undoubtedly the most powerful influence on the fashions of this period came from the Middle East. The appropriation of Algeria by France in 1842 unleashed a spate of North African designs upon fashionable Europe. There were burnouses and kaftans, Algerian slippers and moorish capes and coiffures. As is usual in the first half of the century the influence on jewellery was an oblique one and there was no effort as far as is known to copy or borrow the jewels of the harem. Instead the elaborate knots and tassels of arab costume were simulated in gold or gilt metal and worn as brooches or bracelet centres. This theme of elaborate and sometimes tortuous interlacement runs right through mid-nineteenth-century jewellery. Lithe branches were entwined about an amethyst or a citrine in a deep collet—this kind of brooch needs looking at very closely as the metal is all too often only gilt, and the stone a paste. Gnarled and decayed branches

* *Illustrated London News*, 6th January 1844.

were often incongruously treated in the same way. Gold ribbons, too, were elaborately looped and interlaced, with pendants and festoons of plaited chain hanging below (plate 22a). Brooches and earrings based on two or three interconnected oval chain links were very fashionable at the time, and a brooch of this design formed part of the magnificent parure presented to Grisi the singer by the Czar when she performed in St. Petersburg. At their most splendid, jewels in this design had the rings of blue enamel enlaced with diamond foliage (plate 23b), but most were of gold encrusted with filigree and applied with a fern leaf, and with almandine garnets, of such a deep purple colour they could be mistaken for amethysts, set together like a cluster of fruit. Sometimes the garnets are accompanied by pale lemon-yellow chrysolites. These jewels may still be found as they were sold, as a demi-parure of brooch and earrings, still in their little heart-shaped case of plum morocco and velvet tooled with gold.

Carbuncles, or blood red cabochon garnets are the most typical stone of this time. This gem is often so dense in colour that it is hollowed out at the back to make it paler. A typical arrangement would be of two or three large egg-shaped carbuncles set among diamond foliate scrolls, with a third stone as a drop. The garnets in the best work were mounted so skilfully that the setting is almost invisible, giving the impression that the stone is swelling out of the jewel like a ripe, luscious fruit. Long diamond drops sway from this kind of jewel like pendulous racemes of laburnum or wisteria. The tapered shimmering drops are typical of diamond jewellery in the 'pampille style' as it has been called. In the forties a diamond bouquet occasionally has leaves of dark green enamel, but royal blue is the most usual enamel colour. It is as well to remember that blue has the curious effect of making a diamond look whiter than it really is.

About 1840 the practice of 'colouring' gold came into widespread use. The piece was steeped in a mordant which dissolved out the alloying metal at the surface leaving a lightly frosted layer of pure gold. The idea of leaving a surface plain and undecorated seems to have filled the nineteenth-century jeweller with horror and every visible millimetre was either engraved or flooded with enamel. Enamels were often used in large unbroken areas and as a certain irregularity in the background is necessary if it is to get a purchase this technical necessity was turned to good account. Sometimes the background was engine turned, or 'guilloché', that is to say engraved by machine with a pattern of intersecting spirals. This is often seen on the backs of watches, with or without enamel. Often a sparkling effect is obtained by gouging small chips out of the ground with an engraving tool. This is wonderfully effective with the dark green enamel, which is clear enough for the glints from the bright chisel cuts to reflect right through, but not quite so effective with the denser royal blue shade. A cameo or a miniature encircled by a ring of this enamel is occasionally seen with crisp baroque scrolls curling over it at the four cardinal points. These cuir roulée scrolls which look as though they have been snipped out of parchment are a part of the baroque style which left such a deep imprint on the period.

Towards the fifties the hair was worn parted at the centre and dressed over the ears and a tiara was invented to follow this line, framing the face rather than encircling the head. The design was of the traditional garland of flowers which was often orthodox in every respect save that the two end sprays could be adjusted to hang down the temples (plate 24).

In 1843 flowers and diamonds were often mixed—'the fashion of flowers now being intermingled with diamonds and other precious stones is now completely in vogue'*. Roses and camelias seem to have been the greatest favourites. The 'coiffure lamballé', for example, was a confection of roses and a blonde scarf entwined with a rivière of diamonds.

Cameos returned to favour in 1842. The berthe, a deep band of lace which followed the low décolletage from front to back, needed some kind of accent to its bold horizontal line, and a cameo brooch was ideal for this (plate 23c). Most cameos of this period were cut from shell. Seashell cameos were carved long before, but the earlier pieces were usually small in size and of very thin shell, pale buff or greyish in tint. Now, however, the conch shell was imported for this purpose from the tropical seas of Africa and the West Indies. Each mollusc yielded enough to make one really fine cameo which was taken from the top of the shell. Here the creamy outer layer in which the design was cut was thick enough for carving in deep relief. The rest was used for commercial work, the thinnest sections of all being given to the apprentices. After a suitable oval of shell had been sawn out it was cemented to the top of a stick for ease of handling. The rough brown outer layer was then cut away and the design drawn on the white of the shell with a brass point. Sometimes the subject was biblical—crowded crucifixion scenes were not uncommon—but usually it was selected from respectable classical mythology; Minerva with her owl, helmeted Athene or Mars, Demeter, Flora, or a decorous Bacchante were most common. The design was roughed out in silhouette with files and chisels. At this early stage it was polished all over with sulphuric acid and pumice. The detail was then worked in with the result that the matt-finished creamy white of the carving contrasted with the highly polished cornelian tints of the background. These brooches could be of enormous size, sometimes as big as the palm of the hand. Sometimes the subject of a shell cameo was clad in jewels and costume of inlaid precious stone. These cameos habillés are of Italian origin and quite rare (colour plate Ed).

Coral jewellery was reintroduced to the court of France in 1844 by the duchesse d'Aumale. It was popular for a time in many kinds of jewels, but not until the sixties did the fashion for wearing coral ornaments become a craze.

Seed-pearl jewellery of a particularly interesting kind seems to have been greatly admired (plate 25). The framework or base of these jewels was fretted from a sheet of mother-of-pearl and the pearls, which are not much bigger than confectioners' hundreds and thousands, are sewn to it with white horsehair. A great deal of this jewellery is still to be found, sometimes in quite elaborate parures—a châtelaine brooch with one, two or three drops, a collar, and a pair of long pendant earrings are almost a minimum. The designs are always openwork, of buxom cuir roulée scrolls, honeysuckle motifs, vine, and even hop designs. They are invariably pavé all over with seed-pearls with larger lentil-sized pearls here and there—the latter often turn out to be imitation although this seems

* *Illustrated London News*, 4th February 1843.

to have little effect on the value of the jewel. Such jewels are very fragile and only rarely to be found wholly intact. It is almost impossible to find anyone to undertake repairs to this work, so that this kind of jewel can often be bought cheaply. If the collector has the patience and skill to do it for himself it would be well worth while.

Horsehair jewellery, minutely woven in a kind of crochet work, is certainly rare but it can be found now and again. Sometimes black and white hairs are used for contrast—in the links of a chain, for example (plate 19a). Sometimes the hairs are dyed red.

Staghorn was used for brooches, usually carved *à jour* with the animal at bay in a garland of inter-woven branches. Ivory was treated in the same way, but the greatest test of the carver's skill was the cross on a chain, the links carved from the solid and without a join. Much of this work came from Switzerland.

Jewellery was well represented at the great Crystal Palace Exhibition of 1851, although there were some interesting omissions too. Earrings were not to be seen, and neither were gentlemen's fob seals. Baroque designs proliferated and the jewels of Messrs Levy Prins of Brussels had an eccentric swing to them which was unmistakably rococo. The same kind of asymmetry is apparent in the brooches shown by Ellis and Son of Exeter, although this was imposed upon the design as much by the novel and ingenious method of fastening as by the dictates of fashion. For some reason this style of brooch never caught on in 1851, although it was to make a highly successful comeback in the nineteen-twenties.

A most unlikely material, granite, appeared in the jewels of Messrs Rettie and Sons of Aberdeen and bracelets made of it are not uncommon in the antique market today. The pink or grey rock was fashioned into prisms or cylinders which were capped with silver and linked into bracelets. As the exhibition catalogue says 'the hard and impracticable nature of granite would seem to defy delicacy and minutiae of workmanship, and to preclude it from being an article of personal decoration', a judgement which is hard to fault. However, no collection of Victorian semi-precious jewellery would be complete without a granite jewel.

Bog oak jewels also are another result of the Victorian quest for novelty at almost any cost. Huge oaks, half petrified, lie buried in the Irish peat bogs, and this wood, nearly as hard as rock, was carved into shamrocks and Irish harps and made into jewels. Yellowish green Connemara marble was also carved into jewels and charms.

Fossil marbles from Purbeck were mounted in silver as brooches and bracelets: sometimes the stones were inlaid in elaborately contrasted diapered designs, but this is unusual. The beautiful purple fluorspar found around Matlock and known as 'blue john' or 'Derbyshire spar' was also set into simple jewellery. Spiral ammonite fossils were lapped and polished down to expose the cell-like structure of their interior and also mounted as gems, either in a silver or a jet mount (plate 23d). These materials were prized because they were British, and also because in some mystic way they were felt to be 'educational'. Trivial though these articles are they stand at the meeting of two great Victorian streams of motivation—patriotism and self-improvement. This was also the age of steam and the railways were gobbling up the green English miles like insatiable caterpillars: all sorts of people were now going to the seaside for their holidays, and wherever they went they brought back souvenirs. White Sidmouth pebbles were considered good enough to mount in a precious setting of purple enamel. Visitors combed the Brighton beaches for agates which they took to the local lapidary to be cut and mounted as souvenirs. He, being no fool, would recognize that the dull and lifeless pebble with which he had been presented would turn out to be, when cut, a dull and lifeless gem, and rather than have a dissatisfied, and possibly non-paying customer, he would substitute a cheap and spectacular agate from Germany!

The jewels of Lemonnier* in the Great Exhibition show that the fashion for long cascading drops introduced in the forties was still very much alive. This technique was dazzlingly exploited in the jewels made by him for the Queen of Spain (fig. 3). Typically they were of emeralds and diamonds, for fine emeralds are the glory of Spanish jewellery. Thousands of stones from the Colombian mines were brought back to Spain in colonial times. The tiara is of traditional strawberry leaf form, but a sinuous rope of gems is loosely festooned over it to hang down at the sides. The stomacher brooch is a branch of huge blooms and emerald leaves from which diamond drops hang like glittering Spanish moss. Two aiguillettes—an interesting brooch designed to be worn on the shoulder—show a similarly intelligent use of movement. Beauty of form is of course the basis of good jewel design to which the flavours of colour, texture and movement may be added to taste. Colour must be measured sparingly and precisely, and the same is even more true of movement. The wobble of a badly sprung tremblant flower or the lurch of a badly balanced pendant can make an otherwise lovely jewel look quite comical. And yet with cunning a small movement can light the diamond with a kind of magic fire.

At this time diamond jewels were on a lavish scale. Until 1844 supplies of stones from Brazil, the primary producer, had been insufficient to meet the demand and the Amsterdam cutters had long periods of unemployment between shipments. In 1844 however the rich Bahia fields were discovered and from then until 1856 when production began to fall off supplies were plentiful.

The niello technique is something of a curiosity in modern European metalwork. Russian silver snuffboxes often carry a nielloed scene of the usual troika, with or without pursuing wolves, but otherwise it was rarely used except by a few Paris firms. Niello is a metallic black substance used like champlevé enamel. It is made by heating silver and sulphur together in a crucible; the resulting anthracite black lump is then ground up very finely, the design engraved on the surface of the metal—usually silver for contrast—and the niello melted into it. The effect is that of a dark metal inlay. Good niello work is characterized by a kind of unspectacular elegance, but the bracelet exhibited by S. D. Gass of Regent Street manages to achieve an almost annihilating vulgarity. In spite of the fact that niello is not suited to the miniaturist's technique, the artist, Crewe, used it regardless, to portray the Queen and presumably the infant Prince of Wales on an enormous plaque at the centre. Gass also contributed to the exhibition a pendant with a highly

---

* G. Lemonnier became crown jeweller in 1851. His fortunes declined with those of the Empire, however, and the firm went out of business after the Franco-Prussian war. He died in 1882.

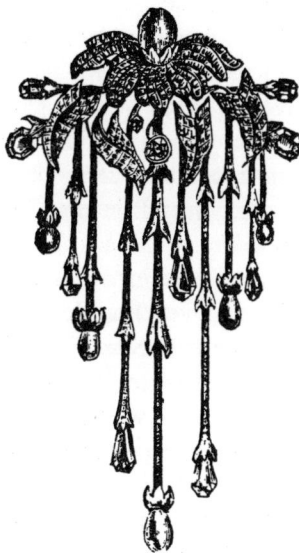

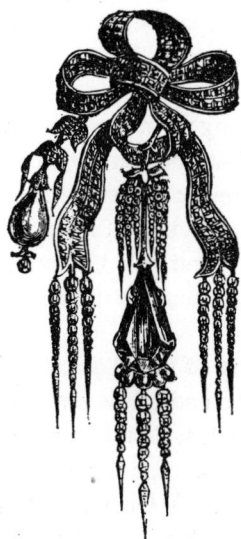

Fig. 3 JEWELS MADE BY LEMONNIER FOR THE QUEEN OF SPAIN
(*Catalogue of the 1851 Great Exhibition*)

allegorical 'Britannia expelling the dragon of anarchy' in diamonds and rubies beneath a gothic arch with pillars of carved garnet. From the technical point of view Gass were very fine jewellers, but this tendency towards florid decoration and over-elaboration was apparent in many of their jewels.

Bracelets with miniatures as their centres had already been fashionable for some time (plate 17a); the Queen was wearing one on the royal visit to Scotland in 1842, and in the following year Princess Clementine wore one with a portrait of her husband at a fête-champêtre at Orléans. Usually the miniature was an oval one and quite large, with sides of superbly engineered scale-like linking. Sometimes the miniature was concealed beneath a hinged cover. Bracelets like this with large box-like centres were called 'cadenas' bracelets (plate 27a). Sometimes, instead of chain, the back was a hoop of curved sections joined together. Bracelet designs proliferated and it was not uncommon for a woman to wear several on each wrist, but little other jewellery. In the early forties the expanding bracelet made an appearance; each of the identical segments of this kind of bracelet was pierced longitudinally with two holes so that strands of elastic could be threaded through it from end to end. Its advantages were obvious: it could be made to fit any wrist, plump or lean, and could be worn anywhere on the arm. Expanding bracelets were being worn well into the fifties on the evidence of contemporary fashion plates and probably into the sixties too. An interesting if not very attractive variant of the expanding bracelet, which probably dates from this later period, was made from plain discs of Cornish serpentine of contrasted brown and olive shades stuck back to back and threaded on elastic. This reversible bracelet was probably made as a tourist novelty.

Around 1850, too, bracelets often sported a pendant which hung from the centre and presumably swung over the back of the hand in wear (plate 26c). Both pendant and centre were detachable so that the bracelet could be worn on a neckchain, or, by attaching pin and hook, as a brooch. The sides were of tubular chain of oval cross-section. Two like this which came on to the market not long ago were set with peridots and pale Ceylon sapphires respectively. The gem most typical of the period, however, is perhaps the emerald, a Spanish fashion set by the Empress Eugenie.

The jarretière bracelet was of strap and buckle form. The strap of fluted gold linking was held by a squarish sliding clasp (plate 27b). The clasp and the end of the strap were nearly always decorated, with perhaps engraving and small emeralds, or turquoise blue enamel and pale rubies. The loose end of the strap was allowed to dangle free and even hung with a fringe of tagged drops to accentuate the effect (plate 26b). Occasionally the strap and buckle idea was taken more literally with a properly spiked buckle and a perforated band (plate 26a).

Following on from the jarretière was the manchette, designed as a broad, slightly tapered cuff (plate 27c). Even on this theme variations were possible: some were fastened with a row of buttons with perhaps one button coyly left undone, others were decorated with diamond laces.

A number of successful diamond bracelets were made in simple designs of overlapping C scrolls or open-centred circles tapering from an elaboration of these motifs at the centre.

The war in Russia meant that even more miniatures and locks of hair were worn in jewellery. The Crimea had another interesting and, for the Western European collector, fortunate side-effect. Time and time again in Britain and France one encounters mid-century jewels bearing Moscow and Petersburg assay marks which are clearly of Russian origin. One can only presume that these were presents brought home by returning servicemen.

The Crimea may have had something to do with the popularity of malachite jewels at this time. Malachite, a beautifully marked green ore of copper had long been mined in the Ural mountains and was traditionally used by Russian lapidaries for inlay work. There is more likely another reason for its popularity in England, however: an important discovery of malachite had already been made at the mines of Burra Burra in South Australia which was said to rival the Russian material in beauty and quality. This is borne out by the inscription on the back of the brooch illustrated on plate 23a which bears the date 1851, though war was not declared on Russia for another three years. Malachite is quite soft as semi-precious stones go and can be fashioned without difficulty. Usually it was inlaid in silver and the surface then ground flat and polished.

Many suites of buttons in gold decorated with enamels or gems were made in the middle of the century. Sometimes they are found stitched on a ribbon of black velvet and it is clear that they were worn around the throat from the evidence of contemporary portraits.

As we have seen, great ingenuity was lavished on the dressing of the hair at this time, and all manner of combs, pins and accessories were invented to keep it in place. Often these were improvised from necklaces, brooches and strings of pearls and beads, sometimes they were made expressly for the purpose. Part of Hunt and Roskell's exhibit at the Great Exhibition was a diamond ostrich feather for the head which must have been one of the first of many jewels to this design made in the latter half of the century. But the ephemeral nature of hair styles meant that the more outré accessories were necessarily expendable. In the mid-fifties two pins were worn connected by a beaded chain and hung with long dangling pendants. The materials were usually gilt brass with beads of blown glass to represent jet, or stained bone simulating coral. An original and doubtless short-lived hair style of 1859 was hung with four pendants, each composed of two joined chain links.

Throughout this period many designs seemed deliberately to fly in the face of nature. At first this was probably a part of the new romanticism and its cult of the mysterious and the grotesque. There was a quest for novelty in almost any form and at any cost. Unlikely and unsuitable things were used in jewellery and designs did things which all the laws of nature and commonsense declare to be impossible. Decayed branches flex and intertwine like lithe and supple shoots, eyes appear without faces, hands without arms. Towards the sixties a more empirical approach became apparent: innovation turned into experimentation and designs became taughter and altogether more disciplined.

4. Second Empire and High Victorian

The 1860s were years of almost reckless vanity: corsets were laced so tightly as to cause broken ribs and even death; crinolines extended to igloo-like proportions, so that rooms which had formerly been spacious enough for twenty or thirty guests were now crowded with half that number. Once again there was an emperor in France, and this emperor, like the last, had a lovely and fashionable bride. Masked balls which enabled women to exchange their stiflingly uncomfortable clothes for garments in which they could actually breathe were very popular. At such a ball in 1860 one lady appeared as the goddess of fire, incandescent with rubies; another, bespangled with diamonds, represented the sky. A good fairy, in a flame coloured mantle to which ostrich feathers had been attached with huge emeralds, also wore a double diadem hung with diamond pendeloques and two immense necklaces; her wand was of gold and carbuncles and even her slippers were semée with gems. In such a glittering assembly who was to know which was paste and which the produce of the mine. The jeweller did a roaring trade; so also did the fabricators of paste and bijoux d'art like Bon who specialized in the counterfeiting of opal and lapis lazuli, and Savary whose 'mock jewels might be worn at a party without risk of detection'. This was an age of extravagance both real and simulated in which presents for new year parties were sometimes hired to impress the other guests and in which, at Anna Deslions' celebrated gambling salon a huge Chinese bowl was kept replenished with gold coins for the use of her friends.

Poured into her stays and stockaded by the touch-me-not perimeter of her crinoline, a woman's most typical characteristics were either invisibly wrapped or grotesquely distorted. Into this physically deprived climate the new hair styles of 1862 which exposed a woman's ears in all their rosy nudity brought the radiant promise of a false dawn. Ears were a focus of desire, gallants raved about them, jewellers vied with one another to produce ornaments which would do them justice. In 1860 the hair covered the ears either partly or completely and when they were worn earrings took the form of spherical or bomb-shaped drops. At this time a Paris fashion correspondent wrote: 'We cannot believe that this yellow invasion of earrings, waistbands and buckles is destined for a long existence.'* How wrong they were: this was no more than a preliminary skirmish, for the real invasion was yet to come. In 1864 the same correspondent had this to say:† 'The spirit of exaggeration which we have so frequently observed is now applied to earrings which have now acquired almost dangerous proportions . . . all forms have been adopted so that now we have the

* *Illustrated London News*, July 1860.
† *Illustrated London News*, 29th October 1864.

triangular, the long, the wide and the round cymbal-shaped earrings, of a fearful weight in gold'. To this list he might have added the lozenge, the trident, the inverted drop hanging from a key-fret or within loops of gold, the Greek amphora, the chandelier, and the innumerable designs of concentric ovals fringed with gold drops (plate 28). If anything stamps a jewel as belonging to the late sixties and early seventies it is this row of little pendants, teardrop, oatgrain or spindle shaped. Most typical of all, however, is a saucy fringe of short tubular chains, each tagged with a little point like a shoelace: these appeared on both brooches and earrings during these years. 'Novelty' earrings took many forms: a gold parrot swinging on its perch, gold flower baskets—even enamelled willow pattern plates. The fashion for large earrings seems to have originated in England.

Very large and elaborate parures were not all that common at this time, and the most usual suite was of earrings and a brooch which did double duty as a pendant. The pendant frequently was of plain oval form with a light incrustation of filigree and could be set with carbuncle, turquoise, pink coral or emeralds. A shimmering fringe gave life to the whole thing which hung from a wedge-shaped loop that could be readily unhooked, allowing the jewel to be worn as a brooch. Very often a spool or bobbin motif was introduced between loop and pendant (plate 30b). Fashion plates sometimes show a woman wearing a brooch like this flanked by the matching earrings on a ribbon at her throat—typical of the ingenuity which the Victorians brought to the wearing of jewels. Usually the chain from which a pendant hangs is a single strand of the Brazilian pattern used nowadays for keychains. The most characteristic necklace used two strands of this 'snake chain', one looped from the other in four festoons terminated with serpents' heads, with a pendant hanging from the centre and one or two more at each side. Occasionally, and very successfully, the pendants are carbuncle amphorae (plate 29). Undoubtedly the most powerful influence to shape the jewel designs of this period was classical Greek, just as it had been a kind of bastard baroque in the years that went before. And just as in the forties and the fifties the approach to design had been romantic, now it was scientific. Jewellers seemed suddenly to awaken to the properties of the metals and gems they were using and to exploit them for their own sake. Now gold was hardly ever smothered with engraving as it once had been. It was still 'coloured', or lightly frosted, but apart from that was for the most part left untouched so that it reflected a soft velvety gleam. Any decoration was in the form of filigree and granulation sparsely applied in the Greek manner. A trick optical effect was often cleverly exploited in the circular brooches that were so popular. The centre of the brooch, a boss of pavé-set turquoise (as in plate 31b), or a bouton of pink coral would be surrounded by courses of decorative wirework, and around this a trough of plain metal would be sunk below the surface so that it reflected the intricacies of the border like a distorting mirror (plate 30b).

Stars were a favourite decorative motif: set with diamonds or half-pearls they formed the centres of nearly every kind of jewel, applied to a domed oval background of gold, ultramarine or sky blue enamel, or inlaid into the surface of a carbuncle or a cabochon amethyst (plate 28). Sometimes, however, it was used on its own as a hair ornament in diamonds or unset gold. These star ornaments of the sixties are inclined to be flat almost as though they have been snipped out with shears. The mounts are frequently all of gold and outlined with a thin border of blue enamel. They should not be confused with the star brooches of the nineties which are more frequently met with and are of a much more elaborate design.

Some jewels, particularly lockets and half-hoop rings around 1860 show an enamelled basket-weave pattern on their visible surfaces (plate 31c). This was also done with diamond openwork. The London firm of Hancock used a similar device on many jewels especially with turquoises and diamonds. The idea was not new, and among the wedding gifts to the Princess Royal in 1858 was a locket-centred bracelet in a diapered pattern of rubies and diamonds. As far back as the Great Exhibition, too, the firm of Emmanuel exhibited 'a small diamond-shaped brooch divided into chequers of rubies, each square separated from the other by rows of brilliants, having something of the effect of a harlequin's coat'. A similar motif forms the centre of the pendant illustrated as plate 30b.

At the 1862 London Exhibition Hancock displayed a tiara of a very open scroll design with nine graduated emerald drops hanging in the interstices. This design probably came from across the channel where it had been revived from a First Empire style. And this was not the only Imperial fashion to return in the reign of the other Napoleon; there was a veritable craze for cameos—not the flimsy shell cameos of the forties and fifties, but cameos of stone like onyx (plate 30d), sardonyx, agate and even sometimes emerald. More often than not the workmanship on these hardstone cameos is technically excellent, the commonest failing being a certain stolidity of posture and expression. Cameo cutting is the art of the Italian just as jewellery is the art of the French and there were some fine engravers working at this time: Neri* and the younger Pistruccit† in Rome, Bassi in Florence and Luigi Isler in Paris. It is in large brooches that one usually finds these gems, sometimes in a plain border of half-pearls with a wisp of blue enamel (see colour plate Ea), sometimes with diamonds.

The agates from which these stones were cut were often artificially stained. Agates are formed in layers and it is these stripes which give the stone its beauty and make it so attractive to the cameo cutter. The opaque white layers are dense and impervious, the translucent parts of the stone more porous. For centuries lapidaries had exploited this property of agate by steeping it in honey which was taken up by the more absorbent parts of the gem. The stone was then heated to carbonize the sugar and turn it black—the white parts into which the honey never penetrated of course stayed white. A modification of this process was used by the lapidaries of Idar Oberstein in Germany to produce 'onyx' for the cameo cutter and for mourning jewellery. Metallic salts were substituted for the sugar to produce other colours when nature had failed to oblige—chrysoprase green, cornelian pink and lapis lazuli blue in particular.

In 1862 a curious gem engraving technique appeared in England and remained in style for many years. This was a kind of crystal intaglio used mainly for studs and cufflinks, although it was set in other jewels also (plate 31f). The design was deeply cut into the

* Paolo Neri, born Rome 1813.
† Elena Pistrucci, 1822–86; Maria Elisa Pistrucci, 1824–81.

back of a crystal cabochon and then painted and backed with a slice of mother-of-pearl. This gives an extraordinary effect, rather like a French paperweight, in which the subject, usually a dog or a horse's head, appears to be embedded in the crystal as though in a kind of aspic. Lambert and Co. of London appear to have been the first to market this kind of jewel. It seems that to begin with the intaglios were the work of one craftsman, a Mr. Cooke, but from the quantity and diverse quality of the jewels to be seen on the market today many others must have followed suit. There is an interesting similarity between the animals on these intaglios and the pastel drawings of winsome terriers and mournful racehorses that street artists do on the pavement outside the London National Gallery, almost as though they were part of the same folk tradition. The price of a well-mounted crystal by Cooke was quoted as being between £7 and £10, so by current standards they were quite dear. Game birds were another favourite subject, and a pair of cufflinks often portrayed mallard, cock pheasant, partridge and woodcock. These are of course men's jewels, but crystal intaglios of flowers, brightly feathered tropical birds and monograms were set in ladies' jewellery. The monograms were of entwined gothic initials tinted white and often set in a rim of gold, studded with small onyx cabochons. This type of jewel was often selected as a royal presentation and when engraved with the cipher and surmounted by a crown was perfect for the purpose. They were imitated by crudely cast glass intaglios, roughly painted. Sometimes, too, a rough print on paper of a fox mask was set beneath a glass cabochon and mounted as a tiepin.

It will already be apparent that there was growing in the sixties and seventies a new adventurousness in the treatment of gems. Small turquoises were often 'calibré-cut' to fit snugly together in target clusters with pearls at their centres (plate 30c): garnets were segmented and fitted together as rosettes, usually with a star at the centre, and used in the centres of both brooches and bracelets. It seems as though the jeweller had ceased to think of gems as mysterious immutable substances and begun to regard them as just another material to be ground and polished into whatever form the design required. Perhaps too the British Queen's love for her Highland home in Balmoral had something to do with it, for this was undoubtedly the cause of the great vogue for jewels of inlaid Scotch pebble which relies on precise lapidary work for its successful execution. This technique uses slices of variously coloured agates and jaspers inlaid in gold or silver (plate 31e). Many large round brooches of the kind the highlander uses to fasten his plaid with were made in this technique, and others formed as thistles, dirks, St. Andrew's crosses and the like. They were a speciality of the Edinburgh workshops. The silhouette of the jewel was cut out in thin metal. This base, or background was repeated in thicker metal with holes fretted out to admit the stones. The two were then hard-soldered together, one on top of the other. The stones—jasper from Ayr, bloodstone from Perth, Pentland pebble and Arthur's Seat jasper from Midlothian—were sliced up on a rotating disc charged with oil and diamond dust. They were then nipped roughly into shape with pincers. For ease of handling each stone was cemented to the top of a stick and ground to shape on a lead disc smeared with emery and water. The stones, still unpolished, were set in the mount with shellac. The rough face was then ground flat and polished on a tin disc with rottenstone and water. The brown or yellow cairngorm that so often occupies the centre of these jewels was set last of all.

The mosaics of Florence (plate 31d) were very popular and lapidary skill of a very high order was needed to make these tiny jigsaw pictures of cornelian, malachite, white agate and lapis lazuli and to sink them into their background of black Belgian marble. Flowers, birds and butterflies were favoured subjects.

The tortoise-shell piqué technique which had been used in the previous century for making decorative boxes was now effectively revived for jewellery (plate 30a). Originally the design was traced on the surface of the dark tortoise-shell with a pattern of gold dots —hence piqué. In the second half of the nineteenth century, however, more sophisticated arrangements of stars, scrolls and bands were in use. The following account, dating from 1872, explains how tortoise-shell jewels were made in America where quite a lot of this work seems to have been done:

'Shell jewellery is made from tortoise-shell. This material is first soaked for forty-eight hours in warm water, and then shaved, cut into pieces which are then joined together until the requisite thickness is obtained and then carved by hand, or inlaid with gold. In this last process gold wire is pressed hot into the shell in any required pattern and is then polished with "list wheels" made of layers of carpet stuff.'*

The very nature of tortoise-shell does not permit the degree of elaboration possible in metal jewellery. Many earrings, however, are similar to designs also intended for manufacture in gold, and creole, loop, sphere and torpedo designs, all with their dainty inlay of precious metal, are quite common. Brooches of convex circular form are just as plentiful and in their quiet way are very pretty in wear. E. L. Samuels of St. Pauls Square, Birmingham advertised an inlaid tortoise-shell demi-parure of brooch and earrings in a velvet case at prices ranging from fourteen shillings to a pound.† At this time it was not uncommon for the cheaper types of jewellery to be sold by mail order. Tortoise-shell jewels were also made with decorations of rich carving instead of metal inlays. These are quite unusual and are generally lockets, crosses and chains in dark and blond tortoise-shell. The pale translucent 'blonde' tortoise-shell was sometimes used for inlay work, but the contrast is not strong enough for it to be really effective.

The traditional use of tortoise-shell was of course in combs and ornaments for the head. From 1862 the hair was brushed away from the ears and gathered at the nape of the neck into a bunch of loose ringlets or a chignon. Later the chignon moved up towards the crown of the head. Sometimes it was encased in a résille—a net of coral or jet beads, sometimes it was held in place by a jewel specially designed for the purpose (plate 32b). In its simplest form this was a tortoise-shell clasp which could be had for a mere two and tuppence, or a suite of buffalo-horn combs. As the style progressed these hair ornaments became more elaborate. A popular design was an arched band of gold, its lower edge pierced in a dentil or arcaded fringe and in 1867 it was festooned with chain and hung with imitation gems or pearls. These jewels were often worn in tandem with a bandeau

---

* *Great Industries of the U.S.*, ed. Horace Greeley, 1872.
† *Illustrated London News*, 21st March 1868.

over the front of the head, but since they were only an accessory to the coiffure they dropped out of fashion when the hairstyle changed. As a result only a few have survived, which could be adapted to other uses, or which are of non-precious materials and not worth the melting down.

Apart from the traditional ornaments for the head, diamonds were briefly used to decorate the hair in a new way. Piesse and Lubin of the 'Laboratory of Flowers', Bond Street, London, sold diamond dust at three and six a box for sprinkling on the hair. Every passing season seems to have brought a new fashion idea just as ephemeral as this. In 1866 the fashionable world was invaded by a kind of brash exhibitionism—there was even an attempt to bring back the high First Empire waistline, but with the full-skirted styles of the time it looked too grotesque and soon disappeared. The jewellers' most striking contribution was the Benoiton, an arrangement of chains descending from the coiffure and festooned across the chest. Endless variations were possible on such an exotic theme. The chains could be caught up and held by a brooch at the neck. They might hang from the sides of a velvet headband applied with three gold rosettes in the style of ancient Melos, or from a humming bird perched atop the head. An awkward jewel which must have endlessly ensnared both fans and cutlery, it scarcely survived the season of 1867. The chains were made of many materials besides the noble metals, such as coral, jet, pearls and even aluminium bronze. It is rare to find one in its original state today as most of them must long ago have been restyled as longchains, necklaces and bracelets. This curious jewel got its name from Victorien Sardous' highly successful comedy *La Famille Benoiton* at that time playing in Paris. The influence of the theatre on fashion in the second half of the nineteenth century was probably even more powerful than that of the cinema today.

Other elaborate arrangements of chain appeared during these years. One, in which a doubled band of chain was looped from the waistband in a casual festoon was revived from 1859, another in which it was noosed around the neck like a lasso and tucked into the waistband seems to have been new. The purpose of the chain was often to hold the watch, which could be enchantingly decorated with Geneva enamels and rose diamonds.

Another watch-chain, the Leontine (plate 33a), was named after a celebrated actress. The braided chain was richly decorated with tassels and coulants of coloured golds, although towards the end of the seventies it was more likely to be in silver. One of the most celebrated chain makers of the day was Auguste Lion* in France who produced a wide variety of reasonably priced chain jewels and did a thriving export business with Britain (plate 33b). Lion dubbed his inventions with ingenious trade names— 'Napolitain', 'Eccossais' et cetera—but the most popular were 'Imperatrice' which was like a coarsely woven ribbon; and 'spiral', which is self-descriptive. It is recorded that Fosse, a contemporary of Lion, combined the spiral chain with an enamel decoration. By this time chains were machine-made and many firms competed in an expanding market, Lejeune and Rouel in Switzerland, Bolzani in Vienna and in England Watherston who manufactured articles of fine quality.

* Auguste Lion, 1830–95.

These were years scarred by wars and military expeditions which, like the Algerian campaigns of the forties, influenced fashion. In 1860 French troops were operating in China. They captured Peking and looted and burned the summer palace. Some of the Chinese Emperor's fine jade was taken back to Paris where it was carved and mounted into jewellery in gold and precious stones by Eugène Fontenay*—huge maybug beetles with elytra of imperial jade, and earrings like Greek amphorae. The last are much more in Fontenay's usual taste as he was renowned for jewellery in the classical manner (fig. 4). Even the defeats of the Franco-Prussian war and the loss of the two provinces of Alsace and Lorraine left their mark in jewels bearing the emblems of the ceded provinces. The passion for 'la revanche' burned so ardently that many Frenchwomen must have cherished jewels like this until the Great War redressed the wrong. Of similar inspiration are those rings in the form of a band of bronze decorated with bay leaves and the arms of the city of Paris and inscribed TOUS AUX DANGER TOUS A L'HONNEUR. These were apparently made by the firm of Froment-Meurice.

The Italian Risorgimento captured the romantic imagination everywhere. The natty little feathered hats of the Italian light infantry were adopted by foreign armies and the first of the brilliant aniline dyes which were to illumine the fashions of the sixties were nicknamed Solferino and Magenta after battles in the war of unification. The Garibaldi biscuit is with us to this day. Warwick and Sons of Regent Street purchased the entire stock of jewellery and cameos from Signor Civilotti (see colour plate Fa), a Roman jeweller, and offered them for sale in London, and at the 1862 Exhibition there is no doubt that it was the great Castellani who carried off the palm in spite of the pyrotechnics of Emmanuel and Hancock and Hunt and Roskell. The passion for coral was just another symptom of this Italomania. The rose-pink variety was most highly priced and very expensive by any standard. One particularly fine parure by Gismondi cost 1,000 pounds and according to the maker most of that value was in the coral which it had taken him twenty years to collect and match. One hundred pounds would be a high price to pay for it today. Generally prices ranged from between one shilling to twenty pounds per ounce for raw, unworked coral. Precious coral, *corallium nobilis*, is found only in the Mediterranean. The biggest, but not neccesarily the best pieces came from the Barbary coast. The deepest colours came from Spain, but the branches were often wormeaten. The finest coral of all was raised from the waters of the straits of Bonifacio, including the delectably tinted and exorbitantly priced pinks. Coral was landed and worked at Leghorn and Genoa—Paravagna and Casella of Genoa employed four hundred hands—but Naples was the traditional home of the trade. The coral boats landed their cargoes at nearby Torre del Greco and it was in the back streets that the precious roseate twigs were sawn, filed and fitted into sprays of roses, marigolds and harebells (see plate 34). Sometimes the branches were left as they were and made into tiaras with less happy results, as their arrid leafless quality is not pleasing. Cameos too were carved from coral and not only of the standard classical subjects: the three heroes of Italian Unification, Cavour, Mazzini and Garibaldi were often represented. The heads of ferocious dogs, bulls and boars were made into tiepins of

* Eugène Fontenay, 1823–87.

Fig. 4 JEWELS BY FONTENAY IN THE PARIS EXHIBITION OF 1867
In the two pendants (*top left* and *centre*), the background to the birds is of jade. The demi-parure (*top right*) is of Chinese derivation, and the rest are in neo-classical taste

alarming size. Coral is a fragile material and most of the more delicate work is sadly chipped and broken now. Phillips of Cockspur Street imported and sold most of the fine coral on the London market.

Souvenirs from carved Vesuvian lava had for some time been made for the tourist—usually bracelets or collars set with several cameos in a cheap mount. This material is usually putty grey, but creams and browns also occur. Very elaborate jewels were fashioned with great skill from this curious substance but they are most rare (plate 35).

If France's Mexican adventure had ended differently it is probable that this too would have affected jewel fashions. In any case it could well be that the fashion for humming-bird jewels could have originated like this. Sometimes the bird was faithfully copied in diamonds and coloured stones, sometimes the poor creature itself was used. Fragile although they are, some still remain, the head and shoulders of the bird surrounded by a gold border gipsy-set with stones, the gem-like feathers scuffed and broken, sad little memorials to the barbarity of fashion and to the unspeakable vulgarity of which the Victorians were too often capable.

South American beetles, too, were used in jewellery, brilliant green insects whose irridescent shell is as tough as many gems, and which were mounted in the same way into necklaces, brooches and bracelets. Pringles catalogue for the year 1876 lists them at prices between one and six and four shillings a dozen as 'Brazilian beetles'.

Insect motifs were important in the jewel fashions of the sixties. Bees are the emblem of the house of Buonaparte, so their presence is easy to account for, but why the unloved and unlovely housefly should put in so frequent an appearance is less easy to explain. Yet there they are, their wings glistening with rose diamonds, their noisesome bodies set with rubies or some other coloured stone, resting nervously on the edge of a plain gold locket as though they had just alighted there, or perhaps more heraldically displayed on a crystal cabochon—three of the latter often hang from one of the necklaces of Brazilian chain described earlier in this chapter. In 1859 a somewhat similar kind of necklace with three golden flies hanging from it was found in the Egyptian tomb of Aah Hotep, and it is just possible that the style originated there.

Sporting jewellery made its first appearance in the sixties and, true to Paris fashion form, it ran to wild excess. Horsey ladies wore earrings formed as a pair of stirrups, or, hideously, a horse's foreleg. If fashion reports are to be believed, horseshoe brooches could be up to two-thirds actual size. Sporting jewels were worn all over Europe, although the style was of English origin (plate 32a).

For the bookish there were jewels inspired by Victor Hugo's latest work *Les Travailleurs de la Mer*; parures of oxidized silver shells, or earrings formed as fish and suspended from the tender earlobe by a fish hook! Ephemeral though this particular fashion was, scallop shells of carved onyx, coloured gold, pavé turquoise or diamonds, and almost all with a pearl at the centre appear in every kind of jewel from necklaces to tiepins (plate 30c). At the London 1862 Exhibition Messrs Thomson and Profage entered 'a necklace of diamonds and pearls with dolphins of green enamel from the mouths of which hang escallop-shaped pendants of pink enamel, each holding a pearl'. At the same exhibition London and Ryder showed a tiara of pearl scallop shells with branches of red coral. These pleasing motifs were to recur until the end of the century.

Diamonds were worn on the grand scale. Three diamond bows of diminishing sizes were pinned one below the other down the front of the dress to form a magnificent corsage ornament (plate 36a). Necklaces in the form of a net of pearls and diamonds covered the throat and breast. Diamond flower jewellery was to be seen at its finest at this time (plate 36b), especially in the work of Oliver Massin.* Massin's success with these designs was due not only to his shrewd observation of nature and impeccable taste, but also to a method he devised for emulating the suppleness of the plant stem. Mounting the flowerheads 'tremblant' on a clock spring was an old idea. What Massin did was to make sections of the stem tubular so that a straight strip of spring steel could be threaded through them. Massin's rose sprays and peacock plumes made in this way were very beautiful and were copied by many French jewellers until the end of the century (colour plate H).

It is interesting at this point to glance back and trace the morphology of the brooch. In the second quarter of the century it was designed along the horizontal axis, that is to say it was wider than it was deep, and often had three drops below. It was usually of complex outline, but roughly in the form of a lozenge or an oval lying on its side. In the sixties emphasis shifts to the vertical axis so that the brooch is now upright, still of broken outline and with a number of pendants hanging from it. It is now prefectly balanced for doing double duty as both brooch and pendant. In the 1870s this 'brooch cum pendant' becomes more simplified and streamlined. Now a plain upright oval, the number of pendants has been reduced to one. Typical of this decade was a plain oval with a border of pavé-set diamonds with larger diamonds at the points of the compass, a pearl at the centre, and another as a drop. This trend towards simplicity became general in the seventies bringing with it an appearance of solidity which in the more commercial kinds of jewellery was often more apparent than real.

Towards the end of the seventies silver jewellery became very fashionable. The discovery of the Comstock lode in the U.S.A. and the release of reserves of silver bullion from Germany due to Bismark's currency reforms, had made the metal more plentiful and caused a slight fall in price, but not enough to account for the great popularity of silver jewels in the late seventies and early eighties. This was more likely to have been caused by the trade depression during which gold would have become too expensive for many people. Women took to wearing great fetter-like bracelets and quite huge silver chains with big silver lockets. The lockets were mostly oval in shape but variously decorated (fig. 5). Some were engraved or applied with a monogram, others with crosses or strap and buckle motifs. Some had a corded wire laid in a vertical groove down the centre like a ship's block and would hang from a chain of anchor cable pattern. Many châtelaines were made. The châtelaine was an eighteenth-century invention consisting of a decorative plate provided with a strong hook which can be used to secure it to the belt and from which were suspended all sorts of useful nick-nacks by chains—memo book, scent bottle, an egg-shaped box of pins, thimble and scissors. Many jewels, particularly brooches, were

* Oliver Massin, born Liège 1829, retired from business 1892.

Fig. 5 A SELECTION OF LATE NINETEENTH CENTURY LOCKETS FROM PRINGLE'S CATALOGUE, 1878

inscribed 'Mizpah': it was at Mizpah that Jacob and his brothers set up a cairn of stones as a sign of their covenant 'the Lord watch between me and thee when we are absent one from another'.

For a while in the eighties women gave up the custom of wearing jewellery altogether. Garments became brisk and close-fitting; pared down to its bare essentials the silhouette of a well-dressed woman now began to resemble that of a man. The woman's emancipation movement was gathering momentum and it must have seemed to the horrified Victorian male that not only did the woman want to take over his role in society, but also to look as much like him as possible. It is a curious fact that over the previous twenty years a fetter-like quality had become increasingly pronounced in certain types of jewellery (plates 37a and b). Felix Duval actually made jewels in the forms of bolts, screws and shackles. One cannot help correlating this trend with the status of the woman in society and in the family. The personal ornaments of a North African or an Indian housewife have the same formidable quality. In some cases a particular jewel symbolizes the marriage bond, and it is not called a bond for nothing. In de Maupassant's day a Norman peasant bride was presented with a massive gold chain which was actually called an *esclavage* and symbolized, wittingly or unwittingly, the servitude into which she was contracting. As we have seen, jewels in the nineteenth century were all too often used to affirm the status of the male rather than the personality of the female. As jewellery was not only designed, but also paid for by men it was perhaps more than just a whim of fashion that made a woman cast off her jewels at this time, just as she escaped from her brassière almost a century later.

There were other reasons too, and there is no doubt that the cheap jewel trade richly deserved the predicament in which it found itself. As mechanization increased, so standards declined. The steam or gas engine came into widespread use in the jewel trade around 1860 and from that time quality deteriorated—this is not Ruskinesque sentiment but simple fact. Unskilled female labour infiltrated the workshops in large numbers. Designs were trivial, workmanship and finish poor. As most of the Birmingham workshops were adapted from dwelling houses it was difficult to mechanize them properly. For the garret-masters this problem was solved by installing the engine in the end house of a block and knocking holes in the walls so that the driving shaft could pass clean through all the workshops and locate in a bearing in the far wall. Power was transmitted to the machines by means of belts. A notice saying 'Power to Let' was not uncommon in the industrial districts of the midlands and the north of England. These workshops were usually too small to cope with all the operations involved in making a jewel, so they carried through one or two stages and then passed them on to someone else. With such haphazard and uneconomical organization the Birmingham trade was bound to feel the draught from its competitors, and this came from several quarters.

In Providence, New Jersey, U.S.A., the jewellery industry was already well established. Back in 1794 Nehemiah Dodge had developed his own method of plating base metals and by 1818 his former apprentice Jabez Gorham had already turned over to machine production. In 1810 a contemporary survey shows that a hundred jewellers were at work there. By the end of the nineteenth century this had grown into an industry with 100,000 operatives. Providence seems to have specialized in the cheaper types of low carat and rolled gold jewellery. Factories were large so that all the operations could be carried out under one roof. Rolled gold (*or doublé* in France) is an alternative method to electrogilding or coating a base metal sheet with a thin layer of gold. A sheet of gold was hard soldered to a sheet of brass. This was rolled out thinly, resulting in a sheet of base metal with a layer of gold on its surface. This rolling process made the metal hard so it was heated in a charcoal furnace to make it more tractable, and then polished on the 'good side'. The jewel was stamped out in two parts, back and front. The fronts were sent to the 'fillers' who melted tin into them with a hot copper bit. This gave support so that the chasers could sharpen up the detail with a hammer and punch, but it was melted out as soon as this was done. The edges were trimmed on an emery wheel, matched to the 'backs' and hard soldered together. After being lightly polished the fittings were soldered in place and the jewel was finished.

In Europe cheap export houses sprang up in France, Austria and Switzerland, but especially in Germany. Pforzheim was the principal centre of the jewellery trade, and like the industry in other major centres, it had its roots in the previous century. In 1767, the Margrave, Charles Frederic, was persuaded to establish a workshop in the orphanage where twenty boys over the age of twelve and four girls could learn how to make watches and cut-steel jewellery. Foremost among the energetic and unscrupulous men who were involved in this venture were Jean François Autran and Jean Jaques Ador. Kindly, idealistic and an ardent physiocrat, the Margrave was a natural prey to these men who, brilliant, creative and fizzing with ideas were dedicated to the single-minded pursuit of wealth and fame. Ador took charge of the business side of the venture and introduced the double entry bookkeeping system, unknown in South Germany at that time. Unfortunately for his partner its subtleties could not conceal Autran's financial sleight of hand, and the two men were eventually arrested for the embezzlement of 15,000 florins. Autran was eventually deported upon admitting liability for the whole amount and Ador was released. On 1st February 1776 Ador set up on his own with a staff of a hundred and ninety workmen. Workshops sprang up all around the town and in other cities too, Hanau and Gmund in particular. The Hanau workshops recruited many goldsmiths and engravers from among the French immigrants who had settled in the district. On the steep watershed of the Rhine valley, running water provided a cheap and convenient source of power. Hydraulic power was also used to turn the grinding wheels in the agate cutting shops of Idar Oberstein. These huge cylinders of sandstone turned in bearings located in the floor of the workshop which itself straddled the banks of some swift feeder stream. The top of the wheel poked through the floorboards and in order to present the gem he was cutting to the whizzing sandstone the workmen had to lean over the work in a nearly prone position, his feet braced against cleats nailed to the floor, his head rammed against a wooden pad. Working in this grotesque attitude set up all sorts of physical stresses and strains and the work was very unhealthy. Originally the agates had come from the local hillsides but the local material had long since been exhausted. It is said that men thrown out of work by the

E (a) A sardonyx CAMEO of a bacchante mounted as a brooch within a border of half-pearls and enamel

　　1860–70 *See page* 54

(b) A labradorite CAMEO of Bacchus mounted within a diamond border as a brooch
　　Late nineteenth century *See page* 70

(c) An opal CAMEO with a strong art nouveau feeling set in a simple gold brooch
　　See page 70

(d) A CAMEO HABILLÉ carved in shell and inlaid with coral, mother-of-pearl and amazonite
　　Italian, nineteenth century *See page* 46

F (*a*) A PENDANT by Civilotti of Rome in Renaissance taste set with a fine agate cameo of Minerva, the mount decorated with champlevé enamels and gem-set

See page 58

(*b*) A PENDANT in late Renaissance style in a design of grotesques, foliate scroll and drape motifs and set with emerald, ruby, pearls and diamonds, the enamels finely shaded with the brush

French, *circa* 1880   See page 90

(*c*) A 'Holbeinesque' PENDANT set with carbuncle and chrysolites and decorated with champlevé enamels

English, *circa* 1870   See page 90

lack of stones formed one of the nomadic German brass bands that wandered like tinkers all over the old and new worlds in the last century. Custom has it that they made their way to Uruguay and while tramping from one village to the next a musician spotted some nodules of agate in the banks of a stream. It turned out to be present in large quantities, enough at least to ship back home and set the lapidary workshops of Idar Oberstein back on their feet again.

Freiburg in Saxony also had its gem-cutting industry which relied upon local stones—blood red pyrope garnets—as its raw materials, and upon local rivers as a cheap and untiring source of power. Here too the industry was long established for it is known that the lapidary guild of the town presented Marie Antoinette with a thousand garnets when she passed through on her way to marry the Dauphin.

The most important centre of garnet cutting, however was just over the frontier in Bohemia. Mostly rose-cut, tiny stones were mounted in large clusters with a cabochon at the centre, and this simple basic motif was built into many designs (plate 38). A succession of such clusters may make a necklace or a bracelet; singly they may form brooches or earrings. There were other designs too: a succession of stars may form a collar or a plain pavé-set hinged band, a bangle. The metal was usually a debased reddish gold with a purity as low as five or seven carat, sometimes it was just gilt brass. These simple Bohemian jewels strike a note of sombre richness which can be dramatic in wear. The principal centre of this work was around Gablonz—the so-called 'Birmingham of Bohemia'.

The city most associated with the cutting of precious stones was of course Amsterdam. At the beginning of the century the Amsterdam diamond-finishing trade was a home industry and the iron *scaife* or cutting wheel was turned manually—often by the cutter's wife. In 1822 the first horse-driven mill was founded. Conditions were primitive, and at first both cutters and horses worked in the same room, the *manège*. Steam began to replace animals in 1840 and one engine could power as many as a hundred mills. The mills were not always operated by their owners: under the *molenhuur* system they were also rented by self-employed craftsmen.

It was not until the mid-sixties that the jewellery industry became truly mechanized. At first there was a kind of honeymoon with the machine. Bensons proudly advertised their steam factory on Ludgate Hill, and in the following year Hancock and Burbrook announced the sale of machine-made jewellery in eighteen carat gold at fifty per cent of the price of the hand-made article. In France Lefèbre was making the settings for stones mechanically and Ferre was producing gallery strip in the same way—both became typical features of late nineteenth-century diamond jewellery. Rigeaud sold rings at thirty-six francs the dozen, the gold value of which was twenty-four francs, and Trux was retailing similar jewels in gilt metal for forty centimes per hundred. The makers of jewellery seem to have become price mad and in their anxiety to undercut their competitors one wonders if they did not forget that jewellery is by its very nature precious and costly. They seem to have overestimated the degree of shoddiness the customer will put up with, and in the process of cutting each others' throats cut their own as well.

5. Fin De Siècle

In the late seventies we see the beginnings of a kind of revulsion against the machine that could almost be described as an industrial counter revolution. What had been hailed as a universal saviour now came to be regarded in some quarters with a sense of unease. To some the machine appeared as a kind of Moloch which gobbled up the workman's health and vitality and in return spewed out an endless stream of identical shoddy goods. Ferocious international competition seemed only to have the effect of lowering standards instead of raising them. Europe was flooded with shoddy jewels of gilt, or gold so debased that it was scarcely worthy of the name, and in order to compete, the British assay offices introduced the nine and fourteen carat standards. A trade depression at this time only made matters worse.

There were signs, too, of a reaction against the constraints and taboos of Victorian life. In some circles this was expressed by a kind of studied eccentricity, especially in dress. As one commentator remarked 'they struck me as striving after some emotional expression, one lady was in red; red gloves and stockings, a serpent coiled around her wrist, red tulips in her hair. What a fuzz it was, what a passionate tangle'. These aesthetic women might wear a serpent on the neck or wrist, or a large string of Russian amber beads, or very often no jewellery at all. Emphasis as far as personal decoration was concerned was on the individual and the idiosyncratic; matched parures, and the glittering christmas tree toilettes of the seventies were considered vulgar. As Mrs. Haweis said 'Machine-made jewellery has increased the vulgar and mistaken craze for "sets" and "pairs" which are in themselves antagonistic to all true beauty, the essence of which is change, variety, freshness'.*

Indian goldsmiths with their eye on the main chance had for some time been employing their traditional techniques and designs on jewels which were suitable for European women to wear, and when Queen Victoria became Empress of India in 1877 these became very fashionable. Lockets and bracelets were embossed with Hindu gods: full-breasted Lakshmi, or elephant-headed Ganesha, in the vigorous repoussé work of Madras (plate 39). Silver flower sprays were made in the exquisite filigree of Cuttack. Tiger claws, too, probably shikar trophies, were mounted up into jewellery, singly as brooches or pendants or a succession of them as a barbaric collar. Sometimes two would be joined end to end to make a brooch with a gold repoussé band set with Kashmir sapphires and surmounted by a tiger. These were the trappings of the Victorian establishment and the intense young ladies of the aesthetic movement craved something more exotic, so for a time the silk

* Mrs. H. R. Haweis, *The Art of Beauty*, London, 1878.

tasselled bazu-bands of Jaipur and the mysterious thali necklaces of Malabar appeared on the pallid necks and arms of these avant-garde young women. It is of course this kind of display that catches the commentator's eye at the expense of the ordinary and the everyday. These manifestations were the indulgence of only a comparatively few women. We can no more take them as evidence of a popular fashion than we can draw any conclusions from the wilder excesses of the Paris collections in more recent years. Paris fashion prints of the eighties show women wearing enormous silver brooches in the form of leopards' heads, rampant heraldic beasts or pendants formed as pairs of confronted cockatoos, but this does not mean that the average Parisienne felt undressed unless she was ornamented in this way.

Crescent brooches appeared towards the end of the eighties (plate 40d). These were arranged so that the brooch pin could be unscrewed and replaced with a double prong of gilt silver and worn in the hair 'a là Diane'. The stones were usually set in three rows, those forming the middle row being larger and set in a slightly raised mount. Sometimes the middle row was of sapphires. Rubies in this particular kind of crescent are less common and emeralds most unusual. The raised middle row may have claws tipped with rose diamonds. Sometimes the stones are quite large and set in a single graduated row. The crescent brooches of the eighties and nineties can be quite magnificent with diamonds having individual weights of several carats and with values well into four figures. At the cheap end of the market many crescent brooches were made and appropriately set with moonstones. The crescent brooch existed in other versions—sometimes at the centre of a bar brooch with a collet-set stone at each end, sometimes with a star between the points. The last two types may be found set with half-pearls, or with brownish Siam rubies.

Diamond stars appeared a little later (plate 40b). They were generally made in parures of five which could be worn separately as brooches or in the hair, or together on a tiara or as pendants to a necklace. A typical star had six points pavé-set with rose and brilliant-cut diamonds with a larger brilliant set in a raised collet at the centre. Between the points the diamonds were set on the end of knife wires in plain, or perhaps husk-shaped collets. Sometimes the star was of twelve alternately larger and smaller points. Coloured stones are very rarely mixed with the diamonds in this kind of jewel. A cheaper version of the star, in gold pavé-set with half-pearls, did quite often have a single diamond collet-set at its centre, however, and like the crescents they were often set entirely with moonstones with silver mounts.

All kinds of jewels were made in half-pearls, sometimes mingled with peridots, aquamarines, pink tourmalines and other coloured stones. Enchanting little necklaces were made in designs of leaves, flowers and scrolls, the soft orient of the pearls highlighted with an occasional diamond. The backs of these necklaces were nearly always of cord-like Prince of Wales pattern chain (plate 41). Half-pearl jewellery was very popular during the nineties and must really be thought of as a substitute for the diamond. In France half-pearls were mounted in silver-gilt together with miniatures of cupids and bergères. Designs were of palmettes and festoons of garlanded leaves and the odd turquoise provided a dab of colour (plate 47c).

Insect brooches were introduced in the early sixties but most of the many butterfly brooches to be seen were made in the last decade of the century (plate 44c). They differ very little one from another and then more in quality than design. Most are set with diamonds, sapphires and Siamese rubies. The coloured stones are made to represent the ocellae in the wings, but they need to be examined with care as they sometimes turn out to be pastes. Sometimes two diminutive insect brooches—bees, moths, or whimsically a spider and a fly—are joined with a chain. These are intended to fasten a lace jabot. Giuliano made a few gold butterfly brooches with enamelled wings but they are far from common. Some magnificent dragonfly brooches were produced (plate 40a) life size, the bodies in diamonds, the wings of transparent plique-à-jour enamel. Terrifyingly realistic stag beetles were also made life size, usually in France (plate 44c).

Longchains returned during the last quarter of the century to carry the watch or lorgnette. Although slenderer than those of the forties, designs were just as varied. Pringles catalogue for 1876 lists several patterns—secret link, cylinder, square-pierced cylinder, facetted belcher, alma or double jack, pierced bead, Spanish tie, and Prince of Wales as available to the retailer. Most frequent are of long faceted oval links and hollow links piereced with stars.

When the first shipment of South African diamonds reached Amsterdam in 1870 the diamond finishing trade there was almost at a standstill. Production in Brazil had slowed to a mere trickle and the Franco-Prussian war had prevented trading in Paris, then the traditional market of the Netherlands cutters. Plentiful material from the Cape of Good Hope caused an unprecedented boom and the average cutter in 1872 was earning thirteen times as much as he got in 1861.

The South African miners sold their stones as fast as they could dig them up with no thought to the effect that this would have on prices which kept on falling alarmingly, and, when the de Beers consortium was formed in 1889, its first reaction was to cut production by forty per cent to hold the prices of rough stones.

Before 1872 it had been necessary to cut a diamond so as to waste as little as possible of the rough crystal. The classic form of the natural diamond crystal is that of an octahedron and in order to form this the cutter simply sliced off the top point of the diamond to give the table and then ground the facets on the sides. A tiny facet was cut on the point of the stone opposite and parallel to the table. The result was the cushion-shaped, or, as they say in American, old mine brilliant. This form did not make the most of the unique optical properties of the diamond. Stones like this were too thick to exploit the exceptional refractive index and dispersion of the stone, and furthermore the large culet allowed the light to pass out at the back of the stone giving the effect of a dead spot. So that the light could enter the stone and be reflected off the back facets and also be split up into the prismatic brilliance of the spectrum, the blazing violets, reds and golds that are the glory of the diamond, it had to be cut circular and a good deal thinner than before and the culet had almost to form a point. This involved as much as fifty per cent wastage of the original crystal which was possible now that stones were more plentiful. The older style of rose cutting belonged more to the early years of the eighteenth century rather than the nineteenth although roses were occasionally mixed with brilliants in a Victorian piece. The tiny pinhead sized stones in many pieces in which the larger diamonds are brilliant cut often turn out to be roses. Many nineteenth-century Dutch jewels were set with rose diamonds in deliberate imitation of an earlier jewel.

Considerable advances were made in the setting of stones at this time. Earlier, the object of the setting had been not only to hold the stone securely but also to make it look bigger than it really was. Now this was no longer neccesary and light openwork claw settings which admitted light behind the stone were increasingly used by the jeweller. Now that diamonds were being cut to a regular shape it was possible to make collets for this kind of setting by machine; stamped collets and gallery strip were already being manufactured in Paris by 1867. The gallery was a tiny openwork balustrade which raised the jewel slightly, allowing the light to pass beneath it and through the back of the stones. These techniques did not come into use until the last quarter of the century.

Although the diamond was a great favourite, a wider variety of coloured stones was in use than at any earlier period. Many of them were not available to the jeweller before. The superb velvety blue sapphires of Kashmir had only recently been discovered, and it was only at this time that the Burma ruby mines began to be worked by modern methods, although the stones must have been known in Europe long before the emissaries of the Burmese monarch made a present of some of these fine stones to the Empress Eugenie.

The exquisite green variety of garnet remained undiscovered until the 1860s when the first specimens were discovered in the bed of the Bobrovka river in the Ural mountains. Naturally, if a jewel set with these demantoid garnets is presented as dating from before the mid-nineteenth century one can draw the obvious conclusion. The colour of the demantoid garnet is similar to that of a peridot, but richer and more brilliant with flashes of red and gold. A buyer should always examine them with a lens and try to pick out the golden filaments of asbestos which are called by gemmologists horses' tails, and are never seen in peridot. The distinction is important as demantoid garnet is much more expensive than peridot, and any stone of good colour weighing more than a carat is quite a prize. Some find the demantoid garnet more beautiful than the emerald. Its most typical use is in the lizard brooches of the nineties. These little reptiles with their pavé-set diamond scales, golden claws and glowing ruby eyes have a brilliant streak of demantoid garnet along the spine. Little tortoises are often given the same treatment, and frogs as well. The frogs may have had a special significance for the giver as this is the Roman emblem of wedded happiness.

It must be the demantoid garnet that Oscar Wilde refers to in *The House of Pomegranates*: '. . . there were carbuncles, both wine coloured and like grass'. These pages are steeped in the fragrant mystery of precious stones—'There were huge tortoise-shells full of pearls, and hollowed moonstones of great size piled up with red rubies . . . ivory horns were heaped with purple amethysts, and the horns of brass with chalcedonies and sards, the pillars which are of cedar were hung with strings of yellow lynx stones', and so on— lynx stones must have referred to amber which was at one time believed to be the solidified urine of the lynx. The precision and delight which Wilde brings to the description of the young Emperor's treasure house reflects the fascination which precious stones exercised at this time.

Chrysoberyl cats' eyes were greatly admired in the eighties and nineties. This curious honey or molasses-coloured stone with its silky reflection was still fairly cheap then. In our own century, however, it has been elevated from the semi-precious to the precious class of gems, and today a good example may be worth more than a sapphire and it would certainly be rarer. Cat's eye looks best when set in a plain mount without details which distract the eye from its subtly changing lights. Often then it was set as a brooch or a pendant in a plain border of brilliants, but it is in a ring that it looks best because the movements of the finger bring the stone to life.

Precious stones were treated so as to enhance their more fantastic characteristics. Moonstones were carved with the benignly smiling face of a harvest moon in a nursery rhyme illustration. Labradorite, which is closely related to the moonstone, shows glancing lights of peacock blue, orange and gold on a dull grey ground (see colour plate Eb). Tiepins were often set with labradorite carved into the form of a wild beast's head, a wolf, a bear, a lion or an ape, the eyes of glittering rose diamonds.

Opal cameos often used the natural markings of the stone (see colour plate Ec). The most effective were cut with the chocolate coloured ironstone of the matrix so that a dark-skinned Red Indian chief could be seen wearing a plumed head-dress of precious opal. The goddess Isis with her bird helmet was an even more favoured subject. The magnificent black opals of Lightning Ridge, Queensland had only recently been discovered. Until then most opals came from Hungary and were of a dull, pinkish white.

The Mississippi freshwater pearl occurs in weird random shapes which often resemble ducks or chickens. These were provided with gold legs and eyes and made into tiepins, as were gold nuggets, the souvenirs of those fortune hunting expeditions celebrated in Victorian mythology. Gold nuggets were also mounted as brooches with a little pick and shovel trophy, and gold-bearing white quartz was cut and set as a gem as well.

Crocidolite is a golden brown mineral with a satiny chatoyancy. European jewellers did not realize, when it first came on the market, that although it was only to be found in one locality in South West Africa, it was present there in huge quantities. At first they bought it by the carat, paying quite high prices. Familiarity, and the discovery that they had overpaid soon brought contempt, however, and this attractive mineral is far more widely used today than it was in the nineteenth century. Occasionally, though, one finds two small brooches joined by a chain, a spider and a fly, the bodies of 'tiger's eye' and 'hawk's eye', the golden and blue-grey varieties of crocidolite.

From New Zealand came deep-green nephrite which was commonly carved in the form of a leaf and provided with the Maori inscription, 'kia ora' in gold. Peridots were an especial favourite at the end of the century, particularly in diamond jewels designed as rococo cartouches with latticework centres and diamond scroll borders. These peridots were often of fine quality, and their soft olive-green colour was perfectly in tune with the moods and fashions of the fin de siècle period (plate 44b).

Bracelets in the nineties were typically of the classical half-hoop design in which the decoration was restricted to the visible part at the front (plates 45a and b). This could be just a single row of stones graduating in size from the centre. Sometimes, as in the crescent brooches, the stones could be set in three rows: a raised row of larger stones between borders of smaller ones. Half-hoop bracelets were not only set with diamonds, but also with rubies, emeralds, sapphires or opals. Also typical are those designs in which a cluster centre is flanked by diamond scrollwork. The back was usually a hinged ring of gold either of keeled or half-round section, or of three slender parallel wires. Chains of large links set with turquoise or opals also belong to this period (plate 45c).

New designs calling for light and near invisible settings for diamonds led to the use of 'knife wires' in jewellery. This type of wire is sufficiently described by its name: the sharp edge, which is always upwards, reflects a thin highlight suggesting wire of a gossamer thinness that would be quite impossible in practice. A very effective necklace design of the time had, at the front, a fringe of single pearls or diamonds in plain or bud-like collets, each hanging on a single knife wire from the necklace chain. Variations on this simple theme were almost endless: the stones could be pear-shaped, the wires with a small diamond in the centre and another at the top. The knife wires might be alternately longer and shorter or even mixed with scroll motifs. Knife wires could also be used on the necklace chain at the back to further the illusion of lightness, short links of it being connected by small collet-set diamonds. These stones, being out of sight during wear, were sometimes rose-cut.

Many diamond necklaces were made in designs of lyre-like scrolls which could be fastened to a light silver frame to double as a tiara when occasion demanded (plate 42). Rivières were as popular as they had ever been, although the stones were now set in light openwork collets and when these were diamonds they were cut in the rounder, shallower modern form.

Some designs bridged the closing years of the nineteenth century and the first years of the twentieth, and the dog collar was perhaps the most spectacular of them. Usually it was formed of a dozen or so strands of small ungraduated pearls with diamond openwork plaques at intervals. Sometimes the dog collar was of turquoise with gold mounts that have the warm nuggetty roughness of Indian bazaar workmanship. Photographs of Queen Alexandra show her wearing a magnificent dog collar, sometimes with an Imperial Russian tiara. Until the late nineties the Imperial Russian tiara was an exclusively Russian style. It was said to have been based on the kokoshnik, the traditional Russian head-dress (plate 43). This design, simple, ingenious and utterly right is, at its best, one of the most radiant creations of the nineteenth-century jeweller. The slim, leaflike motifs were arranged almost vertically side by side. Usually they were set very closely together but sometimes they were inclined a little outwards to look like lancing rays of light. About this time diamonds and pearls were combined with the curious white plumage of the egret in jewels for the head. The jet of feathers foamed from the centre of a glittering fountain of diamonds on tremblant knife wires. Aluminium made one of its sporadic appearances in jewellery in the offering of the French jeweller Coulon at the great exhibition of 1900. This included a

Fig. 6 RINGS FROM PRINGLE'S CATALOGUE, 1896

large plume of diamonds set in aluminium, the lightness of which enabled it to be worn comfortably in the hair.

Bar brooches too (plate 47a) were invented in the late nineteenth century but worn well into the present one. The basic design was a slender horizontal bar of gold, with a decorative motif at the centre and a similar device at each end. There were flowers, swallows, horseshoes, wishbones and sprigs of mistletoe and for the sportswoman whips, crops, hunting horns and fox masks—these designs still appear in jewellers' catalogues today.

Ring designs were both varied and attractive (plate 47b and fig. 6). In the cross-over ring, which is still popular today, the shank was not a complete circle, but wrapped around the finger so that the two ends lay alongside each other and were finished off with two diamonds, a diamond and a sapphire, or perhaps a diamond and a pearl. The same idea was used in bracelets. Half-hoop rings, too, were made in several varieties, one of the most felicitous being set with a row of five round Kashmir sapphires, rubies, or canary yellow diamonds, each individually bordered with small diamond brilliants. In another popular design three stones were 'gipsy-set' in the wider front of a band of gold. The gipsy setting has no need of claws or collet to hold the stone firm as the gem is simply dropped into a recess in the gold, the edges of which are worked over the girdle to hold it in place. The principle is the same as that of the Roman setting except that the surrounding groove is left out. Similar three-stone rings were made in which the stones were 'star-set' in the centre of engraved stars. In this case it is a small grain at the base of each of the star's points that does the work of holding the stone. The millegrain setting was used in all kinds of jewels in the last quarter of the century. This differs from the plain collet setting only in that the setting edge is finished off as a trail of fine beading. The setter obtained this effect by rolling a milled wheel around the top of the collet when the stone was in place. This technique was widely used for coloured stones when the setting was usually of gold.

The simplicity of the gipsy setting made it ideal for men's rings. The most favoured design was a solitaire diamond in a massive band of gold, although the stone could also be set in the head of a gold snake which coiled around the finger. Rings were not only made for the finger, but also to hold the tie instead of a knot. John Millais appears in a painting of 1888 wearing a ring on his loose black tie. This jewel usually took the form of a flat elliptical ring, hinged and sprung to close around the tie, and provided with a spike on the inside to prevent it from sliding off (plates 46j and k). Filigree or galleried borders and a star-set rose diamond made up the decoration. Most men wore tiepins, however (plate 46). The most usual designs were of a single pearl or diamond. Sometimes the diamond was held in a gold eagle's claw. There were innumerable other designs, however —enamelled faces in domino masks, horned devils, bicycles, mallets, trowels, clover leaves, yachts, anchors, golf clubs and so on. Cufflinks were less fanciful, but one does occasionally find a pair in a design of enamelled postage stamps. The most typical were of the orthodox oval form, stamped with a hammer-finish with a coloured stone set near the edge—usually there was a different stone on each panel—ruby, emerald, sapphire and diamond.

The most famous and certainly the most widely collected jeweller of the late nineteenth century must surely be Fabergé. Although the Fabergé family were of Picardy Huguenot stock and in fact much of the inspiration for Fabergé's designs is of the French eighteenth century, he became the greatest of Russian crown jewellers. Fabergé has never since been equalled as a maker of objects of *vertu* and *fantaisie*. He is most famous, and justly so, for his Easter eggs. Eggs were given as Easter presents in Russia just as they were in other European countries. Those which he made for the Russian Imperial family remain as brilliant comments on the exquisitely futile society that produced them. The 1900 pine-cone egg which he made for the Dowager Empress Maria Feodorovna was in the form of a pine-cone of royal blue enamel, the scales edged with rose diamonds. Inside was the 'surprise' which so many of the Imperial Russian eggs contained—an enamelled clockwork elephant, symbol of the Danish royal house from which the Dowager Empress was descended. These can scarcely be called jewels, but miniature Easter eggs intended to be worn on a long chain around the neck were also given. These were made in all manner of materials: sleek guilloché enamels bound with garlands of green gold bay leaves in the French taste; native cloisonné enamels in vibrant flower designs like an exuberant patchwork with gold stitching; or hardstone eggs in chalcedonies both rose and lavender, spinach green nephrite or pink and black rhodonite. Some of Fabergé's other jewels, pendants and brooches particularly, were in the sumptuous rococo style for which he is best remembered, with limpid enamels and crisply chiselled gold. Others, in complete contrast, are simple to the point of austerity. This work shows a predilection for cabochon sapphires and amethysts. The output of the house of Fabergé was considerable and apart from the famous establishment at 24 Morskaya, St. Petersburg it had branches in Moscow, Kiev, Odessa and London (plate 48).

Jewellery during this period was inclined to be frivolous and personal. There were good luck charms without number (plates 47a and e). Shamrocks in green enamel complete with diamond dewdrop and inscribed good luck, lucky pigs, lucky horseshoes and lucky beans, and four leaf clovers eternally preserved between slices of crystal.

The eighteenth-century idea of two hearts united by a ribbon bow reappeared in rings, brooches and pendants. The rings were usually set with rubies, emeralds or diamonds, the brooches with a wide variety of stones: opals, moonstones, chrysoprases, pearls and others. Another characteristic heart design was of red or blue enamel with a white border and a pearl or diamond centre (plate 44d). The pansy was another sentimental motif favoured by the late Victorian jeweller: some had diamond petals and a sapphire centre, others were of suitably coloured enamel with a diamond centre, and in a few the rose-diamond edged petals were left open so that they could be backed with velvet. If you are fortunate enough to find one in carved opal examine it carefully for damage and repair.

In some jewels a date, perhaps of a marriage, birthday or meeting, would be spelt out in rose-diamonds, letters and numerals, on a gold chain as bracelet or collar, or as a brooch (plate 44e). And as new ideas and hopes began to rekindle in the ashes of the century there was talk of the millennium, the old legend of one thousand years of peace and justice and jewels of all kinds were designed around the date 1900, the supposed year of its commencement.

6. Arts and Crafts and Art Nouveau

Until the mid-seventies there was a noisy superficial interest in what the craftsmen of the past did, but very little concern with how they did it—Castellani was the great exception. Phillips would adapt into a bracelet a frieze from beneath the tomb of Henry VII in Westminster Abbey, or lift the design of a cross from a picture by Quentin Matsys. Cathedrals, museums and national collections were ransacked and cannibalized by the jeweller in search of ideas, often with taste and success. When he failed it was usually because the design was unsuited to the jeweller's medium; a pleasing form in carved stone or ormolu does not neccesarily translate with fluency into gems and noble metal. The designs of the finest jewels are as inseparable from the materials of which they are made as a growing plant.

By this time the machine and the professional skill of the craftsman had subjugated the materials almost entirely to the craftsman's will. In France the master *joaillier* O. Massin* could make diamond jewellery in which the mount weighed less than the stones—an average of three milligrams of metal per stone. To some it seemed as though technical efficiency had become an end in itself, that jewels had become a kind of conjuring trick devised to conceal the means by which they were made. Mrs. Haweis wrote:† 'In the old work one is struck by the simplicity of the fastenings—never disguised . . . the Greek and Etruscan gems hang from hooks of wire passing through them . . . the links of the chains are all visible and satisfactory to the eye, there is no feeling of doubt as to how they are held—so annoying in much modern work . . . the artistic effect is better when the fastening is seen rather when it is disguised. You may ornament but not conceal it.' Deceptions of this kind were reckoned by some to be dishonest—even prudish—far better the lovebites of the chisel and the repoussé hammer than bland virgin metal.

The idea was also gaining acceptance that there was more to art than oil paintings in gilt frames! The Arts and Crafts Exhibition Society held its first show at the New Gallery in 1888. The Art Workers Guild was formed, and the Home Arts and Industries Association began organizing village handicraft classes. Probably the most significant event of this kind was the founding of the Guild and School of Handicraft, in the unpromising milieu of the London East End, by C. R. Ashbee. Ashbee himself designed many lovely jewels, including delightful necklaces of looped and festooned chains set with coloured stones. He also made good use of the peacock motif that was so popular in the last quarter of the century. It was probably the wide acceptance of these designs that led to the

* Born Liège 1829, retired 1892.
† *The Art of Beauty*, London, 1878.

dominance of blues and greens, the peacock's colours, in the enamels of the British arts and crafts workers. Also these colours are not difficult to fire—one must remember that these people were mainly amateurs, and it is this amateur quality which is the essence of the jewels, both their strength and their weakness.

There was a revival of enamelling in the 1890s. Its most typical use was in pools of subtly graduated colour trapped in a web of swaying silver scrolls. Enamel pictures were created by Fisher that exploited not only the colour, but also the translucency of the medium so that dreaming female figures seem to float, Ophelia-like, among drifting robes and tresses and shimmering paillons of gold and silver foil.

Henry Wilson* who was an architect turned jeweller, not only made many fine jewels, but wrote a book on making jewellery which was to the jeweller of his time what the workshop notes of Benvenuto Cellini were to the Renaissance craftsman. Wilson's work has a kind of symbolic, almost heraldic quality that draws its vitality from the Middle Ages (plates 49a and c). His designs are raised in bold repoussé work: trees, vines and rose-bushes that have the same irrepressible vegetable energy as the mushroom that pushes up a paving stone. Pruned, espaliered and entwined as elaborately as on a medieval illuminated manuscript, these restraints seem merely to exacerbate their growth to such a degree that the border of roped wire or checkered enamel bulges under the strain of containing them. Perhaps the key to his designs is to be found in his advice to the craftsman: 'Remember always to have a bit of the natural foliage near you as a guide, never do anything without reference to nature or without having made a careful and detailed study of the plant or form, you intend to use' . . . 'avoid sprawling lines; let leaves and twigs be well knit together, let all the lines lead the eye to some central point. You must not imitate, but translate. All art is translation from one state to another.' Some of Wilson's work is religious and allegorical with a strong medieval flavour. Like the pre-Raphaelite painters many makers of jewels strove to recapture the purity, simplicity and single mindedness of the Middle Ages in their work. The influence of the Celtic revival is also apparent in Arts and Crafts jewellery.

From 1890 the designer took a new first-hand look at nature and its rhythms, at the movements of hair, plant tendrils and flowing water. Consciously or not, some designs even seem to evoke anatomical formations of bones or muscles. Marine forms, especially seaweeds and fishes, were well suited to this style which often has a slow-motion sub-aqueous quality (plate 49b). Sea plants sway and dolphins curvet in a tide of silver scrolls and pearly bubbles. Viking longships and lugsailed fishing smacks run before the gale with sails unreefed and filled to bursting. These typify British Arts and Crafts jewellery and may be seen in the work of Kate Allen, Edgar Simpson, Annie McLeish and many other workers. It seems quite possible that the whip scrolls with sinewy curves and abrupt returns that recur throughout all the decorative arts originated in the designers' efforts to represent running water. They occur on both sides of the channel and are, probably more than anything else the trademark of fin de siècle design.

A separate school of design grew up in Scotland, in Glasgow especially, whose leading

* 1864–1934.

light was Charles Rennie Mackintosh.* Unfortunately the jewels which he designed are exceedingly rare. Strong verticals characterize his work and that of the Glasgow designers generally. The superimposed rectangles which were also a feature of Glasgow design had a far-reaching effect on the continent and were widely adopted in Germany. In Herbert McNair's jewels human figures are glimpsed through entanglements of briars and brambles with an extraordinary fey effect.

Silver was the usual material of the British Arts and Crafts jeweller, although aluminium and copper were used on occasion. The stones were rarely of any value and fancy settings were an exception. Usually they were put in plain tubular collets. Turquoise was a great favourite, especially when cut with a network of chocolate brown matrix. Small pebbles of turquoise, uncut, but polished, were often enclosed in a cage of gold wire and linked at intervals on a fine chain for the neck, and long houndstooth pearls from the American freshwater mussel were treated in the same way. Otherwise pearls would be interestingly shaped blisters or baroques which are far more suitable for this type of work than the usual spheres or pear-shapes. Quartz cats' eyes, peridots, malachite, moonstone, lapis lazuli, amethyst, chrysoprase, amazonite, stained chalcedony and operculum were also used. Operculum or Chinese cat's eye is a disc of shell with a translucent green centre which forms the trap-door of a tropical sea snail, *turbo petholatus*. Opals were a natural choice, both white ones and the clear orange fire opals of Mexico. The black opals which were often set in the jewellery of this period need to be examined very closely in case they are doublets. Australian white opal often occurs in layers too thin and brittle to be cut and set in jewellery as it is, so this material is often backed with black glass, partly to reinforce it, partly in the hope that it will pass as the much more valuable black opal.

Ultimately and inevitably the Birmingham manufacturer jumped on the Arts and Crafts bandwagon, but from start to finish it had little effect on the high class trade in Great Britain (plate 50a). Liberty's† of London were of course the exception—a department store that was itself so much in the *avant-garde* of the new arts movement that in Italy it was known as 'Il Liberty'. Liberty's made a range of very pretty gold jewels under the trade name 'Cymric'. Marcus of London made jewels in the new style (plate 50b) and the characteristic whip scrolls appeared in a few diamond pieces, but this was almost the total extent of its influence. It remained a popular art which was to continue well into the twentieth century in England in the work of Wilson and Omar Ramsden‡ and many others.

In France it was a different story altogether. Here the jeweller's attitude had always been more experimental and more creative and he thought of his job not only as a trade, but as an art and a science as well. Art nouveau, as the new movement was called in France, was not so much an underground movement as a palace revolution. Back in the seventies the house of Boucheron had already sowed the seeds of change and liberally manured them with U.S. dollars from the American millionaires for whom Europe had now become a playground and who eagerly snapped up anything new and daring that

* 1868–1928.
† Arthur Lazenby Liberty founded the firm in 1875.
‡ Omar Ramsden, 1873–1939.

appeared on the market. And in the sixties the West came in contact with a society as alien to it as had been that of Mexico—Japan. Japanese design, with its topsy-turvy sense of symmetry, its exquisite sense of the appropriate and its economy of line, had a great influence on the decorative arts. More and more jewel designs were balanced off centre, and this led to a re-examination of rococo design which introduced its own special bizarre note into the mood of the times. By the last quarter of the century all the ingredients were there; it required only some alchemist to combine them in a heady elixir which would cleanse the vision and purify the senses, and that could be no other than René Lalique.

René Jules Lalique* was born at Ay, a small town in the hills on the north bank of the Marne. Although he was taken to Paris by his parents when he was still a baby, all his vacations were spent in the Champagne countryside, and it must have been there that he acquired the deep unsentimental knowledge of the ways of nature that he was to draw on later. From an early age he showed himself to be a fine draughtsman, but at the age of sixteen he was apprenticed to the jeweller Louis Aucoc in whose workshop he learned the practical knowledge that no designer can satisfactorily do without. After two years in England at Sydenham College he studied sculpture and experimented with etching. He began designing freelance and allied himself to a M. Varenne, friend of the family, who placed the designs with Paris jewellers to be paid for with a percentage of the ultimate sale price. The designs were executed in yellow gouache on black paper. In later years Lalique collected as many of them as he could and burned them, but whether this was in order to help future designers or because of the distaste some artists feel for their earlier work, we do not know. Certainly, apart from a certain freshness and impertinence, these designs give little idea of what their creator was to produce later (see plate 51a).

In 1886, with many misgivings he took over the shop and workrooms of a M. Destape who was leaving to manage his vineyards in Algeria. Under their capable foreman, M. Briançon, the workshops were already well staffed and equipped, and the business was a thriving one. From this time forward, Lalique was liberated. One of the greatest frustrations for the freelance designer is the client who says that to his educated eye the design is superb, but that it would never catch on with the public. Lalique was now in a position to find out at first hand just what the public really did want.

In 1887 he set out quite self-consciously to evolve a new style. It was almost like inventing a new language—by 1889 he had laid down the first principals of the grammar, by 1895 he had refined and elaborated it and built up a vocabulary so varied and expressive that every jeweller in Paris wished to be conversant with it. In 1891 he designed the jewels for Sarah Bernhardt in her part in *Iseyl*, and again in 1894 when she was playing in *Gismonda*. The lovely actress seems to have become the spirit of art nouveau, its muse and its apotheosis. The Czech designer Mucha created her posters, and for her Lalique liberated some of his most extraordinary creations.

In his fantastically appointed studio on the rue Thérèse, in an atmosphere saturated with fragrance from the flowers which overflowed from vases in every part of the room, Lalique worked hour after hour, his pencil only leaving his hand when he went to observe

* 1860–1945.

the progress of his glass-making experiments, which he did not only by daylight but at all hours of the night as well. The way in which Lalique used moulded glass in his jewels was typical of his approach (plate 52c). That jewellers then regarded glass in jewels as an ersatz, an inferior substitute for precious minerals did not worry him in the slightest. For him sculpted glass opened up possibilities that could be realized in no other way and he did not give a damn for prejudice.

Lalique was always on the look out for new materials. On his work table lay an immense cow's horn which he had bought at the abattoir. Lalique was fascinated by this object and by the peculiar properties of the material of which it was composed, its blonde translucency and fine organic grain, its strength, resilience and lightness. Eventually he had a section sliced off the end and carved into a bracelet with applications of gold. For once this was not a new idea—in Algeria horn or whalebone bracelets of this kind were traditional. The Chinese, too, used to make exquisite jewels for the European market out of carved horn. Most translucent materials in use at that time were very brittle and heavy; horn was not only tough and light, but easy to work, and it was no doubt this, together with its colour, pallid, faded, autumnal, that Lalique found so attractive. He used it mainly for combs, diadems and other ornaments for the head. The coronal of fern leaves is typical not only in its use of this material but in its design (plate 51b). This is not the crisp green of fresh fern, but October bracken, the stems glistening with diamond frost and broken beneath the hooves of forest deer, the fronds of carved horn, mellowed by autumn. What other material could have conveyed this mood and yet be light and resilient enough to be used, unsupported in such large pieces. The same feeling was suggested by carved horn combs headed by flowerheads so sumptuously overblown that it seems as if the curling petal is about to tumble from the stalk, and others with sycamore leaves and keys, delicate, desiccated, worked from the same material. Jewellers had overworked the motifs of spring and summer, swelling buds and laden vines, until they had become tired clichés. Lalique introduced a new iconography, of langorous death and beautiful decay. All of Lalique's work speaks of his loving but unsentimental observation of nature and his deep understanding of the eternal cycle of birth, ripeness and dissolution.

Of the techniques used in France at this time, that of plique-à-jour enamel is most typical of art nouveau. Plique-à-jour is basically a type of cloisonné, with the difference that the back of the mount is left open so that the light can shine through it like a stained-glass window. This is a very difficult technique and there are several ways of tackling it. One is to secure the openwork mount to a sheet of copper foil either by hard soldering it or by firing it on with a thin layer of flux (colourless enamel). The piece is then charged with powdered enamel and fired in the usual way. Lastly the copper backing is soaked away in acid leaving the enamel, and the high carat gold untouched. Lalique seized upon this technique to reproduce the translucent membranes which occur so often in nature— leaves, fins and the wings of bats and insects. He habitually used gold of a greenish tint and removed the gloss from the surface of the enamel, probably with a light dip in hydrofluoric acid.

There was nothing new about plique-à-jour enamel: it was certainly known to

Benvenuto Cellini and probably to the Byzantine craftsman. Its rediscovery and reintroduction in France is often attributed to Fernand Thesmar.* The claim is also made by Fontenay. In 1852 he commissioned some 'translucent enamel' from Lefournier for the mounts of a fan he was making. These represented castle towers, the stained-glass windows of which were to be in plique-à-jour. According to Massin however, the discovery was accidentally made by Briet while firing a piece of cloisonné, the backing plate of which fell off when he withdrew it from the furnace. Briet's friend Riffaut used this apparent mischance as the starting point for a series of experiments culminating in the superb range of jewels he made for Boucheron. Among Boucheron's exhibits at the 1867 Exhibition was 'a hand mirror into the border of which transparent enamel has been introduced with excellent effect when the mirror is held up to the light'.

From 1895 Lalique introduced the human figure into his compositions, either naked or draped (plate 52a). For some this was the worst kind of bad taste, in spite of the fact that the most revered goldsmiths of the past, in the sixteenth century and even in ancient Greece, had done so constantly. In some the naked female figures, in cast green or yellow gold, are seen struggling upwards while others strive to hold them back. The contrast between these tender female limbs and the violent attitudes in which they are locked is curiously poignant. Sometimes the figures have brilliantly enamelled butterfly wings, sometimes they appear to be struggling underwater. These motifs would carry far too strong an emotional charge if Lalique had not defused them by giving them facial expressions as impassive as that of a Tanagra figurine. The same device, this accentuation of the tenderness of the female form with a note of harshness, he uses on other jewels: a gentle female profile is framed in spiky pine needles, a face smiles beneath an enormous helmet of saprophytic foliage (plate 52b) and again the emotional temperature is lowered by the blandness and relaxation of the features. Contemporaries used the same device, but never with Lalique's delicate sense of when to stop. One may look at Lalique's more outrageous pieces and try to find the magic catalyst that makes these monsters, these knots of serpents, these disembodied fighting cocks vomiting diamonds, these cannibalistic dragonflies so irresistibly beautiful. How he got away with it must always be a mystery, although all but his most infatuated aficionados will admit that he sometimes came unstuck. It is impossible to experiment so daringly without an occasional pratfall, and of these Lalique undoubtedly had his share.

Often when the success of a design depended on fine figure work, Lalique would model it in wax or plaster several times the size of the finished jewel. He would then use a reduction machine to transfer the design to the ivory or glass or even to a punch and die.

Many others worked in the new style that Lalique had invented, but it would be wrong to call them his imitators. He evolved a means of expression that belonged so naturally to the fin-de-siècle period that it would have been mere perversity for others to shun it on the grounds of unoriginality.

Vever was perhaps the most distinguished of his disciples. The house of Vever was founded in the frontier town of Metz in 1831. Ernest Vever fought bravely against the

* 1843–1912.

G (a) An enamelled PENDANT in Renaissance style set with diamonds, pearls and cabochon rubies

(b) A 'Holbeinesque' PENDANT set with sapphire, rubies and rose diamonds and decorated with champlevé enamels

See page 90

H Diamond, sapphire and emerald BROOCHES
French, late nineteenth century   *See page* 61

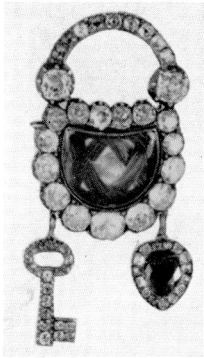

1 (*a*) A diamond PADLOCK with hair compartment centre and with ruby heart and diamond key hanging below English, late eighteenth/ early nineteenth century

See page 18

(*b*) A pair of gold and lavender-blue enamel pendent EARRINGS set with cornelians and pearls

French, *circa* 1805

(*c*) A gold, emerald and rose diamond cluster RING with triple wire shoulders

Circa 1800   *See page* 23

(*d*) A RING of the revolutionary period applied with reliefs of Marat and Pelletier de St. Fargeau (*enlarged*)

See page 18

(*e*) A gold RING set with a heart-shaped cornelian given to Lord Byron by John Edleston about 1805, and the jewel alluded to in his poem *The Cornelian*

(*All pieces illustrated are reproduced life-size unless otherwise indicated*)

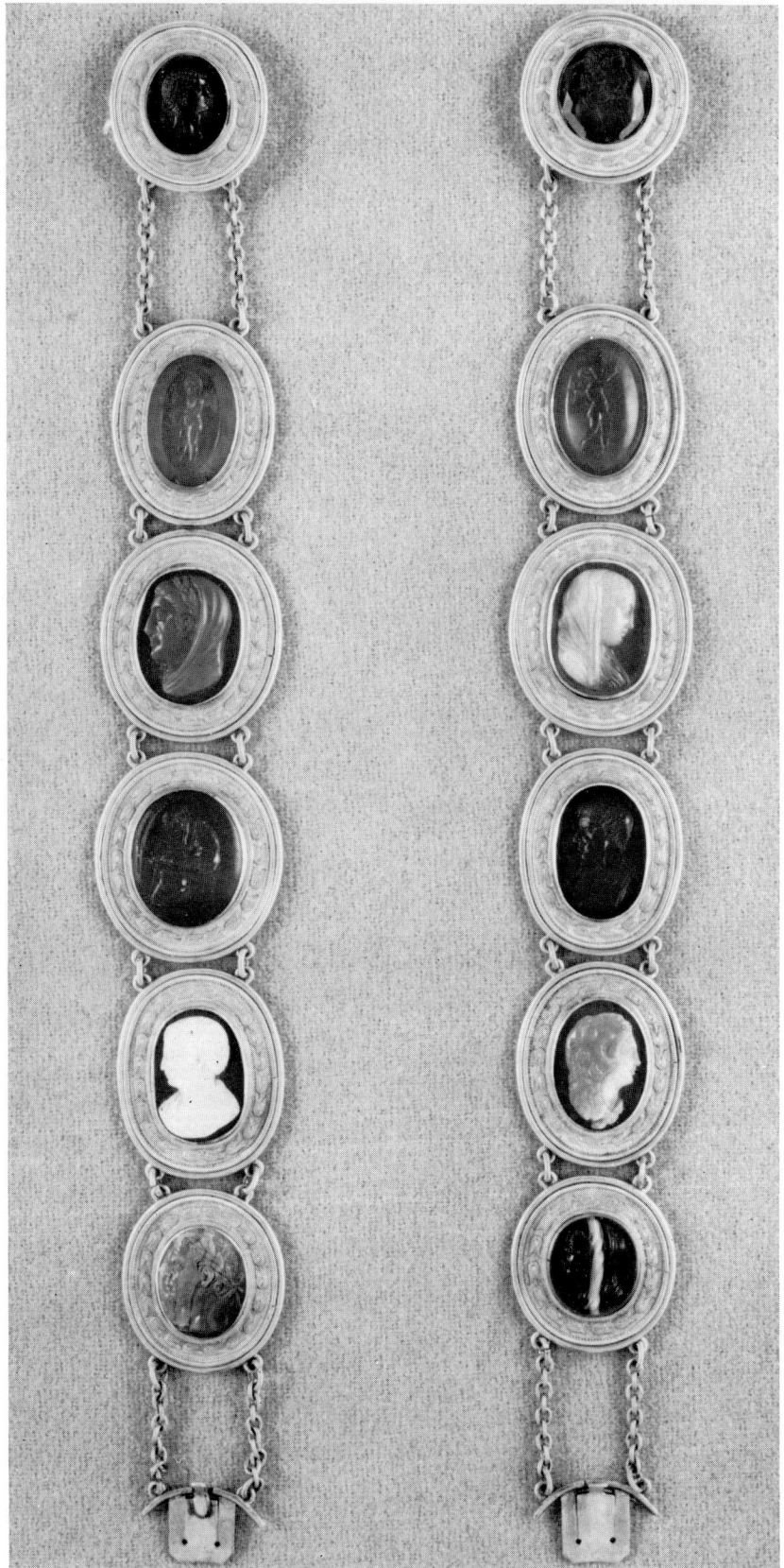

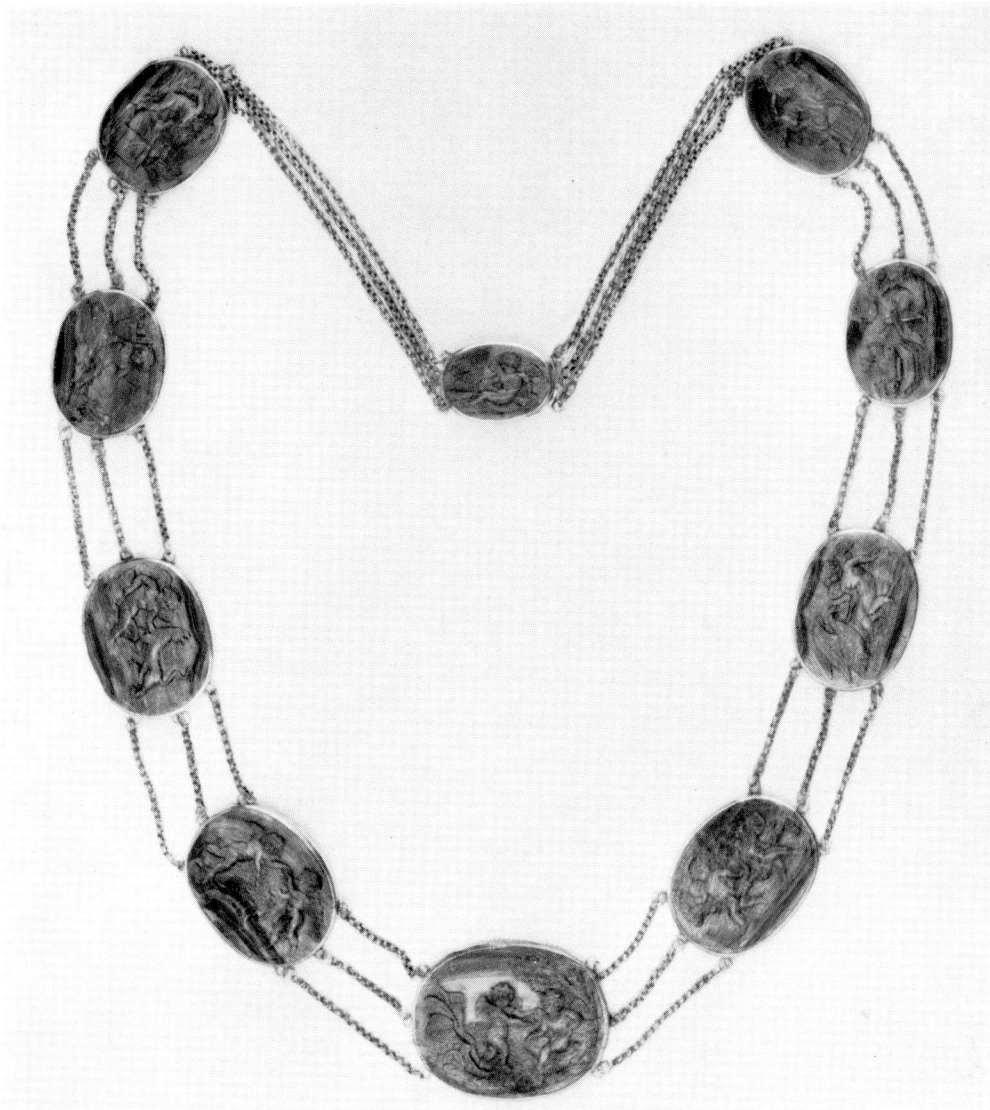

3 A NECKLACE of malachite cameos linked by skeins of fine chain
   Circa 1810   *See pages* 20, 21

2 (*opposite*) A pair of BRACELETS set with cameos and intaglios. The milled gold wire which forms
   part of the outer border, and the garland of husks on a matt gold ground occur frequently in
   jewels of the Napoleonic period. The chains which lengthen the bracelets are probably a later
   modification
See page 20

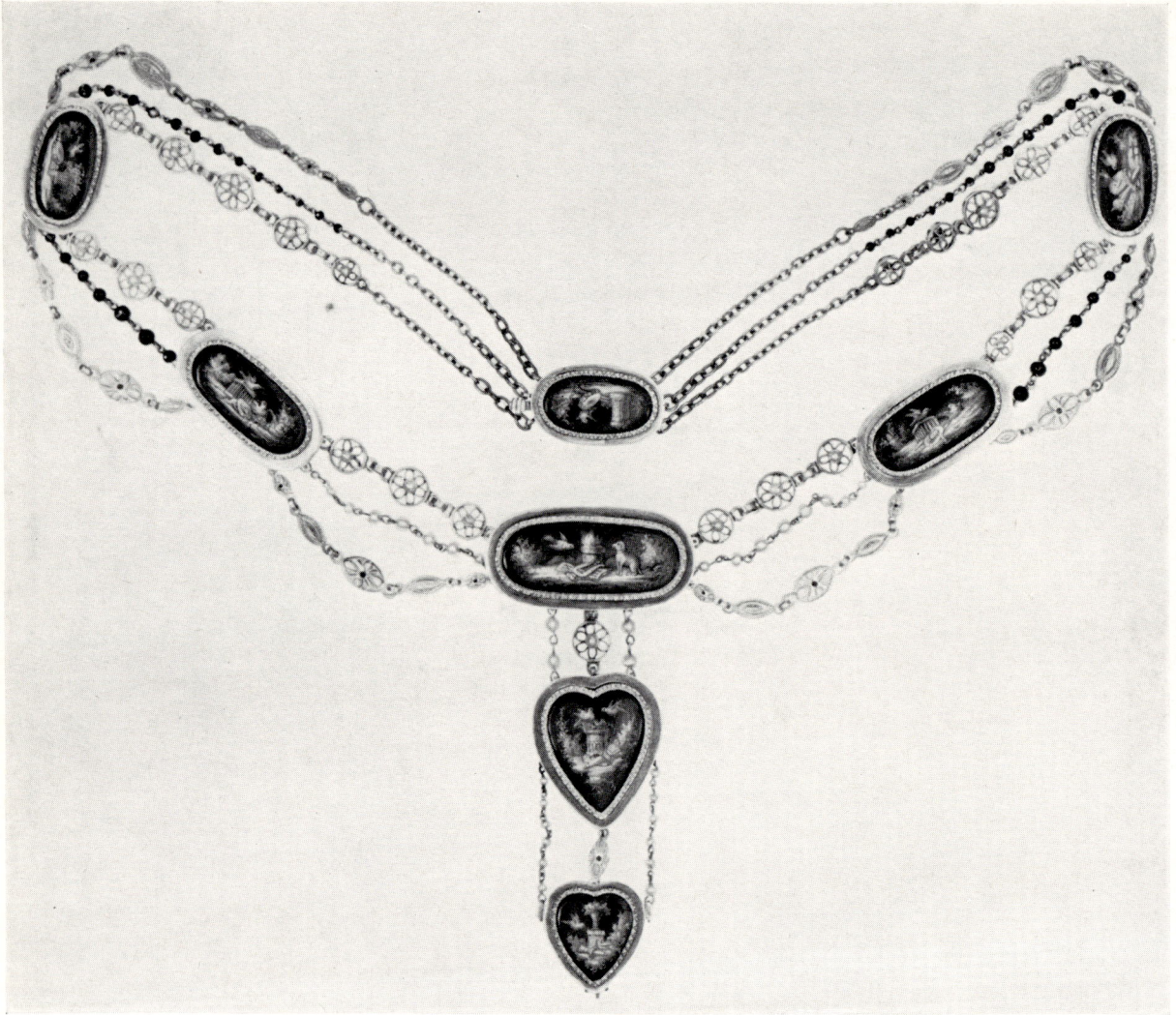

4 A NECKLACE set with enamel plaques painted in grisaille on a royal blue enamel ground with symbols of love, harmony and fidelity, and probably a wedding gift. These complex arrangements of chains are typical of jewels made during the first twenty years of the century (*slightly reduced*)

French   *See page* 23

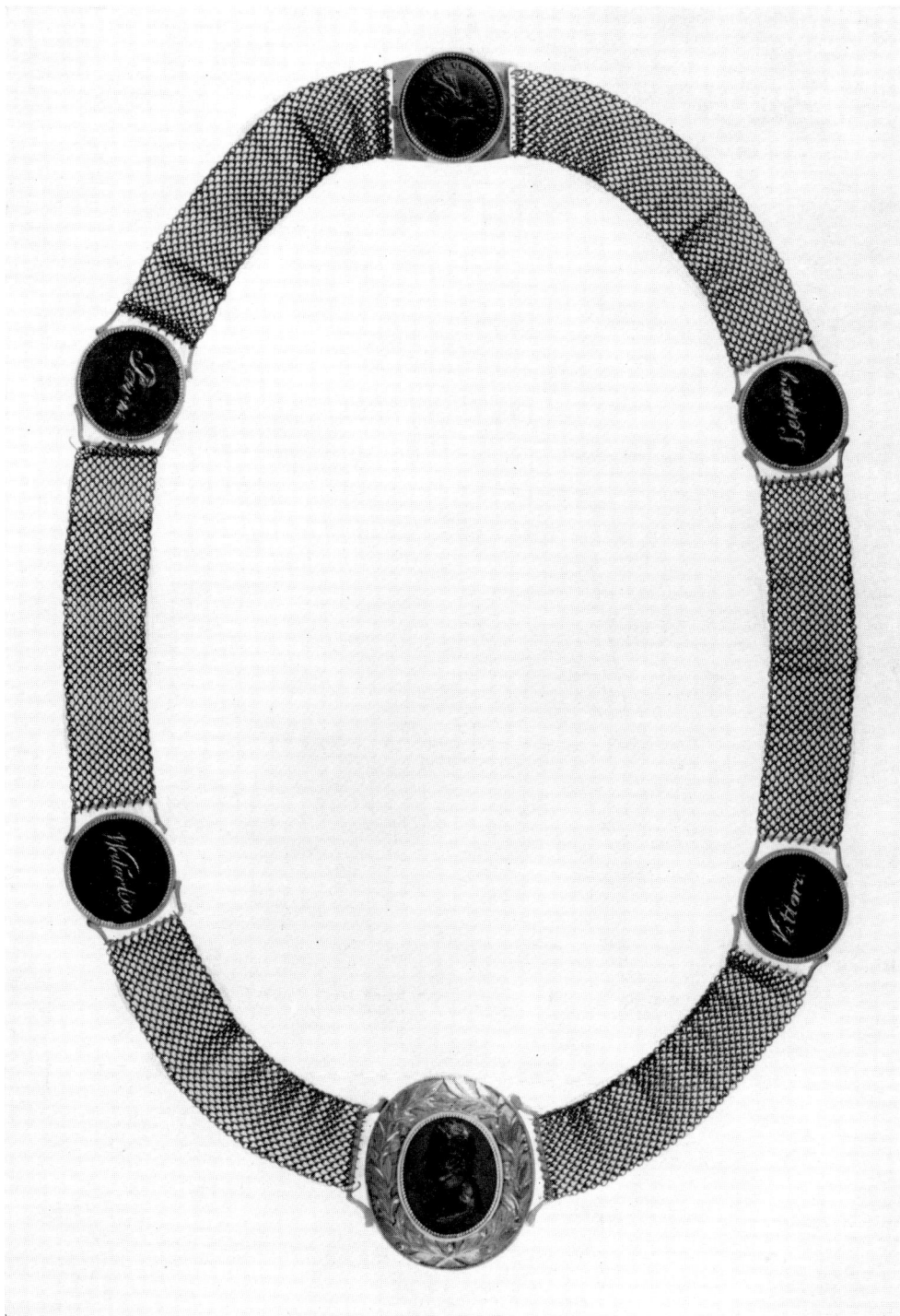

5 A NECKLACE of Berlin iron set in gold with engraved plaques of allied victories, a medallion of Wellington and another with a winged victory inscribed 'Gott segnete die vereinigte herren'

See page 24

6 A paste DEMI-PARURE which may originally have also comprised comb and earrings. The liberal use of milled gold wire places this piece in the first quarter of the century. In the tiara the slender diapered strip at the base and the stylized plant motifs are stamped by machine (*slightly reduced*)

Circa 1820   *See page* 30

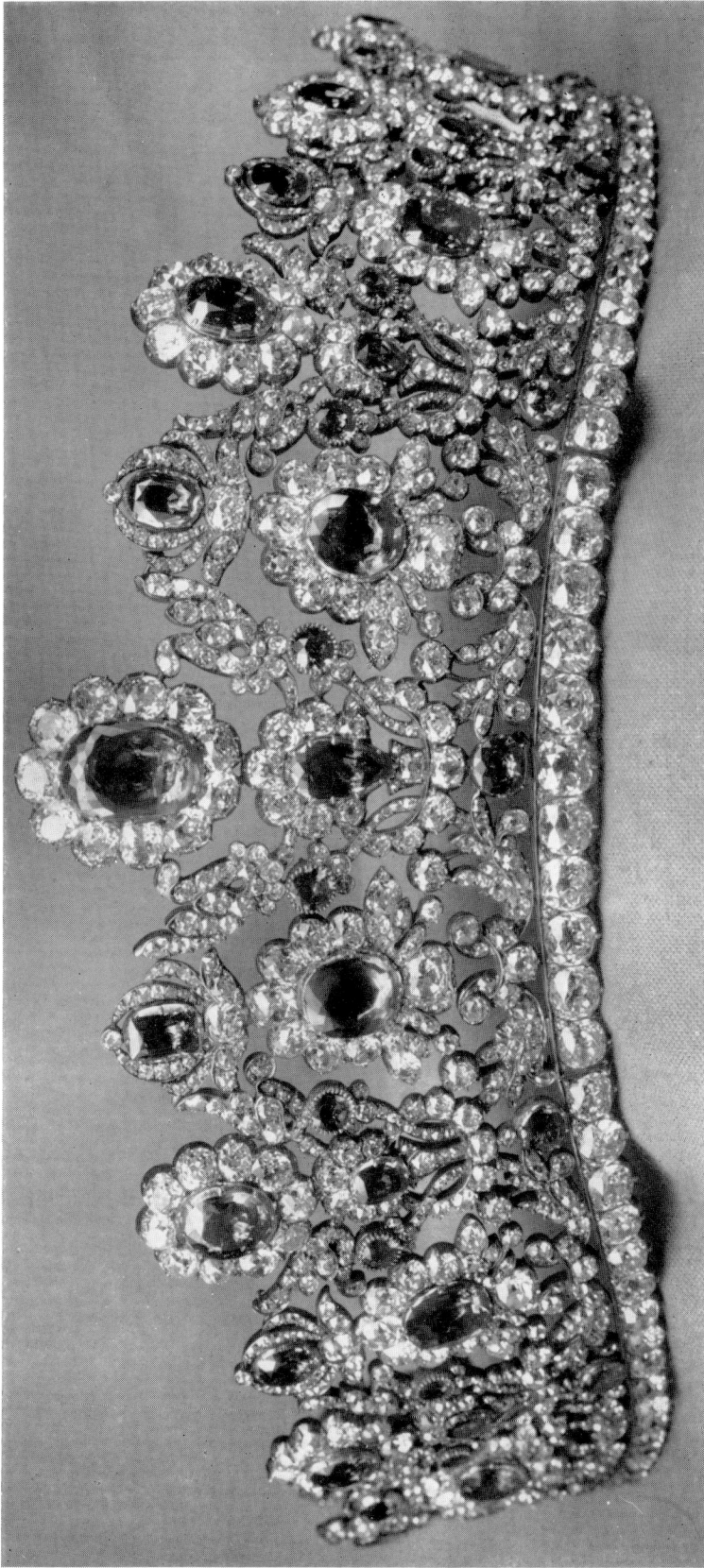

7 A ruby and diamond TIARA, part of the French crown-jewels. Commissioned by Louis XVIII after the Restoration, it was designed by Eberhard Bapst and executed by his brother Charles Frédéric who completed it in June 1816. The cornucopia scrolls at the base of the tiara, spider-like blooms and snapdragon-shaped buds at the top occur between 1815 and 1835

See page 28

8 Diamond chain NECKLACE. Chain designs were numerous, both simple patterns like this and larger and more complex ones. The compact 'marsh plant' motif with its arrow-shaped leaves and looped stems was often used for brooch designs around 1840, and in this case can be detached for wear as a brooch

Early nineteenth century *See page 28*

9 (*a*) The head of a diamond and tortoise-shell COMB in a naturalistic design of wild flowers

Circa 1830   *See page* 28

(*b*) An emerald and diamond BROOCH. The juicy foliate scrolls and the width and symmetry of the design are characteristic of the thirties

See page 28

(*c*) Diamond BROOCH. Many brooches like this one in diamonds were designed around the horizontal axis, recalling the Brandebourg of the previous century, and like it were often worn in suites of three

See page 28

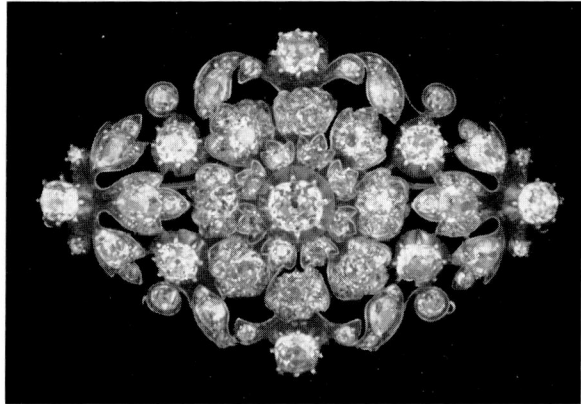

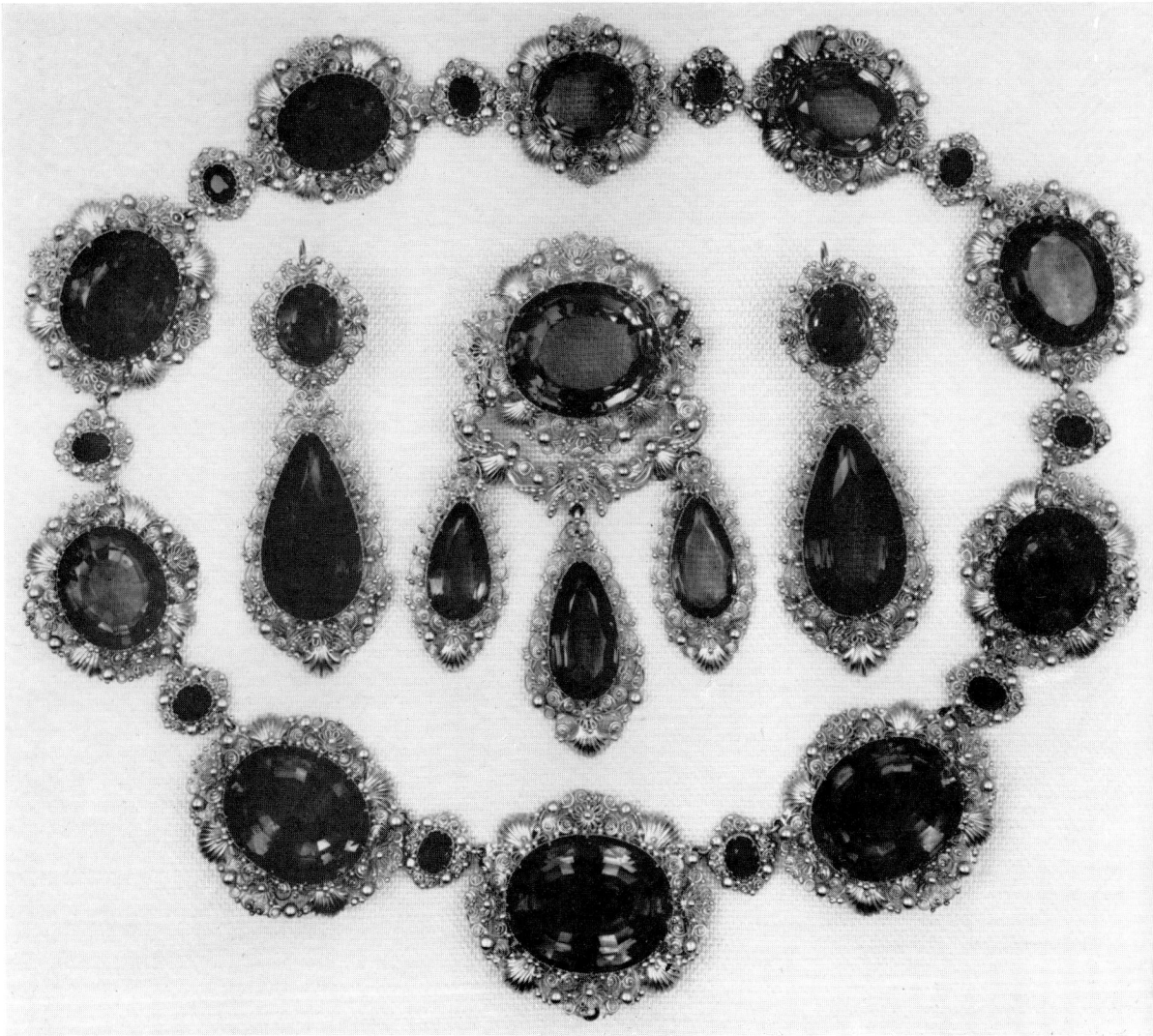

10 and 11 (*opposite*) A gold and amethyst SUITE in the cannetille style. In this case the filigree flowers and tendril scrolls are mingled with stamped seashell motifs (slightly reduced).

See page 29

The BRACELETS and 'chatelaine' BROOCH from the same suite, reproduced actual size for scale and detail

a

b

c

d

e

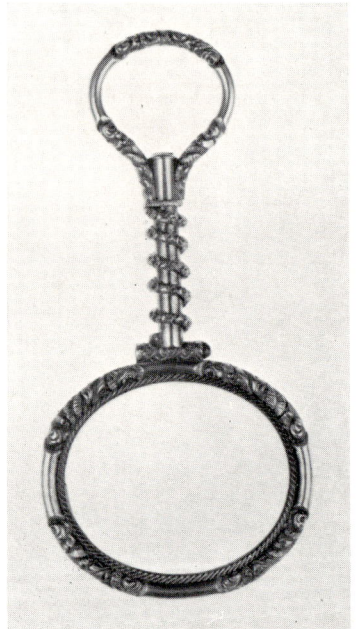

f

g

12 Gold SEALS, 1820 to 1840: (*a*) and (*c*) are characteristic in both size and design, (*b*) a swivel seal, (*d*) is a squatting fox, (*e*) a coiled serpent, and (*f*) is a gilt metal QUIZZING GLASS.

See pages 31, 32, 44

(*g*) A pair of white chalcedony gold and turquoise pendent EAR-RINGS. The milky white chalcedony drops are wound with sprays of turquoise and filigree forget-me-nots
English, *circa* 1835   *See page* 36

13 (*f*) (*opposite*) Embossed gold and turquoise EARRINGS and a gold chrysoprase and pink topaz. BROOCH in the same style,

Circa 1840   *See page* 31.

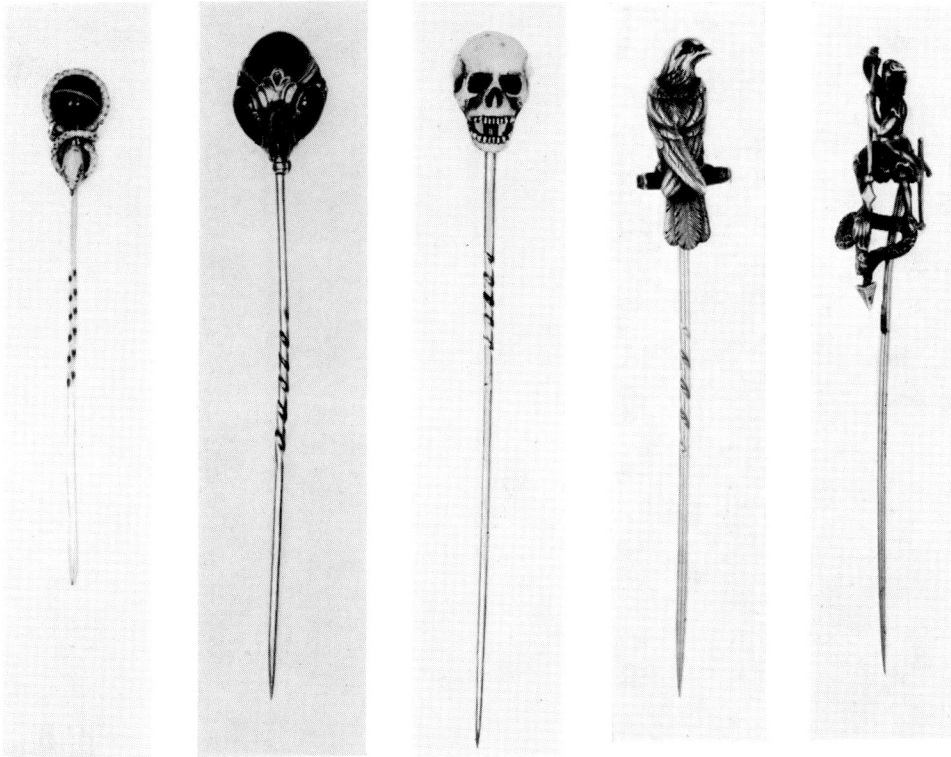

13 STOCK PINS: (a) An enamelled serpent coiled around an onyx apple. (b) A gold and carbuncle pin in gothic style. (c) An exquisitely enamelled skull with a hinged jawbone, French. (d) A falcon, French. (e) St. Michael in gold and silver

See page 32

14(a) Gold, pink topaz, emerald, half pearl and bloodstone MALTESE CROSS

Circa 1835   *See page* 35

(b) A gold and agate MALTESE CROSS with hair compartment centre. Note the chased border of roses and feather scrolls

Circa 1835   *See page* 35

(c) A diamond MALTESE CROSS

Circa 1840   *See page* 35

(d) A Russian diamond and red spinel PENDANT. The small rose diamonds which form the setting edge establish its Russian origin

See page 33

15 A pink topaz NECKLACE and matching BROOCH. The stones are in cup-shaped settings enclosed at the back and have been foiled to enhance the colour. The cross at the centre is fitted with a ring so that it can double as either brooch or pendant

Early nineteenth century *See page* 34

16 (a) A bird BROOCH in contrasted coloured golds set with turquoises and with tremblant wings
Circa 1830   *See page* 35

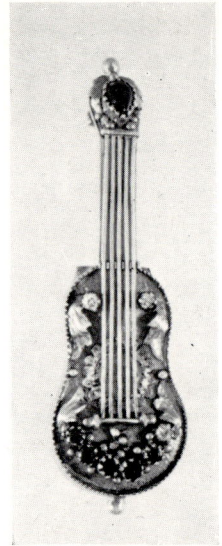

(b) A guitar BROOCH in coloured
golds, the initial letters of the
stones set in the base spelling
REGARD
See page 37

(c) A sky-blue enamel and diamond CROIX-
À-LA-JEANETTE
Circa 1835 *See page* 44

(d) A gold bouquet BROOCH set
with turquoises, amethysts
and half-pearls
Circa 1830   *See page* 31

(e) A half-pearl cluster RING, the
mount richly chased
Circa 1840

17 (a) A sapphire and diamond BRACELET set with an enamel miniature by Henry Bone of Sir John James Scott Douglas who died in 1836 aged forty-three. Compare the cornucopia scrolls which flank the miniature with those at the base of the tiara on plate 7

See page 50

(b) A BRACELET in coloured golds set with gems and Geneva enamels of peasant girls in the costumes of the Swiss cantons. The bracelet is completely reversible and the design is continued on the reverse

Circa 1830 See page 34

18 (*a*) A portrait of Mrs Hogg by Sir William Beechey

See page 30

(*b*) A portrait sketch of the young Lord Beaconsfield wearing his WATCH AND CHAIN in the current mode by Daniel Maclise

National Portrait Gallery   See page 37

19 Early Victorian LONGCHAINS:
    (*a*) Horsehair woven into links of contrasting black and white (*b*) A pinchbeck chain in a popular pattern also common in gold (*c*) Gold, in an unusual design although the hand forming the clasp is typical (*d*) Gold, the stamped links of foliate scroll and key fret design

See pages 36, 47

20 Design for a royal presentation BRACELET by John Bridge, endorsed with the signature of William IV, and part of a list, compiled by the King, of the ladies to whom it was to be given

21 An early Victorian snake NECKLET, the head set with emeralds and rose diamonds
   See page 43

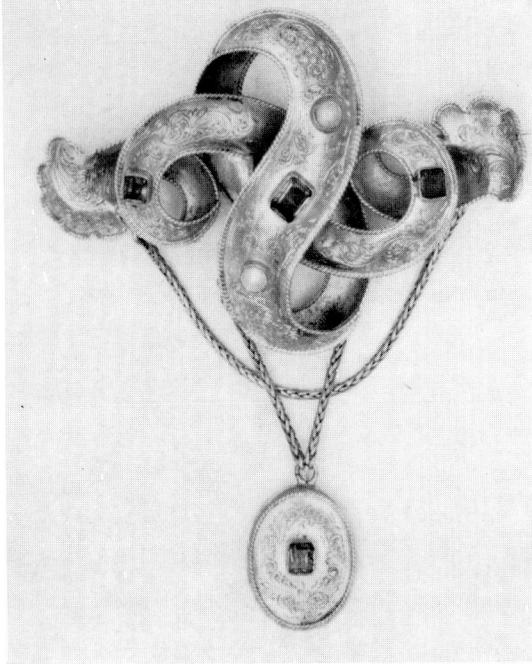

22 (a) A gold BROOCH set with foiled coloured stones and freshwater pearls. The complicated interlacement is typical of mid-nineteenth century design, and so is the rich engraving which decorates it

See page 45

(b) A garnet and diamond BROOCH, the ribbon ends fringed with drops, mid 19th century

23 (a) An inlaid silver and malachite ivy-leaf
 BROOCH dated on the reverse
 26th August 1851

See page 51

(b) A BROOCH—the linked rings are of royal blue
 enamel entwined with diamond foliage

Circa 1850   *See page* 45

(c) A shell cameo BROOCH with swivelled
 centre, the border decorated with cuir
 roulée scrolls

Mid-nineteenth century   *See page* 46

(d) A carved jet BROOCH set with a
 fossil ammonite

Circa 1850   *See page* 47

24 Diamond jewels forming a wedding gift purchased in 1842:

A TIARA in the form of a simple garland of flowers. This jewel may be worn as a simple wreath, or with two sprays pendent at the temples as shown in the illustration. It can also be dismantled into five separate brooches

A stomacher BROOCH and girandole EARRINGS. The chandelier drops on the earrings are interchangeable with the two simpler foliate pendants on the brooch

5 Seed-pearl jewels of the mid-century: a NECKLACE of hop flowers instead of the more usual vine motifs; and a BROOCH of linked ring design (*slightly reduced*)

See page 46

4 (*continued*) A BRACELET. The dainty design of this, the asymmetry of the centre and the slight tilt to the hinges which bring the sides on to it, suggest that this began life as a ferronnière. The chains which hang from the brooch may even have formed the back of the ferronnière in the first instance (*slightly reduced*)

See pages 33, 46

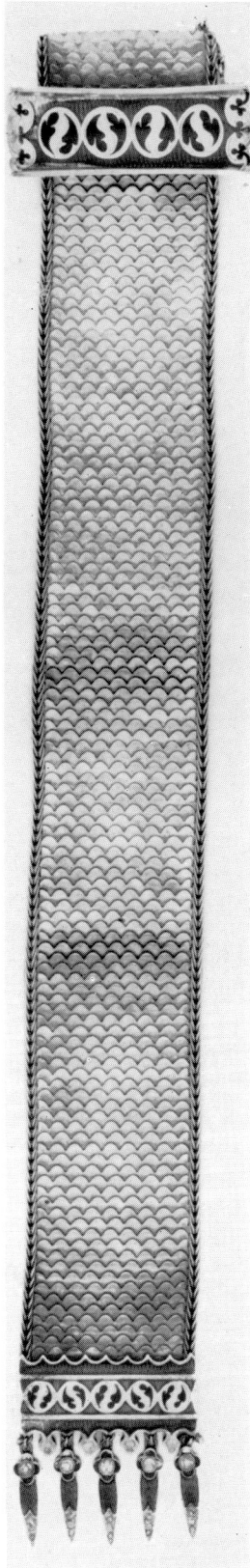

26 (a) (b) (c)

27 (*a*) A gold BRACELET decorated with blue and
white champlevé enamel. Bracelets of this kind
often have a locket compartment in the centre
Mid-nineteenth century   *See page* 50

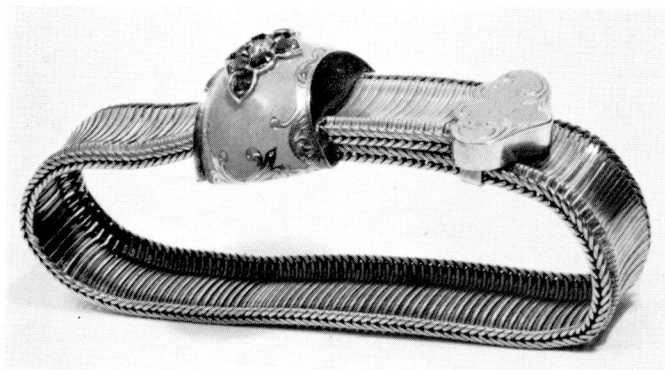

(*b*) A gold jarretière BRACELET decorated
with lavender-blue opaque enamel
and set with rubies
Circa 1855   *See page* 50

(*c*) A gold manchette BRACELET decorated with
blue and white champlevé enamel
See page 50

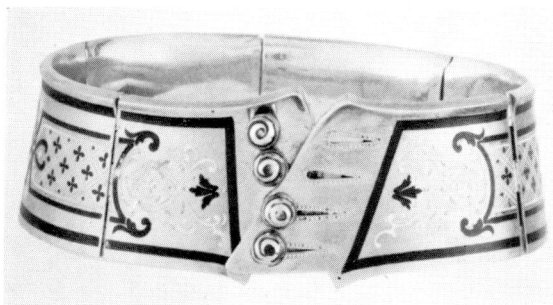

26 (*opposite*) (*a*) A gold and blue enamel BRACELET in which the buckle is not merely decorative but actually
serves as a fastening
Mid-nineteenth century   *See page* 50

(*b*) A gold BRACELET with royal blue, crimson and white enamel clasp and diamond fringe
Mid-nineteenth century   *See page* 50

(*c*) A gold pearl and peridot BRACELET with detachable pendant
Dated 1850   *See page* 50

28 EARRINGS of the 1860s. All are in the lightly frosted or coloured gold which came into use in the middle of the century, but the rich engraving of the fifties has been replaced by touches of applied granulation or filigree. There is a clever use of movement: the interaction of one loop swinging within the other (*top left*); the shimmer of a fringe (*top and centre right*). Star motifs (*centre and lower right*) are typical and bomb-shaped drops (*upper and lower left*)

See page 53

29 A demi-parure of NECKLACE and EARRINGS. Many variations were made on this basic design of festooned Brazilian chain with three pendants. Note that the snake-like chains of the festoons are actually terminated by serpent heads. The amphora pendants show the prevailing classical Greek influence and are set with carbuncles and rose diamonds. Note also the ubiquitous stars, in this case set with half-pearls and rose diamonds.

See page 53

30 (a) A BROOCH and EARRINGS of inlaid tortoise-shell

Circa 1865   *See page* 56

(b) A gold PENDANT with 'boot-lace' fringe and spool surmount. The centre is 'dished' to reflect the pattern of the inner border. The enamel and half-pearl diaper motif at the centre is quite in character with the period, although a star would be more usual

See pages 53, 54

(c) A pair of pendent EARRINGS set with calibré-cut turquoise, the seashell motifs set with rose diamonds and pearl. The fittings have been replaced with modern screws

See pages 55, 60

(d) A gold BRACELET set with an onyx cameo habillé of a Moor within a half-pearl border, the shoulders decorated with black enamel key-fret motifs

1860–70   *See page* 54

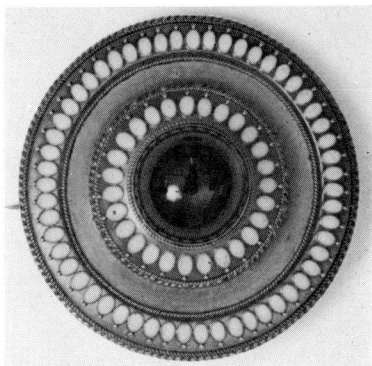

(a) A gold target-shaped BROOCH decorated with white cloisonné enamel and set with a carbuncle

(b) A gold BROOCH, the central boss of pavé-set turquoise
See page 53

(c) A gold PENDANT decorated with half-pearls and sky-blue enamel in a basket-weave pattern
See page 54

(d) In this BROOCH the vine motifs of the border are echoed in the Florentine mosaic at the centre; the leaves are of malachite, the grapes are of imitation pearl and the background of black Belgian marble
See page 56

(e) A gold openwork BROOCH with inlays of Scotch pebble
See page 55

(f) A BROOCH with a tinted crystal intaglio of a tabby kitten in an enamel and diamond border
See page 54

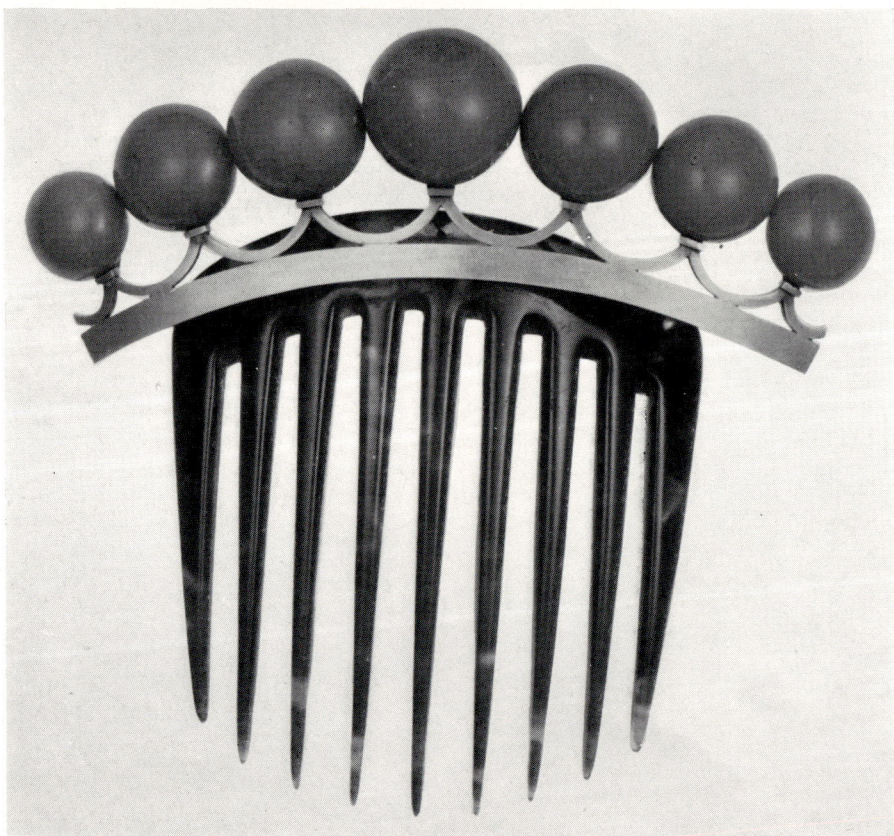

32 (*opposite*) (*a*) A silver BANGLE of horseshoe design with champlevé enamel inscription

Russian, late nineteenth century   *See page* 60

(*b*) A tortoise-shell HAIR ORNAMENT set with coral—a classical design for this type of jewel

Circa 1865   *See page* 56

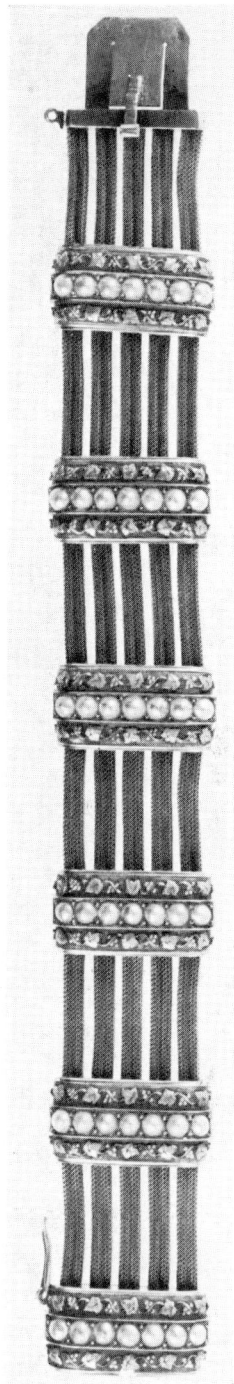

33 (*a*) A silver LEONTINE—a type of ornamental watch-chain much worn by ladies in the 1870s

(*slightly reduced*)

See page 57

(*b*) A BRACELET in contrasting coloured golds set with half-pearls, possibly by Auguste Lion

See page 57

34 A carved coral SUITE
Italian, *circa* 1860   *See page* 58

35 A lava DEMI-PARURE comprising a brooch and a pair of soli-
taires or studs. Carved from grey Vesuvian lava with satyrs and
bacchante

See page 60

36 (a) A diamond ribbon bow BROOCH, part of a suite of three. In the 1860s parures like this were fashionable

See page 61

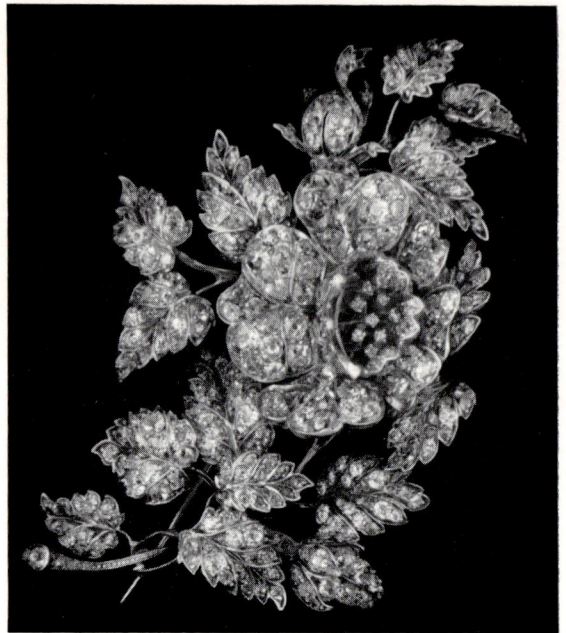

(b) A diamond rose-spray BROOCH

See page 61

37 (*a*) A gold hinged BANGLE decorated with blue enamel
and half-pearls

Circa 1870   *See page* 63

(*b*) A large hinged BANGLE
Late nineteenth century   *See page* 63

38 A Bohemian garnet COLLAR and matching BROOCH
Late nineteenth century *See page* 65

39 A silver NECKLACE of the late Victorian period. The plates are in the traditional repoussé work of Madras, although the beads and fastening are in European style

See page 66

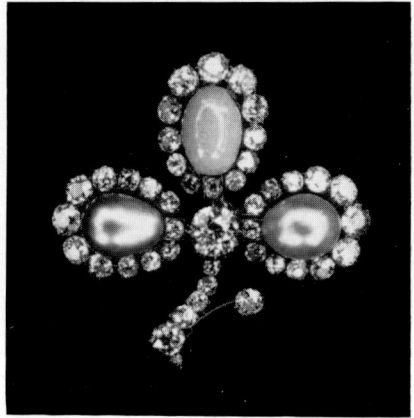

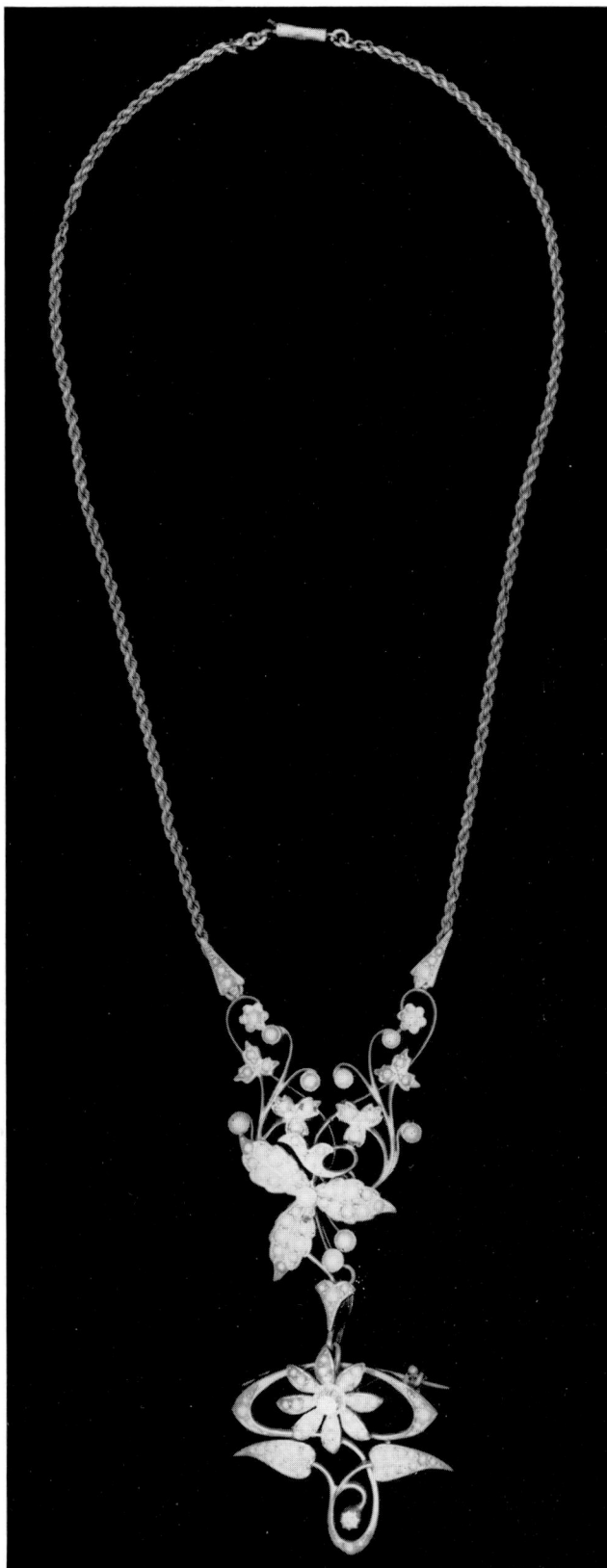

41 A gold and half-pearl NECKLACE
of art nouveau inspiration, the back
of Prince of Wales chain pattern
(*slightly reduced*)
See page 67

40 (*opposite*) (*a*) A ruby and diamond
dragonfly BROOCH

Circa 1890   *See page* 68

(*b*) A late Victorian diamond star
BROOCH

See page 67

(*c*) A late Victorian diamond BROOCH
in the form of a clover leaf set with
pink, black and white pearls

(*d*) A late Victorian diamond crescent
BROOCH

See page 67

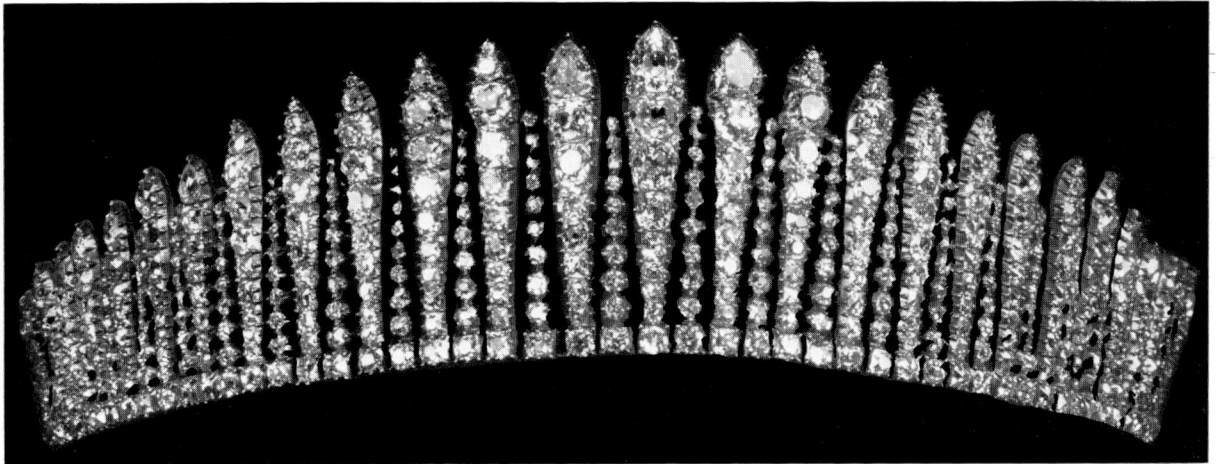

43 A diamond TIARA of Imperial Russian design (*slightly reduced*)
See page 71

pposite) A late Victorian diamond NECKLACE of foliate scroll design, the back of knife-edge wire links and in the ꞓntre a late Victorian diamond BROOCH PENDANT of sun in splendour design

ee page 71

44 (*a*) An enamelled jubilee CROWN PIECE, mounted as a brooch, probably by Edwin Steele of Birmingham

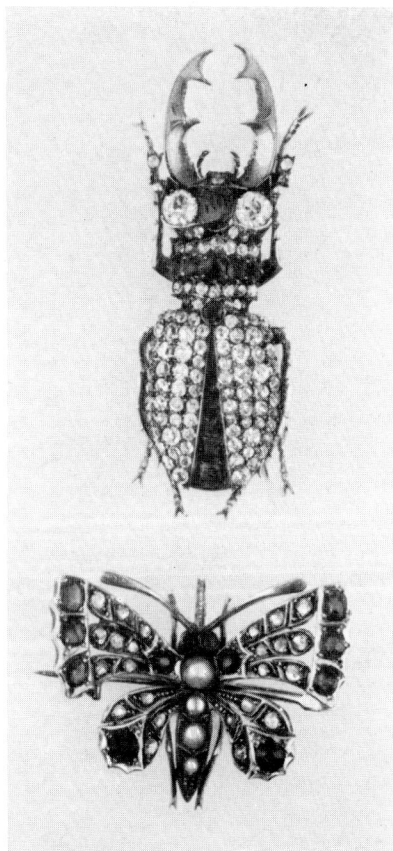

(*b*) A peridot and diamond PENDANT
Circa 1900   *See page* 70

(*d*) A late Victorian PENDANT in rose diamonds, blister pearls and blue and white enamel
See page 74

(*c*) Diamond and gem-set stag beetle and butterfly BROOCHES
Late Victorian   *See page* 68

(*e*) A diamond BROOCH commemorating the diamond jubilee, with enamelled shamrock, rose and thistle, symbolizing 'sixty years a queen'
See page 74

45 (a) A late Victorian gold, ruby and diamond half-hoop BRACELET

See page 71

(b) A late Victorian diamond and split-pearl half-hoop BRACELET

See page 71

(c) A late Victorian opal and diamond BRACELET of curb links

See page 71

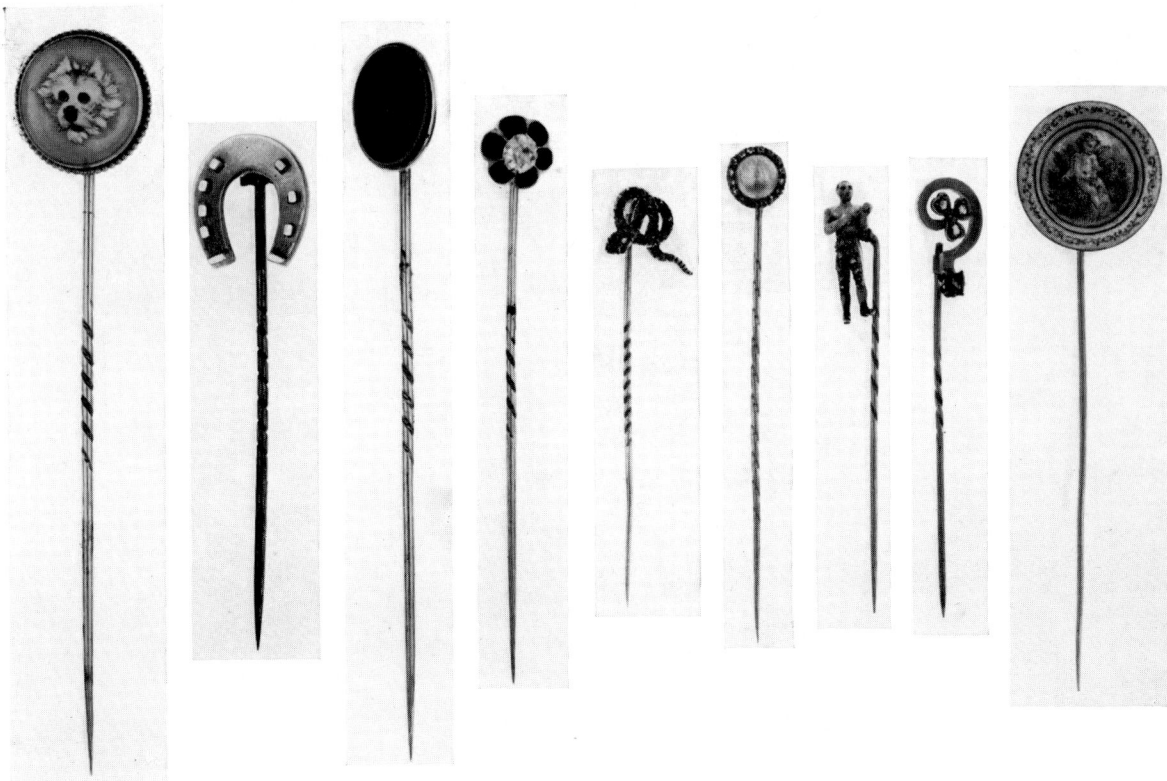

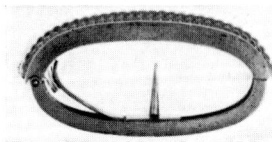

46 TIEPINS worn during the last part of the nineteenth century:
    (*a*) Set with a tinted crystal intaglio
    (*b*) A gold horseshoe—one of the most popular designs
    (*c*) Set with onyx and suitable for mourning
    (*d*) A diamond in a blue enamel setting
    (*e*) A green demantoid garnet snake
    (*f*) A diamond and half-pearl cluster
    (*g*) An enamel and rose diamond prizefighter
    (*h*) A clover leaf and question mark
    (*i*) An enamelled dinner-plate
    (*j*) and (*k*) Two gold rings designed to secure the tie

See page 73

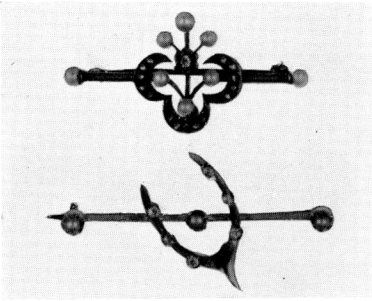

47 (a) Bar BROOCHES
See pages 73, 74

(b) Diamond RINGS of the 1890s in
designs which were made until well
into the present century
See page 73

(c) A BROOCH set with half-pearls
with a miniature of cherubs
mounted at its centre
See page 67

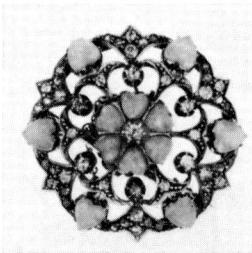

(d) A rosette BROOCH set with
diamonds and heart-shaped opals

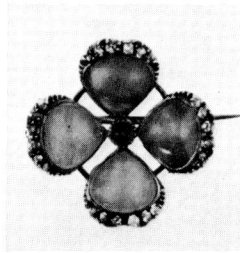

(e) A four-leaf clover BROOCH set with
chrysoprase and diamonds
See page 74

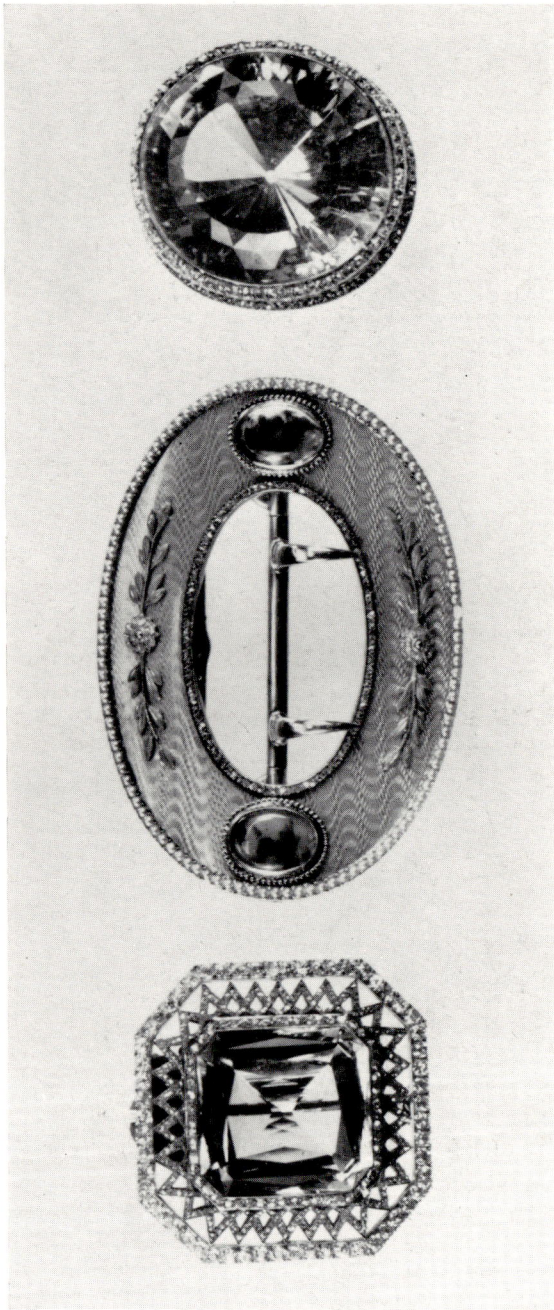

48 (a) A Fabergé blue topaz and diamond BROOCH, workmaster August Holmstrom

See page 74

(b) A Fabergé apple-green guilloche enamel and gold BUCKLE set with moss agates, workmaster Henrik Wigstrom

See page 74

(c) A Fabergé octagonal aquamarine and diamond BROOCH, workmaster Henrik Wigstrom

See page 74

49 (*a*) An allegorical JEWEL by Henry Wilson representing Christ standing flanked by two stags against a tree with leaves of green enamel with the towers of the holy city rising against a background of blue enamel. The border of chequered green, white and mauve enamel is set with star rubies

See page 76

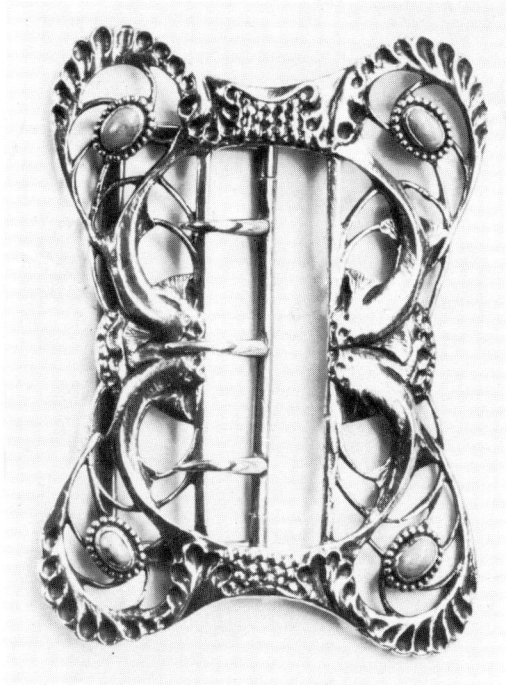

(*b*) A silver and turquoise BUCKLE by C. R. Ashbee in a design of fishes and seaweeds

See page 76

(*c*) A repoussé-work JEWEL by Henry Wilson in a design of interlaced vines bordered by roped wire

See page 76

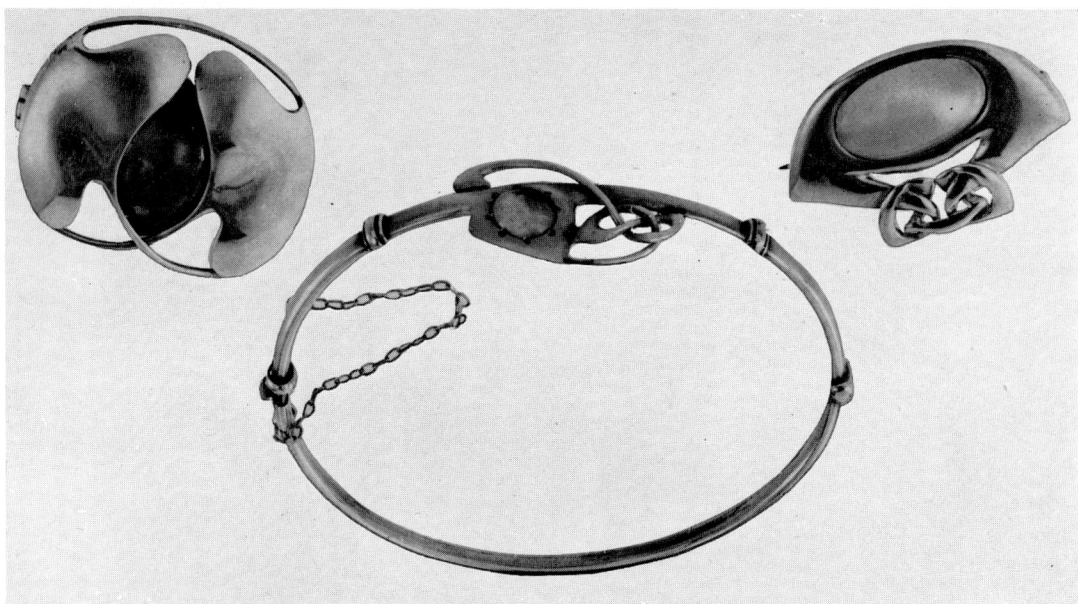

51 (a) A platinum and rose diamond BROOCH made by Lalique before he began his experiments with art nouveau
See page 78

(b) A TIARA of fern fronds in blonde horn with rose diamond stems, by Lalique
See page 79

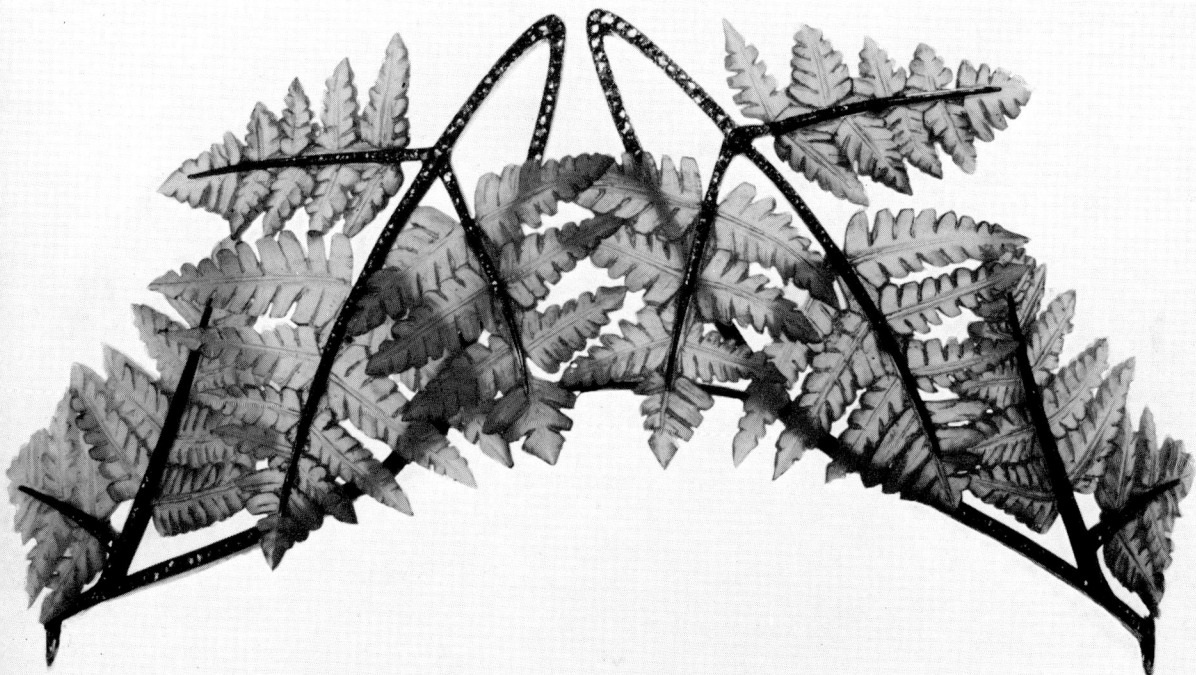

50 (opposite) (a) Machine produced gold JEWELS set with amethysts, opal and moonstone
See page 77

(b) A gold, blue enamel and black baroque pearl NECKLACE by Marcus
See page 77

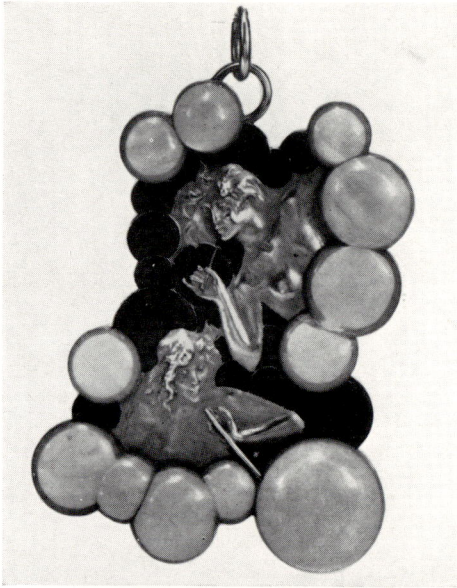

52 (a) A PENDANT of girls blowing bubbles
of opal and blue enamel, by Lalique

See page 80

(b) A PENDANT of a woman in a leafy
helmet of green plique-à-jour enamel
leaves with a baroque pearl pendant
below, by Lalique

See page 80

(c) A BROOCH of carved iceland poppies,
the blooms of blue and white glass,
the leaves and buds of turquoise blue
glass, and the stems set with rose
diamonds, by Lalique

See page 79

(d) A BROOCH of wisteria, the flowers
represented by Mississippi pearls,
the stems of white enamel and the
leaves of plique-à-jour, by Georges
Fouquet

See page 81

53 (a) A PENDANT in gold and plique-à-jour enamel depicting sunrise on a lake and framed by the attenuated bodies of swans, by Lucien Gautrait

See page 81

(b) A gold BUCKLE by Boucheron representing two panthers disputing a cornelian heart, with a lion's mask of moulded olive glass below

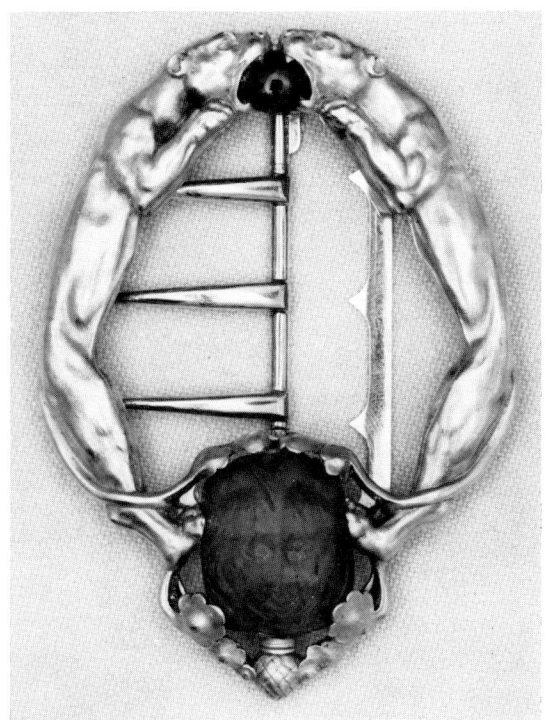

See page 81

54 (a) A half-pearl and gold
MEMORIAL BROOCH
with hair compartment
centre and chased
border
Early nineteenth
century
See page 84

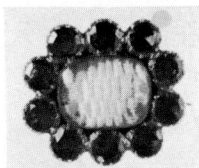

(b) MEMORIAL BROOCH with
hair centre and jet border
Early nineteenth century
See page 84

(c) Inscribed PENDANT in
gold, pearls and black
champlevé enamel,
designed as a Gothic
rosette, *circa* 1830

(d) A serpent BROOCH, its
body of woven hair, the
head, heart-shaped drop
and tail of blue enamel
Circa 1840   *See page* 85

(e) An unusual MEMORIAL
BROOCH in a design of
winged cherub's head of
gold, black enamel and
braided hair
Circa 1840   *See page* 85

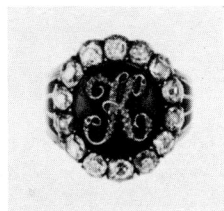

(f) A black enamel and
diamond MEMORIAL RING
Dated 1799   *See page* 84

(g) A black enamel, half-pearl
and rose diamond RING
with feather scroll
shoulders
Circa 1840

(h) A gold MEMORIAL RING,
the swivelled bezel set
with half-pearls and the
reverse enamelled black
Dated 1806   *See page* 86

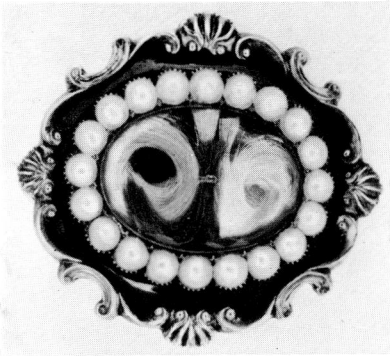

55 (a) A cartouche-shaped enamel,
gold and half-pearl BROOCH
Circa 1840   *See page* 85

(b) A black enamel, onyx and
half-pearl BROOCH, dated
1868, with the circular
outline, key-fret and Celtic
cross motifs common at this
time
See page 86

(c) An onyx and half-pearl PENDANT showing the
miniature at the reverse
Circa 1870   *See page* 86

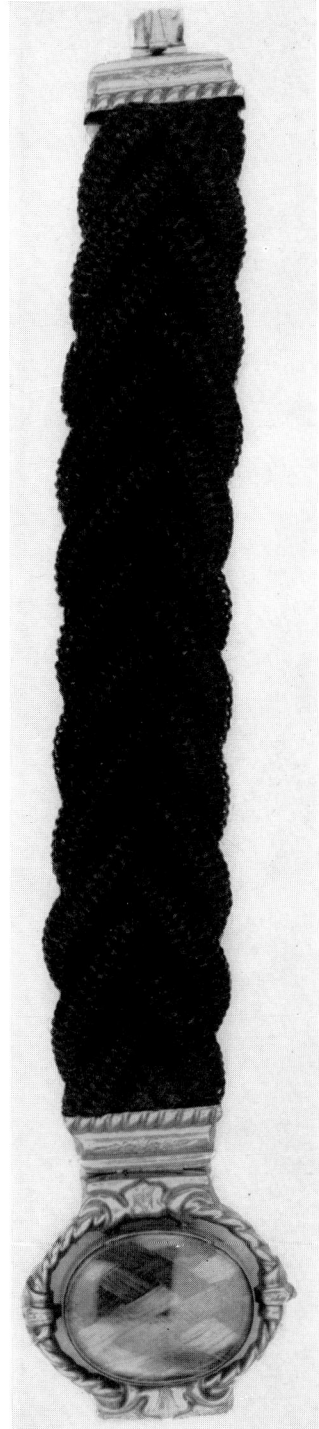

(d) A BRACELET of braided hair
Mid-nineteenth century
See page 85

56 A NECKLACE by Giuliano showing a subtle use of black and white enamel. Note the 's' shaped clasp on

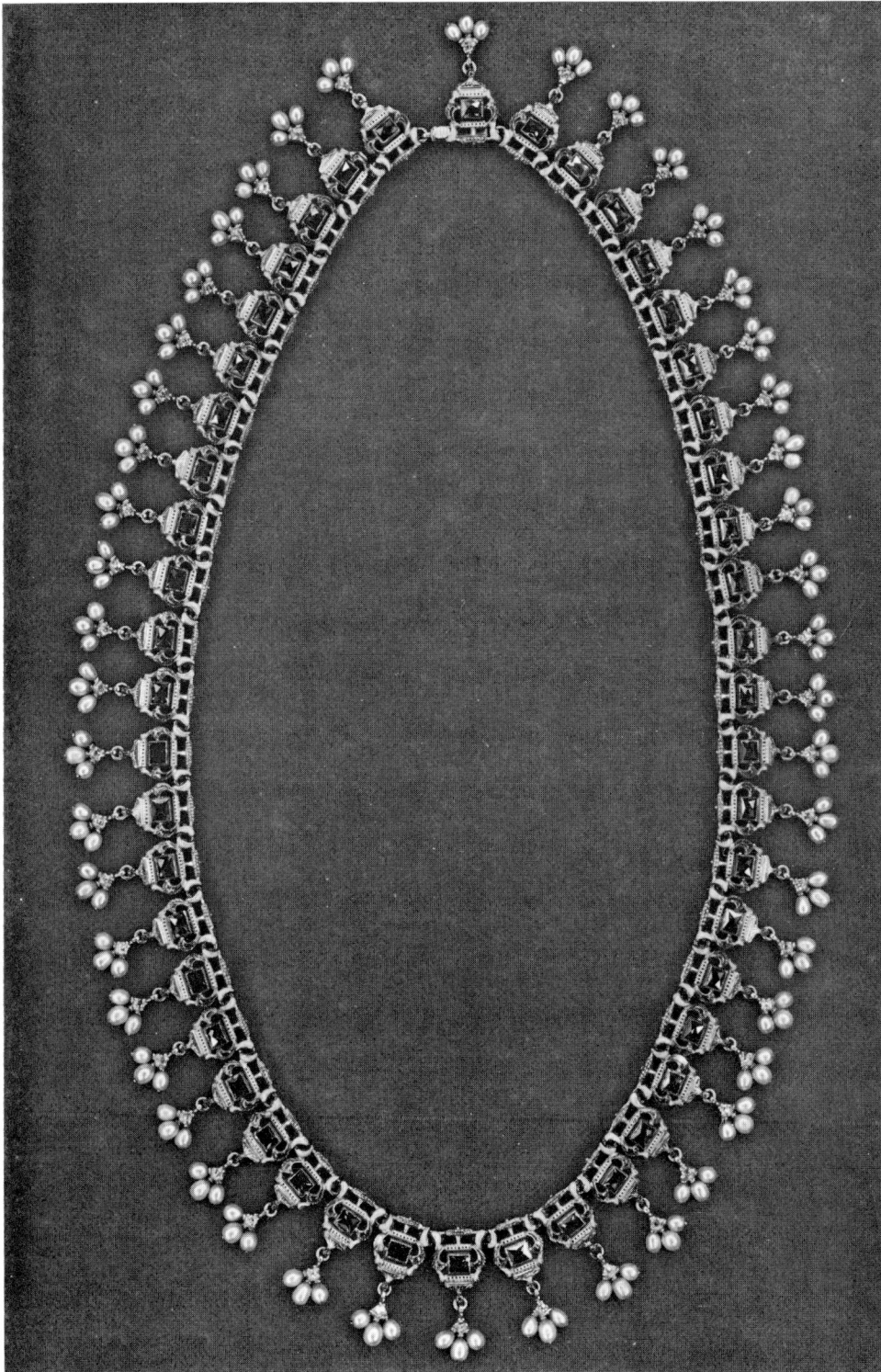

57 A NECKLACE by Giuliano, enamelled and set with cinnamon stones and pearls
See page 89

56 (*continued*)
which the little oval panel containing the signature is just visible
See page 89

58 Amphitrite; a DEMI-PARURE of pendant and earrings, by the brothers Fannières in gold and silver decorated with diamonds, pearls and black enamel set with a fine sardonyx cameo

See page 90

59 (*c*) (*opposite*) A gold NECKLACE in the Greek style. The beads between the dolphins are encrusted with granulation and capped with blue champlevé enamel. The brooch is in the same style and probably by the same maker

Probably Italian, late nineteenth century (*reduced*) *See page* 91

59 (a) A PENDANT which accurately reproduces the late sixteenth-century style, enamelled in crimson, blue and white and set with emeralds and pearls

See page 90

(b) A JEWEL of slightly earlier inspiration enamelled in black, scarlet and opalescent pink and set with demantoid garnets, pearls and diamonds. Demantoid garnets prove that this piece was made after 1860 and the use of opalescent enamel indicates a probable date of manufacture in the 1890s

60 A gold NECKLACE in the Hellenistic Greek style, by Giuliano (*reduced*)
See page 92

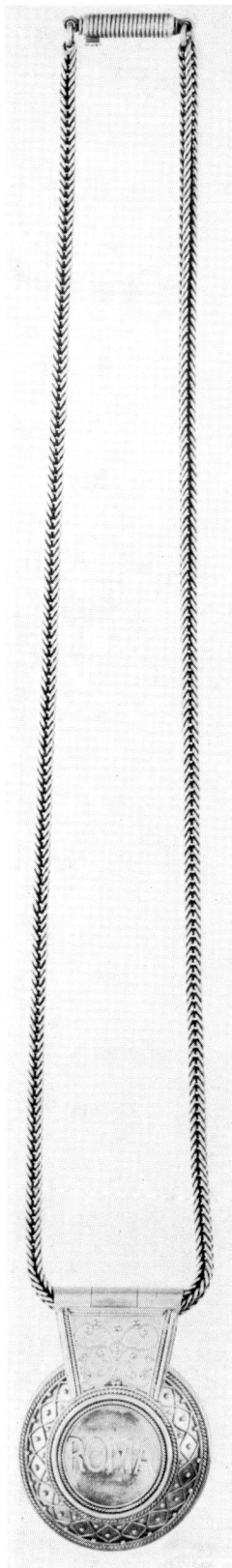

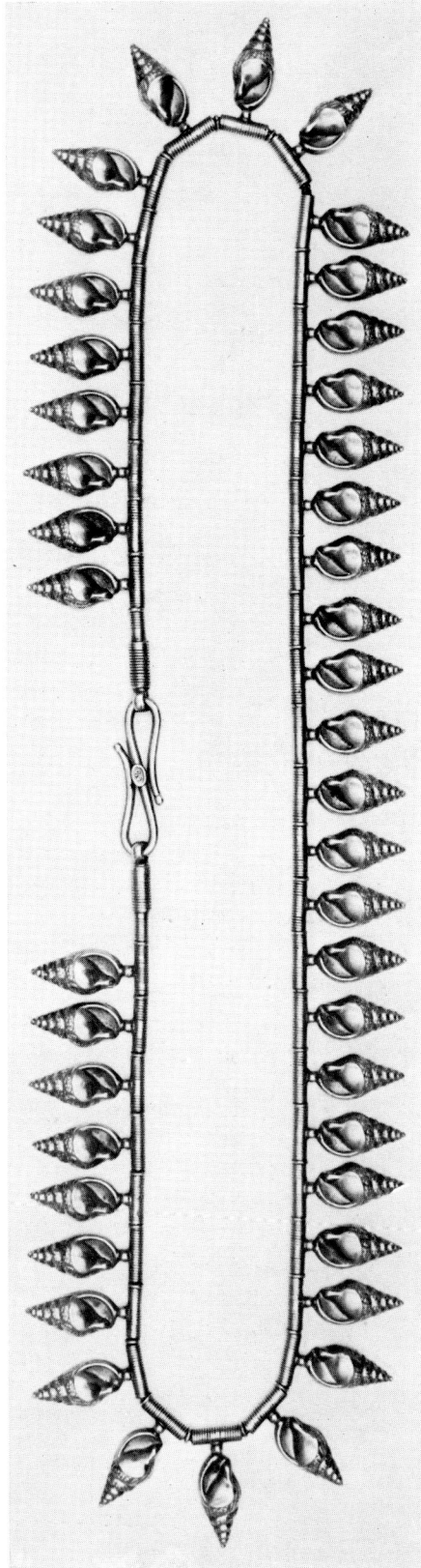

61 (a) A gold LOCKET inspired by the bulla worn by Roman and Etruscan youths, by Giuliano

See page 92

(b) A gold NECKLACE fringed with murex shells in Greek taste, by Giuliano

See page 92

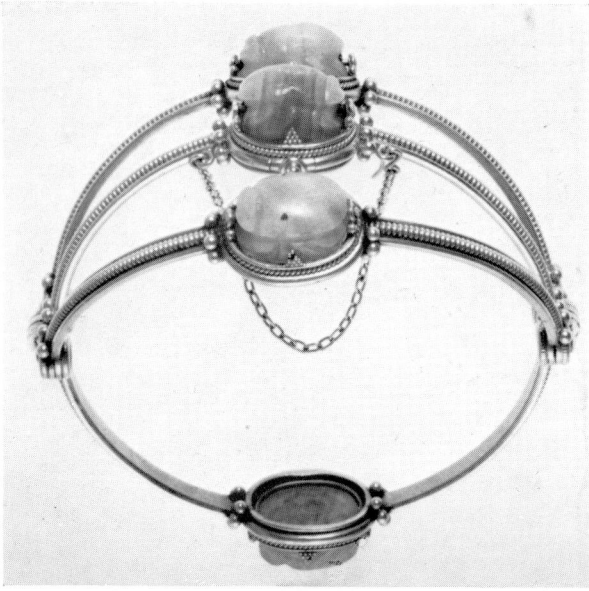

62 (a) A gold BANGLE in four swivelled parts set with grey agate scarabs carved in the Etruscan style, by Castellani

See page 92

(b) A gold and Roman mosaic BROOCH with Greek inscription, by Castellani

See page 92

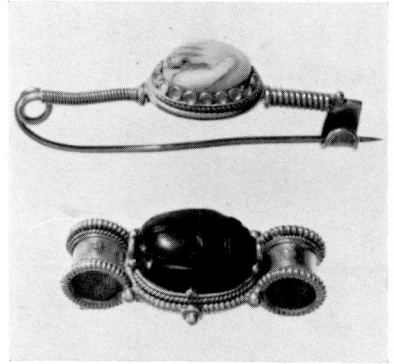

(d) A gold safety-pin FIBULA set with a cameo carved with clasped hands, and a gold BROOCH set with an Etruscan scarab, both by Castellani

See page 92

(c) A silver repoussé Medusa head BROOCH, by Melillo

See page 94

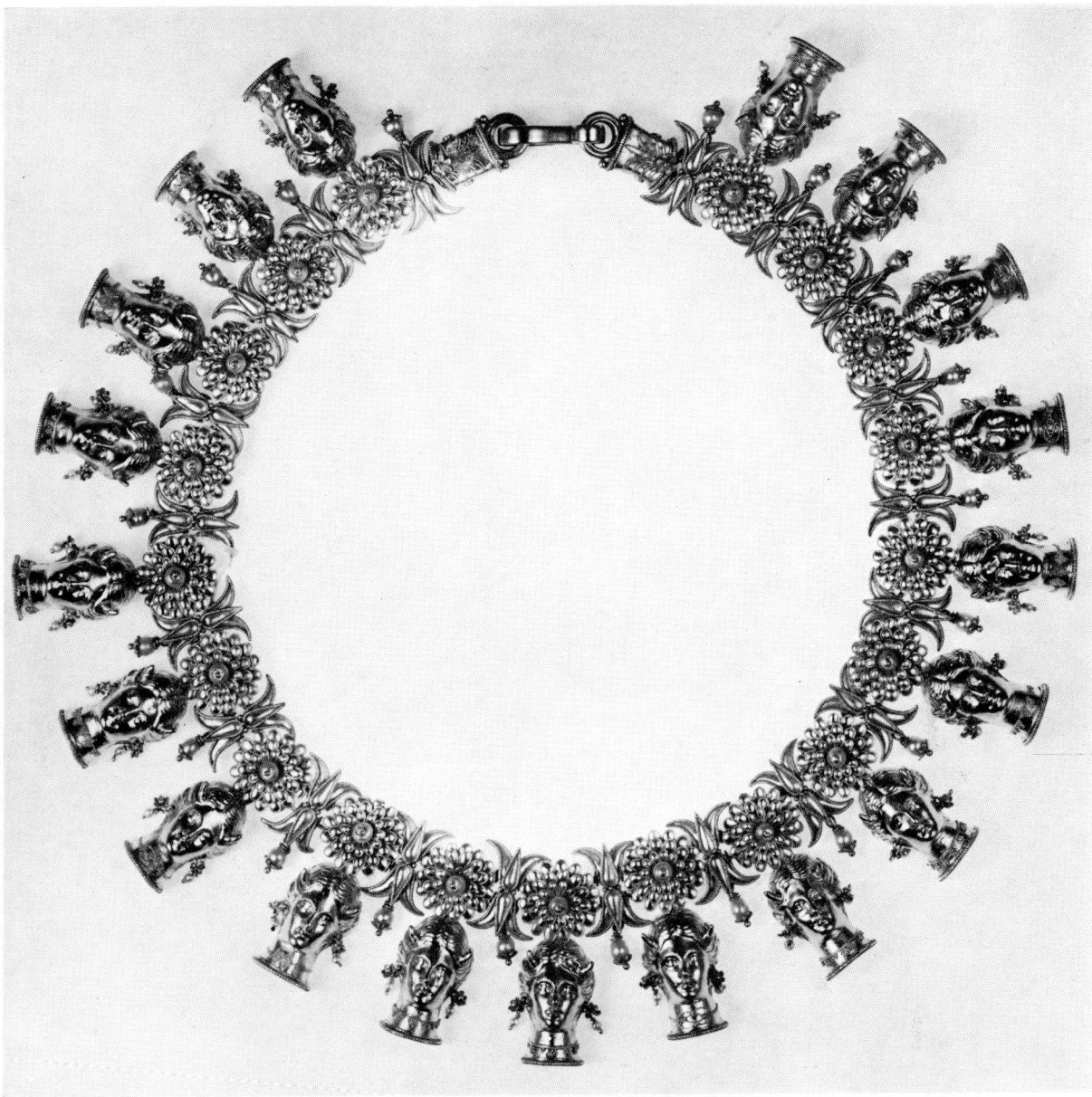

63 A gold NECKLACE in the style of ancient Greece, fourth century B.C. Late nineteenth century, probably by Melillo
(*slightly reduced*)
See page 92

64 (a) A PENDANT by Castellani set with a grey chalcedony cameo, the border of cloisonné enamel set with four cabochon emeralds

See page 92

(b) A gold BRACELET centred by a rosette motif borrowed from the ancient mediterranean world, by John Brogden (*slightly reduced*)

See page 94

(c) A gold, blue and white enamel, rose diamond and pearl BROOCH in eighteenth century taste, by Childs and Childs

(d) Front and reverse of a gold and cloisonné enamel LOCKET in Japanese style by Lucien Falize, Paris

Circa 1876   *See page* 97

65 (a) An 'Egyptian' PENDANT in
gold and Roman mosaic

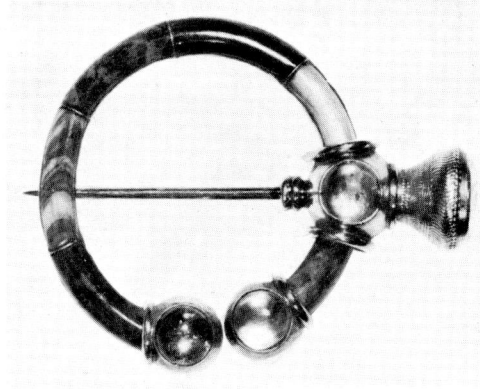

See page 94

(b) A Celtic penannular BROOCH of inlaid
Scotch pebble

See page 95

(c) A pharoah's head PENDANT,
the face of carved almandine
garnet, the collar and head-
dress set with rose diamonds
and hung with pearls

See page 94

(d) A die-stamped gold BROOCH and matching
EARRINGS in Egyptian style

See page 94

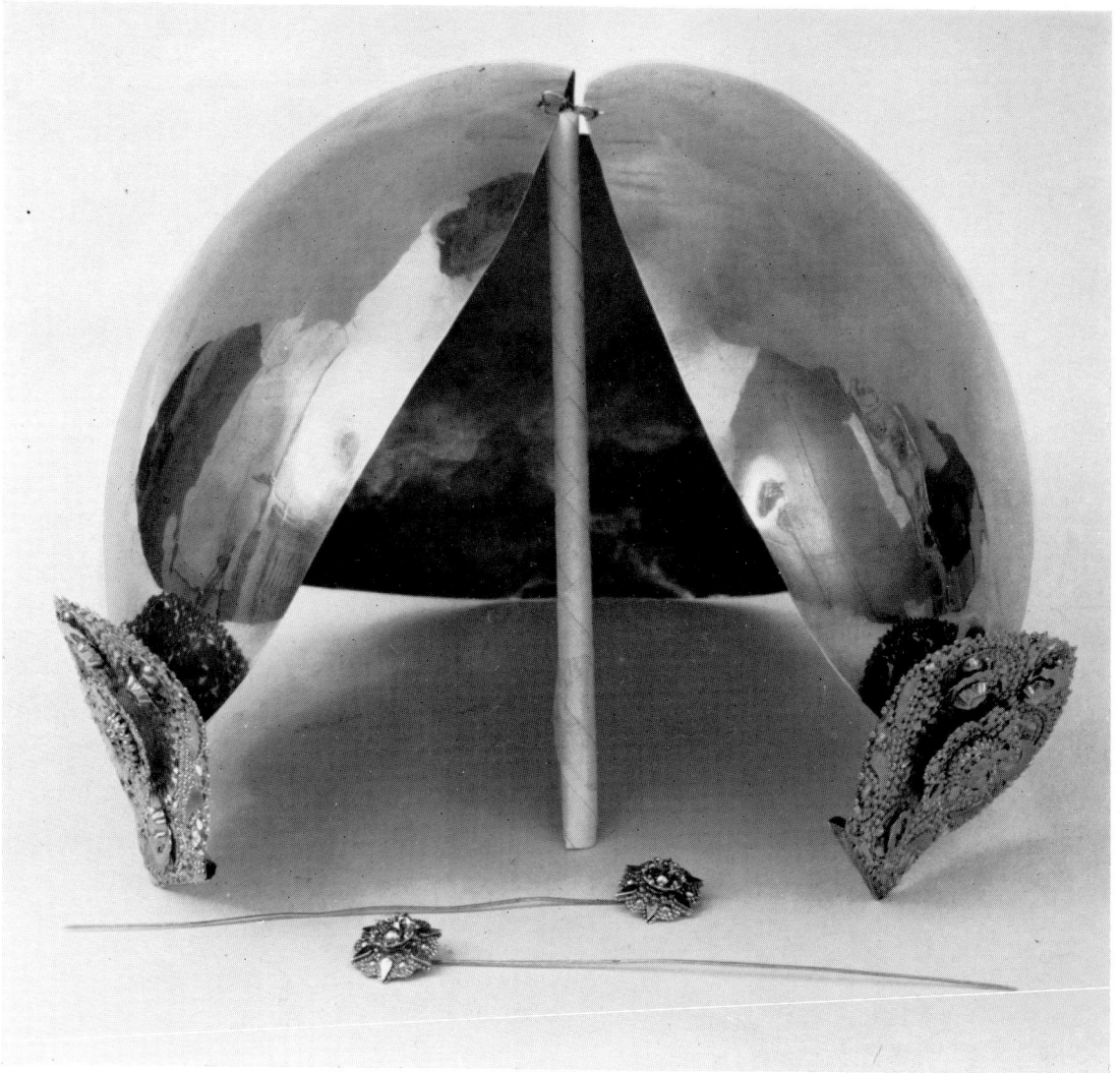

66 The gold HELMET worn by a Frisian girl beneath her lace cap. The cleft from brow to crown proves its descent from the seventeenth-century *oorijzer* in which most Netherlands regional head-dresses originated. The two rosette-headed PINS were used to secure it at the temples

See page 99

67 (a) Rose diamond 'NEEDLES' worn at the forehead with the Frisian head-dress

See page 99

(b) The owner's grandmother as a young girl wearing the ensemble. The helmet is worn *beneath* the lace cap

See page 99

68 A coral bead CHOKER with gold filigree clasp. Netherlands (*slightly reduced*)
See page 99

69 (*opposite*) A SØLJE from the west of Norway, made by Lorenz Reimers of Bergen in 183

See page 9

70 A pair of gold EARRINGS. Italian, actual size
  See page 101

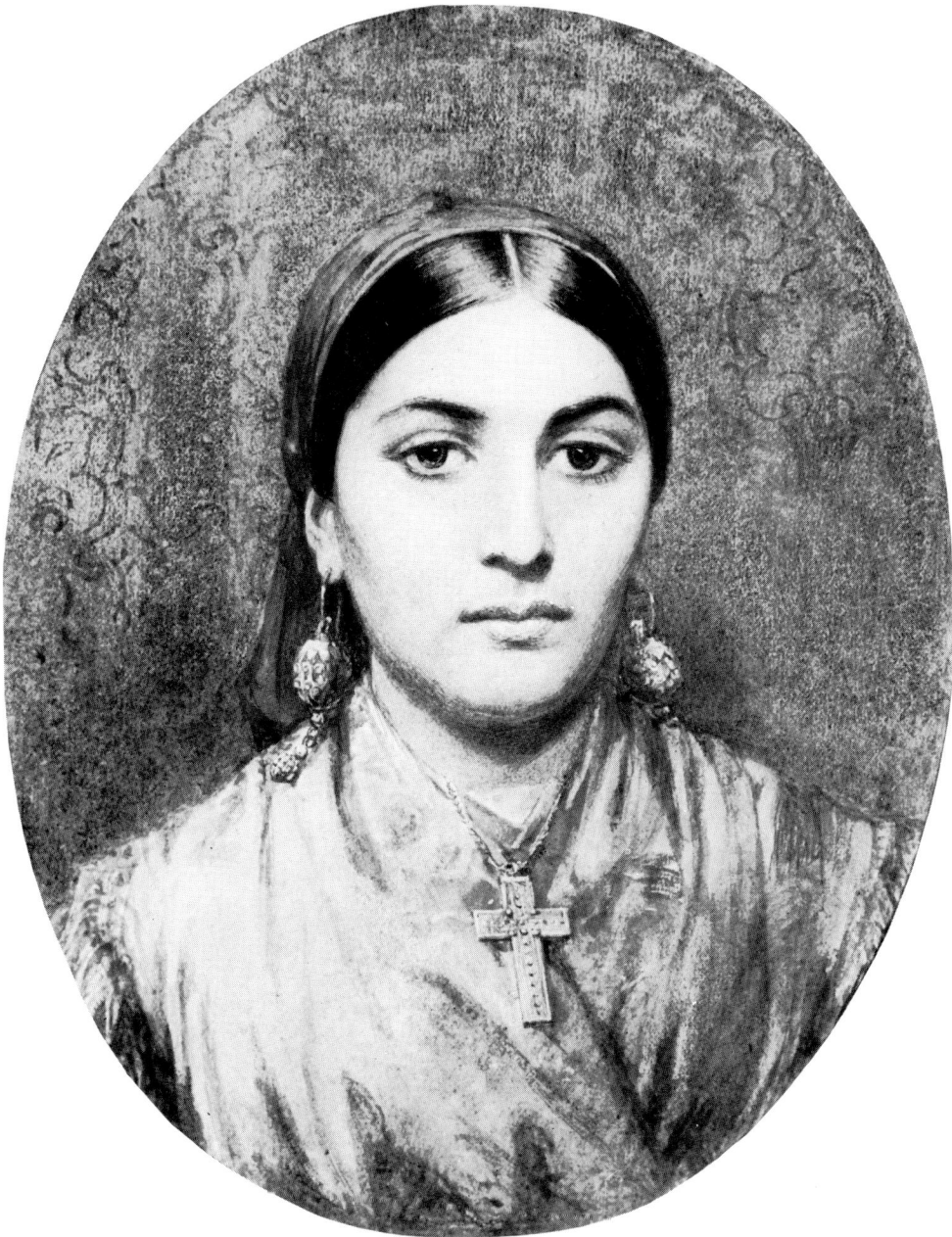

71 A portrait of the original owner wearing the EARRINGS
See page 101

72 A Portuguese MARRIAGE JEWEL in gold filigre
and cloisonné enamel (*very slightly reduced*).
Although inflated almost beyond recognition,
the outline of the eighteenth century heart an
ribbon bow motif is still discernible

See page 102

Prussians as a *franc-tireur* in 1870 and had to run for his life to Luxembourg when the French armies collapsed. When France lost Alsace Lorraine, Vever lost his business. He moved what he could to Paris and bought the business of Baugrand who died during the siege. His sons Henri and Paul followed him into the business.* Both had behind them the jack-of-all-trades background of a provincial goldsmith's workshop which was less narrowly specialized than a slick metropolitan concern. This gave them the right approach to the new style which was emerging in 1895. Vever produced some exquisite jewels, but they are rare. A pendant, which came on the auction market some years ago, represented a spray of Spanish jasmine, the petals of carved opal, the wilting stem sparkling with the subdued light of rose diamonds, the leaves of plique-à-jour enamel. In Vever's pendants the oval rose-diamond loop runs through one of the natural interstices in the design with a simplicity which Mrs. Haweis would have no doubt found pleasing. After Lalique, Vever was perhaps the finest worker in the art nouveau style and he lacks the ferocity that Lalique sometimes brings to his jewels. Several pieces were designed for Vever by Eugène Grasset† who is perhaps better known as a book illustrator, and these suffer from the 'flatness' which sometimes results when the graphic artist designs for the jeweller. In these designs too there is so much symbolism at the expense of wit that they come uncomfortably close to the ridiculous.

Georges Fouquet‡ (plate 52d) had several collaborators, among them Alphonse Mucha.§ Mucha's contribution to the new movement was as original and almost as important as that of Lalique. His posters of robust girls with hair flowing wildly in the style known as macaroni by his detractors (for whom Mucha's greatest fault was that he was not a Frenchman), were a part of the Paris street scene. They appeared in several of the jewels he designed for Fouquet. Mucha also decorated Fouquet's shop in his own exotic style with its piquant overtones of the eighteenth century. The surroundings in which jewellery was displayed were given a great deal of thought and Lalique's stand at the 1900 Exhibition was as much a work of art as its contents. At times Fouquet's work does not seem quite to free itself from the habits of the previous decade—his scrolls seem to have the chiselled tightness one associates with the 1880s, they do not seem to pour in the true art nouveau fashion. Fine although his jewels undoubtedly are, there is at times a hint of formality which restrains them from real lift off. Many others were working in Paris in the new style, of whom Joe Descomps, Gautrait (plate 53a), Gaillard, Boucheron (plate 53b) were among the most important.

Medallions struck from dies like a coin were used in jewels either as they were, with a brooch pin or a stud-fitting soldered on the back, or set like a gem in a more elaborate mount. Whether struck in silver or gold the best of these can be very fine indeed. The subject was almost invariably a female head, a Cybele or an Isis, sometimes just a girl of

---

* Henri Vever, 1854 to 1942, author of the standard work on French nineteenth-century jewellery; Paul Vever, 1851–1915.
† Eugène Grasset, born Lausanne 1841, died 1917.
‡ Georges Fouquet, 1862–1957.
§ Alphonse Marie Mucha, born Ivancia, Moravia 1860, died Prague 1939, designed for Fouquet between 1898 and 1905.

the nineties wearing the hairstyle and the dress of the period and often *habillé* with a
diamond dog collar or earrings. These are usually French, but they can be Swiss,
Austrian or German.

In Belgium the most celebrated jeweller in the new style was P. H. Wolfers. Phillipe
Wolfers* entered his father's workshop at the age of seventeen. He was a restless soul,
never content to work in the same threadbare styles year after year and he experimented
all the time. Between 1880 and 1885 it was rococo, with a flirtation with Japan in 1882;
from then until 1890—flowers. Inevitably he was drawn within the mesmeric influence of
art nouveau. Many of his jewels in the new style made ingenious use of the ivory that was
then being imported from the Congo. Although Wolfers' work was mainly in the French
style his choice of gems was different—he tended to use brilliant-cut diamonds where the
Frenchman would use roses, and the powerful tints of rubies and emeralds are to be seen
often in his work. Precise and delicate although his jewels are there is nothing ethereal
about them, and the naked female figures he uses in his designs are creatures of undoubted
flesh and blood. Wolfers made his last jewel in 1904: after that he worked on sculpture.

The influence of art nouveau spread further than the French speaking countries. In
Vienna jewels were made using plique-à-jour enamels, rose diamonds and semi-precious
stones in designs very like those that were current in France. In Spain Luis de Masriera†
worked in the French style. But in the last few years of the century something different
emerged, crisp, taught and vigorous, a Teutonic style which was ultimately to oust art
nouveau. With certain interesting national differences it grew up in Austria, Germany,
Holland, Denmark and Norway. In Austria where the new movement went under the
name of *Sezession*, Elsa Unger, Otto Ceschka and Prutscher were making jewels of a more
formal kind in which plant motifs were so stylized as to become a sort of ideograph.
Circular motifs became important; some jewels were decorated with stencil-like perfora-
tion and the metallic foliage and 'sausage roll roses' of what has come to be known as art
deco were already in evidence.

In Germany the *Jugendstil* (youth style) found its expression in even more solid and
robust designs. Like so much of German decorative art at this time they are almost uncan-
nily modern, and the uncompromising chunkiness and angularity of jewels by Morawe or
Fahrner seem more at home in the tough twenties than the dreamy nineties. Van der
Velde,‡ the Belgian designer, was working in Germany at this time and designing
jewellery. Brisk and sure, these designs are of calligraphic scrolls set with both cabochon
and facetted semi-precious stones in strong colours. Herman Hirzell used mosaics to
depict the plant motifs on his brooches as Cooke was doing in England. *Jugendstil* was
more closely related to British Arts and Crafts than to French art nouveau and many of
its jewels show the rectangles and verticals of the Glasgow school.

Around 1900 some Dutch designers were making brooches based on a plain square
form. Lambert Nienhuis produced several successful variations on this theme in the first
years of the new century. Quite symmetrical and with the simplest of decorations in
pierced openwork or champlevé enamel, they were most attractive.

* 1858–1929.   † 1872–1958.   ‡ 1863–1957.

Jugendstil, Sezession, Arts and Crafts were all amateur styles that required few tools and a modest repertoire of techniques. French designs, however, were strictly professional, drawn up by men who had done their stint as apprentices, to be made by several highly skilled specialists—a single jewel might involve the participation of a modeller, a chiseller, an enamellist, a lapidary, a polisher and a diamond setter. Their special flavour is due to the use of special techniques beyond the reach of most amateurs, gem engraving, cire-perdue casting and plique-à-jour enamelling especially. In most countries the two streams of design coexisted, even intermingled at some points, but it was mainly the skilled professional jeweller who worked in the French style and the architect, the sculptor and the amateur in the other.

In France the Paris Exhibition of 1900 was the climax of art nouveau. After that its decline was swift and inevitable. The experimentalism of 1895 was replaced by a frenzied search for novelty. What had once shocked and delighted the senses, now bored and enervated. The delectable langours of 1895 became the ennui of 1905. The public needed an aesthetic dose of salts, and they found it in the decisive forms and refreshingly astringent designs of Vienna and Berlin.

7. Mourning Jewellery

Mourning customs and rituals were an important part of nineteenth-century court and family life. In addition to the epidemics arising from bad sanitation, childbirth and the habit of tight lacing took its toll from the female population, and wars, colonial service and intemperance from the male. Death was too frequent a visitor in the home to be ignored, almost a member of the family, and the custom of wearing deep mourning must have helped people to come to terms with it. Jewellery had been a part of mourning costume since the seventeenth century. It was not, like clothing, purely a sign of grief, but also a reminder of the deceased and often contained a lock of hair or a portrait miniature. It was usual for a will to allot a small sum of money to provide mourning rings not only for family and friends, but also for the solicitor or his head clerk. This was one of the recognized perquisites of the legal profession. In *Great Expectations*, Mr. Wemmick 'appeared to have sustained many bereavements; for he wore at least four mourning rings, besides a brooch representing a lady and a weeping willow at a tomb with an urn on it. I noticed too that several rings and seals hung at his watch chain'—all bequests from those of Mr. Jaggers' clients who had died from judicial causes. Pip's estimate that he had them for forty or fifty years cannot have been wide of the mark, because the brooch he described was of an eighteenth-century design.

In the first twenty years of the century mourning rings generally had a bezel of rounded oblong form set with a cabochon of crystal with woven hair beneath it. Often this would be encircled by a snake with its tail in its mouth, the body deeply engraved with cross-hatching like the checking on a gunstock, but sometimes the mount would be a simple Roman setting, or it might be edged with diamonds (plate 54f). The shank could be of flat unadorned metal diminishing towards the back of the finger, or of five or so wires soldered side by side and splaying out at the shoulders where they are brought on to the bezel. Often the metal was a reddish coloured gold. Many small, oblong brooches of this kind were produced (plate 54a and b), frequently with borders set with gems, facetted jet or onyx, half-pearls, coral, garnets or even brilliant-cut diamonds. These were often used to secure a black velvet ribbon at the neck or the wrist. Another very popular style of ring had for its bezel a round hair compartment with a slim border of blue and white enamel.

Round or oblong pendants of about $1\frac{3}{4}$ inches diameter and hung by several light chains from a round ring were in wear around 1815. The snake border is usual on these, often with black enamelled scales. There may also be a champlevé enamel inscription in gothic characters. Usually this is a simple IN MEMORIAM. There was simply not enough room on jewels for the elaborate eulogies which were usual at this time. The great interest of the these inscriptions is the date: they always carry the date of the deceased's birth, and even more important, his death. In most cases this allows us to fix the date of the jewel, although it is not unusual for it to carry a date some years later than its manufacture, because it was a piece of the deceased's jewellery bequeathed as a memento. When the jewel replaces an original which has been lost or stolen the date of death will be earlier. All the same, dated mourning jewels provide a useful document of fashions as they reflect trends and techniques current in ordinary jewellery. When a small mourning brooch, for example, has a slim border heavily chased with flowers, scrolls and seashells and bears the date 1830, it is reasonable to assume, when a similar type of ornamentation occurs on a seal or a ring, that they too, date from around this time.

After fashions changed in 1820 a new kind of mourning ring came into use. This took the form of a wide band of black enamel with a champlevé inscription and chased floral borders of the kind we have described. The name of the deceased with the dates of his birth and death were engraved inside. It pays to look carefully at these inscriptions—even check them against the Dictionary of National Biography. If the dates tally the find could be an interesting one. During the first half of the century these inscriptions were usually engraved in copperplate script. Cameos of black and white onyx carved with a forget-me-not were set into rings between 1830 and 1860. Occasionally these were mounted in a brooch, or more rarely at the centre of a cannetille bracelet-clasp designed to be worn on a band of black velvet. Such bracelets were made in pairs and date from around 1840.

From the 1830s small compartments of glass or crystal were built into the back of every jewel whether for mourning or not, and in the middle of the forties a kind of brooch was devised in which this hair compartment was of large size and occupied a central position at the front. It had a background of opalescent white glass on which the hair was arranged in elaborate patterns. Some of the finest were formed of a cartouche of royal blue or black enamel with a scroll border and hair compartment centre (plate 55a). By this time the working of human hair had become an occupation in itself* (plate 54d and e, plate 55d). In Pringle's catalogue for 1877 it is interesting to note that hair braids for rings were offered at tuppence each or one and threepence a dozen, suggesting that by 1877 mourning had become such a perfunctory affair that it was no longer absolutely necessary to wear the hair of the deceased. These hair rings took several forms (see fig. 6). In the simplest the hair was held in place by the flanged edges of the gold hoop. Sometimes the hair was concealed by hinged covers or placed in a hollow ring where it could be glimpsed through decorative holes pierced in the gold.

In 1862 photography was still a novelty and mourning jewels were often set with photographs instead of painted miniatures. 'Dewdeneys registered revolving brooches in

* Advertisement in the *Illustrated London News*, 11th February 1860: 'H. Rushton & Co. beg to inform the nobility, gentry and clergy that they beautifully work lady's or gentleman's own hair and elegantly mount in solid gold, hair bracelets, brooches, rings, pins, studs, watchguards, Albert chains, necklaces, etc. of the newest possible designs, thirty per cent cheaper than any other house in the kingdom. A book of specimens sent post free to all parts of the kingdom on application—manufactury 43 Northampton Rd. Clerkenwell.'

solid gold to show either likeness or hair at pleasure of wearer' retailed at upwards of forty-five shillings each. This type of brooch was formed by an upright oval frame of gold enclosing a miniature compartment with glass at front and back and pivoted at the centre. These brooches may be found in gold or gilt metal. This idea was not a new one and had been used in rings at a much earlier date (plate 54h).

In the seventies and eighties British mourning jewellery acquired a stark and lugubrious simplicity (plate 55b and c). The gothic letters were replaced by a bald sans serif character and the design of the jewel was plain in every sense of the word. Oval lockets and ring bezels were flooded with black enamel and naked of any decoration save a latin cross or a brittle forget-me-not inlaid with half-pearls or rose diamonds. Although these jewels are often superbly engineered they have a crematorial quality about them which is repellent.

In France women bore their grief with a sense of style. A mourning bracelet of 1858 was composed of linked silver medallions enamelled black; another took the form of a band of gold decorated with borders of black champlevé enamel stars and ivy leaves and inscribed 'Je meurs ou je m'attache'. During the sixties and seventies elaborate diamond châtelaine brooches were worn, the gold mounts dimmed with black enamel contrasting sharply with the whiteness of the diamonds in their rose-shaped collets.

Although in the eighteenth century white memorial jewels were known, in the nineteenth century they were generally black and this determined the nature of the materials used. The sombre and unreflecting shade of Berlin ironwork made it a natural choice. Black onyx, sometimes dramatically relieved with a streak of white, was used in many mourning jewels. A plump oval of onyx with no surrounding setting formed a pendant, the front applied with a pearl cross, the back scooped out to receive the hair compartment. Crosses, too, were cut from slabs of black onyx and garnished with a sprig or a star in diamonds or pearls. For the evening a lady wore three rows of large jet or onyx beads with a low-cut gown, her shoulders masked with black gauze. Jet was of course the gem which became almost synonymous with mourning. It had been used in jewellery in the remotest antiquity when it was mined in Asturias, Spain. In the nineteenth century it came from Whitby in Yorkshire. Whitby jet was used in every kind of jewel, lockets, necklaces of beads, bracelets, hair ornaments and costume trimmings—even in rings although it was too soft to be ideal for this purpose and soon rubbed down to an insightly matt surface. Jet could easily be worked with saws and files and great skill was often employed in its fashioning. Chains were carved without a join, out of a solid block of jet, fine cameos were engraved, usually of a veiled lady. Although jet was comparatively cheap—half-a-crown a pound in the mid-seventies it did not lend itself to mechanical production methods. Imitations soon appeared. Glass was probably the commonest, but glass could not be made completely opaque, and when held up to the light this 'French jet' as it was called shows a purplish translucency at the edges. Ebonite was an early form of plastic formed by vulcanizing rubber with an excess of sulphur. Borneo rubber and powdered sulphur were pressed out with heat in a tinned metal mould, turning black in the process. The presence of free sulphur caused it to decompose and turn brown in time, and this usually gives it away. In the Paris Exhibition of 1876 a Mme Gagné displayed jewels which simulated jet with a composition of wood powder, suitably coloured and pressed in a mould. As with ebonite the subjects were usually 'cameos and bas reliefs'.

As the century passed the obligations of mourning became less and less exacting. Formerly two years was the period of mourning for a parent; by the late eighties only one year. A lower mortality rate and the agitations of the Cremation Society brought about a change of attitude towards death, and by the death of the Duke of Clarence in 1892 mourning jewels were little worn, with serious results for the jewellery trade as it was not considered proper to make a display of ordinary jewels either.

At their finest, mourning jewels have a kind of subdued charm which can be most effective in wear. At their worst they represent the Victorians at their most awesome. Certainly as a touching and eloquent social document they have great appeal for the collector.

8. Jewellery in Earlier Styles

The people of the nineteenth century not only had a naïve confidence in the future, but also an obsessive interest in the past. The styles of many earlier periods were imitated by the nineteenth-century jeweller. The most typical of them of course is gothic. The Waverley novels and the Houses of Parliament testify to this gothic revival, and the decorative arts felt its influence right through the century. The jeweller made few attempts to copy the work of his medieval counterpart and his inspiration was mainly literary and architectural. The likeliest explanation of this is that medieval jewellery is very rare indeed. Charlemagne forbade the practice of burying it with the dead and most of it had been broken up and restyled by the Renaissance. This, and the fact that the great museum collections did not exist in the early nineteenth-century meant that the jeweller simply did not know what a medieval jewel looked like. Most cities had gothic buildings of one kind or another, however, and the tales of Arthur and the paladins would have been known to him in the nursery. Consequently in the jewels of the first half of the century ogives and quatrefoils abound, but of the roped borders and prickly leaves beloved of medieval goldsmiths we find hardly a trace. Only ignorance of the originals can account for this as many designs would have been perfectly suited to Victorian taste. The jewels designed by A. W. N. Pugin, architect of the British Houses of Parliament and carried out by Hardman of Birmingham are in a simple but very effective architectural style. The jewellery of the forties showed the gothic influence more strongly than that of any other decade, although this was to prevail right until the end of the century. A very typical motif for brooches or necklace links was a kind of cartouche of matt gold edged with a raised moulding, fluted and cusped in the gothic manner. The sumptuous style of this type of jewel agrees with the sombre tones of the carbuncles with which they are often set.

Some fine tiaras were made at this time in an arcaded design of pinnacled arches set with agate in a cannetille setting enlivened with small trefoils of red enamel. Tudor roses, in light pressed metal, frequently make up the links of the longchains and bracelets that were so fashionable in the forties. Rose motifs often formed a brooch perhaps with a foiled emerald at its centre. This type of jewel needs close examination before money changes hands, for the excellent jewellers of Madras are known to have worked to this design, no doubt to please their English clientele.

In France Froment-Meurice sometimes worked in the gothic style. In some of his jewels gothic architecture forms the backdrop to a historical tableau of knights, saints or angels. Froment-Meurice made some fine jewels also in the Renaissance style which gave scope to his Frenchman's understanding of finely coloured enamels.

In the 1850s the gothic style gave way to Renaissance as a source of ideas for the jeweller, but in designs to which Benvenuto Cellini would not have accorded more than a fleeting glance of recognition. The rolled leather scrollwork of baroque decoration is here in abundance, for the most part inundated with minute engraving and blue enamel.

It was not for another thirty years that the Renaissance style was to come into full flower in the work of Carlo Giuliano*. Giuliano must share with Lalique the distinction of being the most creative jeweller of the nineteenth-century period. The great difference between them is that while Lalique invented the idiom in which he worked, Giuliano took the style of the late sixteenth century and rearranged it to suit his purpose. In his skilled hands the fine enamels and delicate scrolls of Renaissance jewellery were re-blended to suit late nineteenth-century tastes. Lalique was the iconoclast, the ruthless innovator whose daring explorations sometimes tempted him into error; Giuliano was the traditionalist, his techniques tried and time proven, his designs poised, witty, and in unerring taste. For all that the genius of both was founded on the same rock: an unswerving dedication to the pursuit of beauty. Both shared a contempt for mere monetary value, and neither cared whether a stone was worth five pence or five pounds per carat; all that mattered was what it could bring to a jewel in terms of light, colour and emphasis. The good designer needs courage: either the courage to do what has never been attempted before or the courage not to do the obvious. Giuliano dared to suppress colour almost entirely by covering his gold surfaces with white enamel finely shaded with black. The black enamel is not applied in a graduated wash, but in fine closely spaced lines like the hatching of a draughtsman's pencil or in spaced points, like ermine (plates 56 and 57). Sometimes the order was reversed, white on black and occasionally the black enamel was replaced by ultramarine blue. Most designs were of fine scrollwork, delicate as lace, enamelled black and white and with the only colour provided by the gems—pink sapphires, green garnets, cinnamon stones, peridots, pearls and diamonds. The diamonds, usually small and brilliant-cut were scattered singly over the piece to act as dewy highlights. Like a true Mediterranean—the Giuliano family originated in Naples although they eventually came to work in London—his finest jewels were ornaments for the neck, necklaces and pendants. A typical pendant was in the shape of a lozenge, and several necklaces were of light festonné links. An interesting necklace was of half a dozen or so rows of small pearls united into a broad band by mounts of a distinctly moorish flavour, in pierced scrollwork decorated with black enamel touched with white. In these jewels Giuliano, like the sound engineer he was, included a strand of gold chain among the pearls to take the strain off the stringing.

Giuliano used enamel on such small areas that counterenamelling was not necessary. The backs of his jewels were always finished with meticulous care, but rarely carry any embellishment but his signature, the initials C.G. or C & A.G. in relief on a tiny oval plaque which appears to have been stamped out separately and soldered to the jewel before the enamel was fired. Sometimes signatures are seen stamped into the body of the

---

* Born Naples, emigrated to London and set up business at 115 Piccadilly. Died 1912 and was succeeded by his sons Ferdinando and Frederico.

jewel itself, but this was usually on Giuliano's more commercial productions of which examples turn up from time to time, three-wire bracelets undistinguished except for the excellence of their making and especially for the precision and invisibility of the hinge, that shibboleth of the working jeweller.

Only rarely did Giuliano attempt a deliberate copy of a Renaissance jewel, although whenever he did it was always brilliantly successful. In any case the heavy chains, the carcanets and côtières of the sixteenth century would have been out of harmony with the airy spirit of the late nineteenth century. Giuliano also made jewels in the Greek style, but apart from their superb craftsmanship there is little to distinguish them from the work of any one of half a dozen makers. In this style Giuliano confined himself, like Castellani who preceded him, to accurate reproduction and there is little of the brilliant improvisation that characterizes his Renaissance pieces.

In England during the seventies were made those simple and charming pendants which the auction catalogues persist in calling 'Holbeinesque' (colour plates Fc and Gb). Oval in shape, a largish stone of powerful colour, a carbuncle, a sapphire, an emerald or a tourmaline was mounted at the centre within a wide border decorated with a simple floral pattern in red, blue and green champlevé enamels, and with diamonds or pale yellow chrysolites at the four cardinal points. A drop was invariably hung below, and the reverse, although without a signature or a maker's mark of any kind, is always decorated with fine foliate engraving. These and other simple designs were directly inspired by early Renaissance jewels. Pendants with a little tableau of mythological figures posed within an architectural niche were a late sixteenth-century idea (plate 59a).

In France at the end of the seventies and on through the eighties, the strange chimerical beasts of late Renaissance design, the sphinxes, cockatrices and other heraldic fancies were finely chiselled in gold or silver jewels, sometimes decorated with enamels (see colour plate Fb). Falize of Paris made superb brooches and pendants in this style, and the enamellist Grandhomme painted miniature portrait enamels of historical beauties to set in them, the creamy flesh tints delicately graduated, the shimmer of a silk headdress caught with a paillon of gold foil submerged in the translucency of the enamel.

The brothers Fannières* were among the finest ciseleurs in Europe—it was they who sculpted the figures on the Prince Imperial's cradle. Consequently they relied on form rather than colour for their effects (plate 58). They seemed to prefer working in silver as gold was over rich in colour for their purpose. Enamel was only used in the most sparing manner possible. Carved agate cameos were used in their work and brilliant-cut diamonds provide the highlights.

The most familiar nineteenth-century jewellery in Renaissance taste was made in Austria out of gilt silver enamelled and set with semi-precious or imitation stones. St. George and the dragon was a favoured design and eagles and pelicans were almost as popular. The body of the jewel was roughly cast and touched up with the chisel in the most perfunctory fashion, the enamels were crude and cloudy and the electro-gilding so thin that it only remains in the hollows having rubbed off everywhere else. The stones were

* Auguste, 1819–1901; Joseph, 1820–97.

often doublets. A doublet is composed of suitably coloured glass with slices of semi-precious stone, usually garnet, on the top. The slice of garnet is so thin that the colour of the glass is dominant and only a reddish twinkle gives it away in certain lights. Doublets are more durable than soft paste because of the protective layer of hard garnet. Pale green emeralds mined near Salzburg and the most baroque of pearls are also set in this kind of jewel. Grades of quality are distinguishable even in this crude stuff and in the worst the enamel may be imitated by paint. Paint is softer than enamel and less lustrous so that its appearance will give it away. Austrian or Hungarian assay marks will usually be seen on the fastening.

It was the Italian Castellani* who brought to the study of ancient Greek, Roman and Etruscan jewels an approach to the past which was quite different from anything which had gone before. Until then the modern jeweller, convinced that the ancient craftsmen had nothing to teach him about technique, had looked upon past styles simply as a reservoir of design ideas. The idea that an unclad, untutored Minoan goldsmith, to whom a modern Swiss needle-file would have been worth its weight in emeralds, was initiated into craft secrets of which the nineteenth century with its metallurgists and steam presses was ignorant was quite risible. Castellani discovered, with what must have been something of a shock, that this was indeed the case. Research and experiment as he might, however, the secret of Etruscan granulation remained to him a secret. The Etruscans, that mysterious nation who inhabited parts of northern Italy in early Roman times, were metal workers of legendary skill, and the decorative technique which they brought to near perfection was that of granulation (see plate 59c). Many other nations have practised it since, but never with the same skill, although Castellani came closer than anyone to discovering the secret. The Etruscans obtained beautiful effects by covering the surface of the metal with an encrustation of infinitely tiny spherules of gold. Light as hoar frost or the bloom on a plum it is so delicate that one has the sensation that the mere touch of a finger will dissipate it. To produce the minute globules of gold by mixing coarse filings of metal with powdered carbon and heating the mixture in a crucible was not difficult, but to arrange the dust-like particles on the surface, to secure them in place, and then to solder them without obliterating the exquisite texture with molten solder took knowledge and skill of a different order. Castellani claimed to have discovered the secret technique not by archaeological methods, or in some forgotten document, but actually in use in a remote village in the recesses of the Appenines. There must be more than a grain of truth in this. Castellani carried out painstaking researches into European peasant jewellery, and we are fortunate enough to have his collection on show in the Victoria and Albert Museum in London. He certainly employed peasant goldsmiths at his workshops in Rome and found them more patient than city craftsmen. But if Castellani discovered the secret his work, fine although it is, does not confirm it. His jewels have a robustness and a solidity that is more Roman than Etruscan and his granulation work was a shade too coarse. It was not until the 1930s that Littledale discovered how the Etruscans could have done it. The tiny grains were stuck

* Fortunato Pio Castellani, 1793–1865. On his retirement in 1852 Fortunato handed over the business to his two sons, Alessandro (1824–85) and Augusto (1829–1914).

in place with a mixture of copper-salt and animal glue. Heating released the copper which amalgamated with the surface layer of the gold and effected the join.

Castellani's contribution lay in the new approach that he brought to the jeweller's problems. Not only did he try to worry out for himself the trade secrets of the ancients, he plagiarized their designs wholesale with enormous success. Like Giuliano, he took the Etruscan bulla, that curious lentil-shaped pendant once worn by youths, and fashioned it as a ladies' locket (plate 61a). He made pretty copies of those fibulae (brooches) that look like a safety pin (plate 62d). Many jewellers followed his example in making necklaces in the ancient Greek style of a strap of woven chain with a fringe of small grain-like pendants fastened to it with minute rosettes (plate 60). An infinite number of variations were possible: the pendants could be of seed, teardrop, seashell (plate 61b), or amphora motifs, or even spheres of lapis lazuli; the rosettes could be either plain gold, or enamelled blue and white; or instead of hanging from a band of plaited chain each of the pendants could be headed by a short tube (chenier) decorated by a coil of wire through which a light chain could be threaded (plate 61b). These designs had a profound influence on jewellery design between 1860 and 1880, and the rows of small pendants which fringed the jewels of this time, especially the earrings, probably derived from the same source.

Castellani used mosaics in some brooches with a strong Byzantine feeling. A Greek religious inscription was inlaid in a blue or green mosaic ground and set in a plain mount. These brooches were flat and quite small, and their shape was that of a very simple disc or rosette (plate 62b). He made good use of engraved gems, particularly Etruscan scarabs (plate 62a and d). The agate cameos, however, would have been cut to special order (plate 64a).

Castellani is known to have made crowns of gold leafage in the ancient manner, and exhibited three of them at the London Exhibition of 1862: one of oak, one of oval leaves and a superb 'crown of Gaeta of enamelled bay leaves'. The English jewellery at the exhibition attracted some unfavourable criticism because of its over lavishness and its emphasis on monetary values at the expense of aesthetic qualities. 'Castellani', as one commentator wrote, 'was true to art and puts to shame our amethysts and carbuncles, glowing and fiery and extensive as a current jam tartlet.'* Castellani's work is usually signed on the reverse with two Cs entwined back to back in a lozenge-shaped panel.

Naturally there were many others who worked in the classical manner, and Giuliano himself made a number of fine jewels in this style. Not surprisingly it was a style in which the Italian jeweller excelled—it was after all to Italy that the first tourists came and it was up to him to try and satisfy their insatiable appetite for souvenirs. Many jewels are inscribed 'ROMA' no doubt with this in mind. Giacinto Melillo is especially worthy of note because he combined excellence of workmanship, faithfulness to the classical spirit and a certain lightness of touch (plate 63). Melillo used the moulded glass birds of ancient Greek jewellery as the inspiration for miniature enamelled peacocks and parrots that are prettier than the originals.

In England Phillips made 'Greek jewellery with medallion female heads in English

* *Illustrated London News,* 7th June 1862.

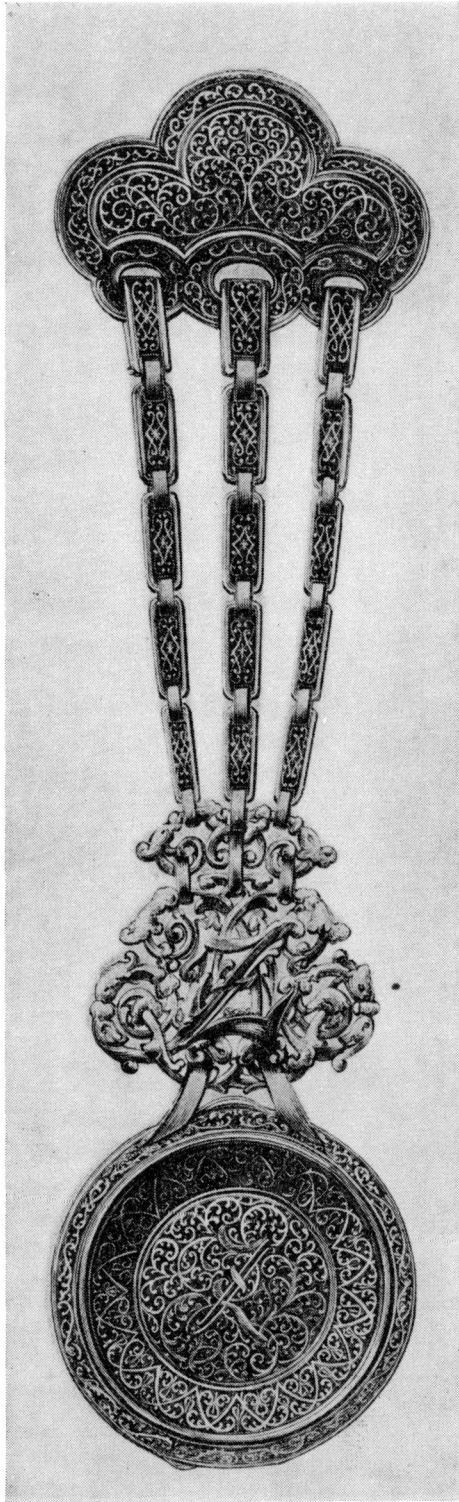

Fig. 7 A GOLD CHÂTELAINE BY BOUCHERON
SHOWN AT THE 1867 PARIS EXHIBITION

porcelain enamel'. Both Melillo and Hunt and Roskell, and doubtless other jewellers too, made round brooches embossed with Medusa heads (plate 62c). In Ancient Greece the originals of these jewels were not only brooches but also necklace centres and hair ornaments.

Richard A. Green of the Strand received an honourable mention at the 1862 Exhibition for his brooches set with corals, cameos, carbuncles, turquoises and enamels 'after the Roman and Etruscan order' priced between two and twenty pounds. Many English jewels of this style and period are decorated with oval cloisons of opaque white enamel sparked with tiny beads of glowing vermilion, and brooches are sometimes decorated with rams' heads, a motif which in Greek jewellery is usually associated with bracelets and earrings.

In France, Eugène Fontenay chose the classical style as a springboard for some fine extravagant fantasies, particularly his necklaces, deeply fringed with elaborate pendants. During the seventies Boucheron invented a type of decoration which bears a striking resemblance to a Roman decorative technique. This consists of a fine pattern of scrollwork pierced *à jour* in thin gold sheet, like the *opus interasile* of Rome and Byzantium (fig. 7). This work was widely copied in Europe, especially in Austria and France although it does not seem to have found great favour in England. Usually it was in highly polished red gold although examples die-stamped in silver are quite common.

In the middle of the century excavations for railway and canal systems and improved agricultural methods uncovered fragments of our past life almost daily. Archaeology was advancing from a haphazard treasure hunting operation to something like a science. As a result more and more models became available from which the jewellers could draw their inspiration direct. Ancient styles proliferated and it is from this period that nineteenth-century classical jewellery dates.

Towards the end of the century there was a great fad for all things Egyptian (plate 65c, d), probably because the Suez Canal had made the Middle East 'news'. This was not the first time. Napoleon's Egyptian campaign of 1798 had made jewellery based on Egyptian decorative ideas briefly fashionable. Egyptian designs also sometimes appear in the champlevé enamel of the 1830s, but it was not until the sixties that they began to assume real importance. Phillips actually copied jewels that were found on mummies, and at the 1867 Exhibition entered his scarabaeus necklaces in richly tinted enamels. Occasionally a jewel in the Egyptian style was done in Roman mosaic (plate 65a), but the skilful inlays of precious mineral which gave ancient Egyptian jewellery its colour were mostly simulated with cloisonné enamel. The style reached its climax in the nineties. Most nineteenth-century Egyptian style jewellery dates from this time and designs were of hawks' heads, papyrus, winged scarabs and the like decorated with opaque enamels of ultramarine, green and brownish red. Faience scarabs, sometimes genuine, but more usually faked to meet the new demand, were the most frequently chosen gems.

Assyrian designs also belong to the second half of the century, particularly after 1860. Rosettes were popular as brooches and bracelet centres (plate 64b), and wide-hinged bangles were decorated with processions of kings, djinns and sphinxes in the style of a bas-relief.

In England, curiously enough, we seem to have neglected our own native styles of decoration to go whoring after foreign ideas. There has been little effort to copy the superb garnet inlay work found on ancient Jutish work in the Kentish burial grounds, probably because modern workmen lack the skill, the time and the patience to do it successfully. Copies of St. Cuthbert's cross were made with the cloisonné garnet work done in red enamel, but nothing else is known. The Alfred jewel in the Ashmolean Museum at Oxford has been extensively copied. Some reproductions were of good quality, others were crude with the cloisonné enamel work imitated by a crude print on paper protected by a slab of glass.

Ancient Irish penannular brooches were imitated in Birmingham with varying degress of success, but it was in Ireland that the finest were made (fig. 8). The two firms of West and Waterhouse produced fine copies of these magnificent Irish ring brooches then on exhibit at the Royal Irish Academy, including the biggest and the finest of them all, the Tara brooch, which had been discovered near Drogheda. Waterhouse worked in gold and silver and nielloed bronze set with Irish gems. The same firm adapted the curious leech-like objects, which have been variously identified as both currency and dress fastenings, into brooches. The ring-headed pins of the ancient Irish are also known to have been copied by Waterhouse. West made brooches of Wicklow gold set with Irish pearls and sapphires. Wicklow was once an important source of gold and as late as 1842 a nugget weighing five and a half ounces was found there by a labourer. Edward Johnson, also of Dublin, made bracelets of a plain hinged gold band, the front applied with the wearer's initials in the ornate entwined style of an ancient Irish manuscript.

The Scots too, took advantage of their heritage to make copies of their own historical jewels. Although the metalworking tradition in Scotland was leaner than in Ireland there were still superb brooches to imitate—like the one found in Loch Buy for example. Celtic crosses were made as pendants both in gold and silver. All of these jewels were set with cairngorms, amethysts, crystals or pebble, or pearls from Scottish streams. These pearls grow in a kind of river mussel, and although inferior in both beauty and monetary value to the oriental pearl, the fashion for Scottish jewellery in the sixties was such that they were suddenly in demand. There was only one fisher at that time earning a full-time living at the pearls. He lived at Killin and his entire stock was bought by the Marquis of Breadalbane. Otherwise the pearls were gathered by children in the height of summer when the waters were low, and they were only too pleased to receive from threepence to a shilling for anything they found, according to size and quality. In 1863 an enterprising Edinburgh gem dealer, Mr. Moritz Unger, realized that this simply would not do. He announced that he would take unlimited quantities of freshwater pearls at a fixed scale of prices, and, as a contemporary commentator wrote 'young and old, both male and female rushed like ducks into the water and waded, dived and swam until the excitement became so intense as to be called the pearl fever'.* Half-clad highlanders of both sexes became as plentiful as trout in the Tay, Teith, Doon and Garry and the glens stank with the mounds of opened mussels that putrified on their banks. Doctors expressed their concern at this

* *Illustrated London News,* 17th September 1864.

Fig. 8 Three IRISH RING BROOCHES BY WATERHOUSE OF DUBLIN
Shown in the London Exhibition of 1851

reckless exposure of the body to the elements in all weathers, whereupon Mr. Unger issued all of his regular suppliers with a sensible waterproof costume. The buyers came from London and Birmingham—they even came from Paris and Vienna. But it was too good to last. Mr. Unger had not only created the supply, he had also inflated the demand. The bubble inevitably burst, prices fell and the Highland pearl fishers dwindled to a mere handful.

In Scandinavia, naturally enough, the most important style was that of the Viking period, and there it was just as significant as, say, gothic in England. Jewels were made in the curious Nordic style of fantastically entwined beasts, others bore the staccato forms of runic inscriptions. Christesen of Copenhagen made a speciality of this type of work, and also imitated the filigree and granulation work of the Vikings (fig. 9).

Few historical styles were left unexplored by the Victorian goldsmith—Chinese, Japanese (plate 64d), Scythian, Byzantine—the jeweller drew his inspiration from all of them at one time or another. The only exceptions were the pre-Columbian American cultures which were probably thought to be improper.

Fig. 9 TWO BROOCHES AND A BRACELET IN VIKING STYLE BY CHRISTESEN OF COPENHAGEN
Shown in the Paris Exhibition of 1867

9. Peasant Jewellery

The kind of jewellery worn in the countryside and in the provinces was often very different from that worn in the capital. The difference was not simply one of value; it was a question of design. The jewellery displayed by a farmer's daughter in Friesland was different in every way from that of a shopgirl in Amsterdam.

We use the terms 'peasant jewels' and 'peasant costume' for want of a better name for the country people who wore these things were often quite well-to-do. The aristocratic landowner was tied to the capital by obligations of court and state and his wife dressed like a townswoman. The wealthiest farmer and the humblest labourer had this in common: the chances were that neither of them had ever visited the metropolis, or indeed travelled further than the nearest market town, except perhaps during their army service. Women very rarely came into contact with the latest fashions. True they may have caught occasional glimpses of the lady of the manor, but to take her as a model would have been 'aping the gentry' or 'having ideas above one's station'.

When, for reasons which were rarely clear, a metropolitan fashion was adopted by country people, the results could be bizarre and unforeseeable, for such was the power of rural conservatism that it could remain for a very long time indeed. Christianity was brought to the Laps by medieval missionaries and they have worn a colourful adaptation of medieval dress ever since. One pattern of bead used in Spain goes back twelve hundred years. Once a style arrived it was there to stay, but that does not mean to say it did not develop in its own peculiar way. In most cases it became so grotesquely exaggerated or distorted that it is hard to pick out the original elements of the design. And when folk in neighbouring communities spoke different dialects it is not to be wondered at that their jewellery evolved from its common root in different ways. This was not just because communities were isolated from each other by mountains and water, it was also an intense expression of the kind of feeling for a place and its people that one gets in Rupert Brooke's poem *Grantchester*. It was a manifestation of local pride.

A head-dress peculiar to the country districts of Holland is a classic example of the way in which this kind of ornament developed. In the sixteenth century a kind of close fitting cap was adopted by women all over the Netherlands. A bow of spring wire held it to the head like a pair of wireless headphones. This was called an *oorijzer*—ear iron—and on this simple device the jeweller lavished fantasy and ingenuity of an almost obsessional kind. The terminals which were allowed to project at the temples were finished with large brilliant oblong plates in some districts. In other localities they were coiled like springs or corkscrews. It has been suggested that this last fantasy represents the false locks of hair which are in fact worn in other districts. Although for many years it had been made of precious metal it was still called an *oorijzer*.

In Friesland the *oorijzer* achieved a kind of apotheosis (plates 66 and 67). Instead of blossoming at the tips the whole of the originally slender wire grew flatter and wider until it covered the whole head like a golden bathing cap, its metamorphosis traceable only by the cleft which ran from the forehead to the crown. Women often owned two, silver for weekdays, and gold for the Sabbath. This extraordinary ornament was worn half concealed beneath a cap of lace with embossed metal leaf motifs at the sides and a pair of pins at the forehead. In Alkmaar one pin, or as it is called locally needle, was worn, by married women on the left, and by spinsters on the right.

In the fishing villages of the Dutch coast the men wore gold clasps on their shirt collars and embossed silver discs in their belts. In Scheveningen and Katwijk, however, old coins were used as belt fastenings. Coral beads were worn by the women of many districts, either a single row of large beads or several rows of smaller ones, as a choker necklace with the gold filigree clasp at the front (plate 68). Coral beads were worn by country women all over Europe, and especially by children as a protection against the evil eye.

The exuberance of the peasant jewellery worn in these dour lands of the protestant north is astonishing. The women of south-eastern Norway wear huge saucer-like brooches or *sølje*, sometimes a good four inches in diameter. Their resemblance to the medieval wheel brooches of the Hanseatic towns of north Germany is very striking. The centre is left open to accommodate a pin fastening of the ring-brooch type masked with the crudely moulded figure of a saint or an angel, and all around the outer rim are set rough medallions of heraldic beasts, spread eagles and lions set in high cylindrical collets.

Up the West coast, cracked with great Fjords and scattered with tiny field-sized farmsteads, the finery that appeared at weddings, Christmas and the seventeenth of May was of almost oriental magnificence. Here the *sølje* was hung with glittering pendants almost as though to entrap the sparse sunlight and send it out again multiplied and strengthened. In the Westlands this jewel often took the form of a concave silver disc, its outer edge crimped like a pie crust (plate 69). Over this was inverted a silver filigree flower spangled with pendants of three distinct patterns: concave discs, maltese crosses and leaves, the last sometimes embossed with strange peering faces that probably go back to Viking times. Other designs take the form of an open circle with pinned centre hung with ring-shaped pendants.

A Norwegian bride was literally loaded with jewels, silver plaques set with mirrors stitched to her dress, a magnificent *sølje* at her breast, and towering above it all, the bridal crown. These were just used for the wedding and were often owned by the parish and loaned for the occasion. The pendants on these bridal crowns are usually formed as a crimped leaf with toothed edges. Generally the crown was of the usual pinnacled form, although in Voss it was round and flat with circular pendants hanging from the edge.

Until the nineteenth century, Norwegian guild rules forebade the silversmith to work in the country districts. When this law was relaxed many workmen who had finished their apprenticeships in the towns established themselves in the valleys where some of their descendants are still at work.

Most Swedish traditional jewels took the form of a heart surmounted by a crown and hung with pendants. This motif originated in the seventeenth century and also occurs in Norway, and—without the pendants—in Flanders, Germany, and in the Luckenbooth brooches of Scotland. In Denmark the most splendid regalia was worn at Laesoe. The black silk bodice was decorated with four big round gilded plaques supporting pendent balls or crosses. The hooks and eyes which fastened the bodice were cast in the orginal gothic designs. Although Danish by race the people of the island of Heligoland are politically Germans. The women of this sprayswept Baltic isle wore a wide band of silver openwork pinned across the breast.

The jewels nearest in conception to those of Scandinavia were to be seen in South Germany. Elaborate girdles are typical of this region, and hanging from them may be seen the disc and oakleaf pendants of the Norwegian bridal crown. In the Black Forest, as has so often happened, woodworking techniques have influenced the making of jewellery, and some of the figures which ornament these jewels would be quite at home on a cuckoo clock. This kind of 'fretwork' decorates the Bavarian betrothal ring, a wide gold band pierced with flowers, hearts and birds, probably meant to be turtle doves. It has also been suggested that the filigree to be found in South Germany was introduced from Switzerland, but this is arguable. In Bavaria also a kind of dog collar was worn by the girls. Made of several rows of chain, the oblong clasp, either of silver or nickel, was set with gaudy pastes and imitation pearls. The German equivalent of the Norwegian *sølje* was the *brust spange*, a large flat brooch with ring and pin centre.

In the ethnographical patchwork of what was then the Austrian Empire design varied greatly from region to region. Along the Dalmatian coast, now part of Yugoslavia, Byzantine influence was pronounced, especially in the women's head-dresses fringed with coins and with long pendants hanging down the cheeks. Here both men and women wore earrings. Large hairpins with round heads were worn right through the empire. In Dalmatia the heads were spherical and of silver filigree; at Pilsen in Bohemia, now Czechoslovakia, they were hemispherical and of silver gilt. Here they were used to support the head-dress, and could only be worn by girls of blameless reputation. In many regions domed silver waistcoat buttons were worn by the men.

Throughout the provinces of France a single theme recurs—the *croix-à-la-jeanette*. Typically this takes the form of a cross hanging from a heart. It has been said that this name originates from the custom of buying or giving these jewels on the feast of St. John. The *croix-à-la-jeannette* was worn round the neck on a plain black ribbon. In Savoy a cross and heart pendant of enormous size was worn by the women.

Norman jewels usually represent the Saint Esprit, the dove of the Holy Spirit with a heart or a cross hanging from its beak. They were mostly made in Rouen of thin gold pierced with lace-like decoration and mounted with pastes or rock crystals in large conical settings. More recent examples are of silver set with white paste with a quite unnecessary garnish of luridly tinted imitation coloured stones.

The jewellery of Belgian Flanders is closely related to this northern French work both in design and technique. Some ornaments take the form of a heart surmounted by a crown, others of a large cross of several sections suspended one below the other. The decoration is pierced scrollwork of hair-like minuteness scattered with rose diamonds in small rosette-shaped settings. The metal of these settings always contrasts with that of the scrollwork background: if the background is silver, the settings are always gold, and vice versa.

Long cruciform stomachers are also worn in Italy. Pierced from gold sheet in scrollwork designs they were set with small facetted garnets and the most baroque of pearls. Huge pendent earrings were worn in Italy as in all of the Latin countries. Light in weight although large in size they resembled a ship in design (plate 70 and 71).

Because of her maritime contacts with the orient Venice has for centuries been famous for filigree work, and it is probably the descendants of these Venetian goldsmiths who have kept the art alive all around the shores of the Adriatic and even in the Greek islands. Some of the pendants of this coastline were in the old *nef* design of a galleon under sail. The stones in most common use were small pearls, often pendent in grape-like clusters. Colour and contrast were introduced with coarse opaque cloisonné enamels on the flimsy gold mount.

Enamelling of this type was also practised in Hungary and in Sicily. In Sicily it was in dramatic black and white, and used to frame shell cameos of biblical subjects. The village of Piani dei Greci in Sicily illustrates the peculiar ways of peasant jewel design. The inhabitants of this place were originally from Albania. Fleeing from Turkish religious persecution, they brought their traditional costume with them. Photographs show them wearing sumptuous gold embroidered dresses with immense silver-gilt girdles of a palm's breadth with a clasp as big as a tea plate. These styles had ceased to exist on the mainland five-hundred years before, but wearing them helped the people of Piani dei Greci to keep their integrity and the Greek orthodox faith which had taken them from their old home.

Due to North African influence Spanish jewellery is often very elaborate. In some districts where women excelled in singing to the guitar this was said to be because the weight of their ornaments prevented them from expressing themselves properly in the dance. On Ibiza women wore across their breasts festoon upon festoon of spindle-shaped filigree beads over a huge filigree cross. In Catalonia earrings were so long that they brushed the shoulder and so heavy that they were often supported around the top of the ear for fear of tearing the lobe. These Catalan earrings are interesting because, although they present superficially the outline of a leaf, when examined closely they will be seen to conform to the classic eighteenth-century girandole design of a ribbon bow and three drops. The stones, often emeralds or topazes and sometimes diamonds, were set in plump mounts, gold for coloured stones, silver for diamonds, outlined with thin borders of crimped gold. Although cheap touristic copies in cast silver sometimes turn up this Catalan jewellery is often of very high standard. In the Salamanca region beautiful jewels were made in gold and massed seed-pearls.

In less prosperous regions jewels can be made of plated copper, but although the workmanship may be coarse they are no less interesting for that. A strong religious element has always been a part of Spanish jewellery and reliquaries abound. The picture of the saint may be no more than a coloured print on coarse paper protected by a glass and surrounded by filigree. The Virgin of the Pillar is a favourite subject.

In Galicia jet has been mined and worked into ornaments since prehistoric times. This material is of good quality although said to be softer than Yorkshire jet. Long jet earrings and a bead necklace must have provided an effective accent to the embroidered chemisette and scarlet wool skirt of the Galician woman.

Some Spanish rivers and arroyos even yielded alluvial gold, and in the summer time when the temperature of the water was tolerable women used to pan it out with vessels of cork or zinc. This metal was often close to twenty-four carats fine and they used to sell it to local working jewellers. The goldsmith's was a family concern located in one room of the house. Designs were taken from hand-drawn pattern books. One is often astonished at the regularity of the floral rosettes which form the basis of many of these jewels. This was due to a simple device called the *vitola*, which was a simple gauge or jig cut out of a strip of sheet iron with one edge straight and the other cut into steps numbered one to five. The thin ribbon of metal used to outline the petals of a rosette was wrapped around the appropriate step on the *vitola* and pressed flat at the edges so that when the metal was unwound the amount needed for each petal was not only measured out, it was also partly formed. The patterns in the book were numbered V.1, V.3, or whatever, according to the *vitola* measurement to be used.

As one approaches the Portuguese border, Portuguese influence becomes more and more apparent in the designs, and in fact much of the jewellery worn by the women of the frontier districts of Extremadura was made by Portuguese workmen. The *reloj*, or clock earring, was worn on both sides of the border. Although of large size these jewels were quite flat as they were pierced from sheet gold. The name comes from the open rosette at their centres which vaguely resembles the dial of a clock, although when viewed at arm's length their origin in the heart and ribbon bow designs of the eighteenth century is undeniable. The same basic motif can be traced in the immense filigree pendants which form part of a bride's regalia and which can be the size of a hand (plate 72). These were sometimes embellished with black or blue and white rosettes cleanly done in cloisonné enamel. Maltese cross pendants were made in the same technique. In Portugal jewels were principally made in the towns of Braga and Gondomar. Crescent earrings were worn all over the peninsula. They have their origins in the remotest antiquity, and although they were at first intended to represent the magical new moon, they were called *arracadas*—horseshoes.

Today, peasant jewellery can be met with far from its country of origin. Nineteenth-century tourists carried many pieces away as souvenirs, and there even seems to have been a Bohemian craze for it some sixty or seventy years ago. Emigration, too, must have been responsible for landing many jewels on the velvet-lined trays of antique shops, far from the village workshops where they first saw the light. So that if the collector knows what he is looking for and searches diligently he can build up a collection without having to travel very far.

10. Collecting

Few antiques are bought to be put to their original use; often the very purpose for which they were made has been half forgotten. Good porcelain or glass one simply does not dare to use at table except for best. This is one of the things that makes antique jewellery so collectable, for few collections languish in a cabinet gathering dust. The delight of a jewel is in its wearing. Jewels are not designed to be viewed behind glass, they are companions to the body and the dress, created to foil the tint of the complexion, to follow the curve of the neck, to flash with the movements of the hand and the rhythms of the breath. Of course wearing exposes them to wear and damage, but nothing lasts for ever and in any case nobody would wear their most cherished pieces every day. Rings are of course the most prone to damage, and the bigger they are the more likely it is that they will strike some hard object which will jump a stone from its setting or chip an enamel.

Enamel is only glass. It is not only soft, it is also brittle, and if the background is distorted even momentarily it will flake off. With enamelled rings, the enamel is usually the background to some decorative motif set with diamonds which projects sufficiently to buffer any violent collision, and the edge is often protected with some sort of border. It is virtually impossible to restore damaged enamel to a perfect state. That involves stripping the piece down and refiring it and not many people today can be trusted to make a good job of it. Once repairs were cobbled up with a splash of paint with unsatisfactory and obvious results. Now plastic resins are made for this purpose which can be closely matched in colour and translucency to the original. Well done repairs of this kind are hard to spot, but if one holds the enamel so that the light reflects off the surface a slight unevenness will often give the repair away. The point of a pin gently applied will catch in a resin repair while it will skid off true enamel. Few antique dealers will stand unprotestingly by while you conduct this sort of test however—some customers do not know their own strength. Try asking if as far as he knows the enamel has been repaired; a good dealer will give you a straight answer. While most dealers are good all-rounders their knowledge of some fields may not be complete, and he may well have bought something in good faith which is not what it seems to be. Sometimes one comes on a piece of antique jewellery which was never enamelled to start with, but which has been doctored with a coat of plastic resin to make it more attractive and apparently more valuable.

Some stones are soft and fragile in wear—pearls, moonstones, labradorites, opals and demantoid garnets especially, and strictly speaking they should not be set in rings. However, the beauty of a stone or its suitability to a particular design often quite rightly outbalance practical considerations like this. Provided they are not worn every day it is a long time before the lustre of the stones is dimmed by wear, and when that happens it is usually possible to have them repolished.

Labradorite has a very pronounced cleavage—a tendency to split along predetermined planes. This tendency endangers cameos—especially the noses or other salient or unsupported parts. Shell cameos are too soft to be mounted as rings and were rarely mounted as such in the nineteenth century. Women's rings after 1820 were usually small, and large rings, especially those set with a single stone, should be suspected if presented as antique. There was a tendency for rings to be larger at the end of the century. The setting of the stone may be perfectly all right and in such cases the jewel probably started life as a brooch or part of a necklace, but was made into a ring by the simple addition of shank and shoulders at some later time. Examine the colour of the gold exactly to see if it matches—it is very difficult to match the colour of gold precisely, although a light 'flash gilding' will usually hide the discrepancy. Grey traces of lead solder nearly always indicate a repair or an alteration although these are sometimes masked with a flick of gold paint.

Obviously a jewel in its original pristine state is the prize that the collector seeks, but sometimes the vicissitudes through which a jewel has passed in its career can be very interesting. Large parures are often split up on the death of the first owner to share amongst the children. So people are left with one earring, or half a necklace and the earring becomes a pendant and the half necklace a bracelet. Sometimes jewels were altered to accommodate a change in fashion. Thus ferronnières passed out of vogue and were made into bracelets. It is not unknown for a filigree parure of 1830 comprising pendant earrings, brooch and cross to be made, with the addition of a few inches of tubular chain, into one of the large dangling châtelaines that were all the rage in 1850. In cases like this where a restoration job can be only partly successful it may be more interesting to leave the piece as you find it. Jewels tend to absorb the characteristics of their owners and the ages through which they pass.

Good antique paste jewellery is very desirable—good antique diamond jewellery very much more so by an amount which far exceeds the additional value of the stones. It follows then that an unscrupulous person might replace the paste in such a piece with diamonds at some considerable profit. It is impossible, however to remove a stone from a closed setting and to replace it with another without leaving some trace of the operation having taken place—for one thing it is not possible to find stones which exactly fit the settings in every case. Over the years stones are almost inevitably lost and replaced, so one or two replacements are to be expected, but where every stone has been reset the piece can scarcely be called antique. Nineteenth-century settings for paste jewels seem to have been a little coarser than those made for diamond jewellery at the same period. The layer of gold with which they are backed is usually thinner and of a lower carat. The first sight of such a piece should tell you that something is wrong even if it takes a little time to work out exactly what it is.

Sometimes the situation is in reverse and a stone has been taken out and replaced with something less precious. The disturbance of the setting edge will usually be apparent under a strong lens, although sometimes the entire setting will have been taken out and a new one dropped in with the stone already *in situ*. The reason for this lies in the movement in the price of precious stones in this century and especially during the post-war years. Rubies, sapphires and fine emeralds have soared in price and cats' eyes, alexandrites and black opals have increased so much that they can hardly be called semi-precious any longer. In most cases it will be stones like this which will be taken out to be replaced by spinels, amethysts, pale Ceylon sapphires and so on.

Composite jewels made up of bits and pieces from different places and periods are becoming more and more common today. Here again discrepancies in the colour of the metal and the presence of soft solder will often tell you all you need to know, but disparities in style and technique can be even more revealing—obviously a Bohemian garnet cluster does not belong at the centre of a blue enamel and half-pearl brooch and the Geneva enamel back of a watch has no business to be masquerading as a pendant. Nowadays the prejudice against mourning jewellery is fast disappearing, but once upon a time the temptation to replace the crystal hair compartment of a memorial brooch with something more saleable obviously proved too much for some jewellers.

Few nineteenth-century jewellers signed their work and with only a few of them does it assume the same importance that it does with silver or paintings, but a credible mark by Fabergé, Castellani or Giuliano can make a big difference to the market value of a piece. Very often it is not so much the case of a downright forgery of a stamp so much as doctoring. A signed and geniune piece which is damaged utterly beyond repair may have its mark carefully removed and placed upon another piece in a similar style—or even on an unsigned work by the same man. Sometimes a piece may be signed in two places leaving the unscrupulous dealer with a signature to spare for some unsigned but in his opinion deserving work. Unfortunately jewellery lends itself more readily to this kind of sleight of hand than silver where the old mark has to be sawn out and the new one sweated in leaving a solder line which nothing can entirely disguise. The mark on jewellery is often placed on one of the fittings—the loop of a pendant, the pin of a brooch, or the shank of a ring which can easily be changed round as it is with the mark untouched. In the case of Giuliano and Castellani the mark is not punched into the body of the jewel, but stamped separately on a little panel or cartouche of gold which is subsequently soldered on to it. This of course simplifies doctoring. The difficulty is that the signatures of many nineteenth-century jewellers really are signatures, actually engraved with the burin into the metal of the jewel, and much easier to fake, by any competent engraver, than a punch. The real test with these as with all other pieces must be the quality of the design and the workmanship. As soon as one knows what to expect from Lalique, Wilson or Castellani marks recede in importance. Work of this unique quality does not need a signature to plead its case, for good wine needs no bush in jewellery as in everything else.

Hallmarks, or to be more correct, assay marks, are another matter. These can be of value not only in establishing the country of origin, but also date of manufacture—sometimes down to the very year. Most European countries require articles made of precious metal to carry a stamp indicating the place of manufacture and the percentage of pure metal. Sometimes in addition it must carry a letter corresponding to an alphabetical sequence which shows the date of manufacture. Often too the maker is obliged to append his own sign, and very frequently special marks are applied showing import or export.

Until the French Revolution most European assay marks were based on the carat. Pure gold was regarded as 24 carat and purities were expressed as fractions of this. 18 carat is eighteen twenty-fourths pure gold. This system is still in operation in Great Britain today. Elsewhere, although a decimal system has been in almost universal use since the first half of the nineteenth century, the standards employed by the goldsmith are the ancient ones of 22 carat, 18 carat and 14 carat which are expressed decimally as ·920, ·840 and ·750. Russia remained an odd man out. There the measure was the zolotnik. Pure gold was at 96 zolotniks and other standards were 84, 72 and 56. In Great Britain all gold work was in 22 carat until the 18 carat standard was introduced in 1798. These were the only alloys in use until 1853 when it was thought necessary in the face of growing competition from abroad to introduce 15, 12 and 9 carat golds. In 1932 the 12 and 15 carat standards were replaced by 14 carat. In Britain the law does not require all articles to be marked and a number of classes of jewellery are exempt including rings and lockets, although they must still conform to one of the legal standards.

Recently, since the introduction of new investment casting techniques, it has become possible to cast large numbers of exact copies of an antique jewel with every detail, including assay marks, faithfully reproduced. However the crispness of the punched mark becomes a little blurred in the casting process, and sometimes a minute spherule of metal will be there to show where the molten gold has filled an air-bubble in the investment mould. When jewellery has been cast with the hallmark the intention can only have been to deceive and defraud, and this intention is all that separates the fake from the 'reproduction'.

Today much jewellery is being made which imitates very closely the jewels of the past—much the same thing as was happening a century ago, and for much the same motives—to give the customer what she wants. The firms who produce this kind of jewellery do not set out to deceive the public today any more than they did in 1870. Most of the reproductions are in high Victorian style and are being manufactured in the northern Italian cities of Milan and Turin. Although the manufacturer and the honest retailer sell this jewellery for what it is there are others who augment their stocks of antique jewellery with pieces of this kind. The buyer should look out for modern Italian assay marks. Remember that almost all machine-made jewellery of the last century was die stamped and not cast. Bear in mind too that the modern manufacturer is seeking to supply a modern demand from modern women wearing modern fashions of dress and hairstyling and his designs may reflect this. If a pair of stud earrings, designed to be clipped on to the lobe and not to hang below it, is decorated with all the trimmings of the 1860s they still cannot be right. They must either be adapted from other jewels or else be a reproduction because women only wore long pendent earrings at that time.

Where a modern designer is asked to design a jewel in antique taste—a pastiche, as it were—he often succumbs to the temptation to lay it on too thick so that 'typical motifs' jostle one another in such profusion that they appear to be in danger of falling off the edge.

This is more apparent with pieces in the First Empire and Georgian manner as a tendency to overdo things is also a Victorian characteristic.

Reproductions of nineteenth-century jewels were extensively made in India, especially the cannetille work of the thirties. This Indian work lacks the regularity of finish one sees in European jewellery and the gold is of a higher carat, and consequently richer in colour. Many of these Indian copies are set with carbuncles and sometimes the stones themselves are inlaid with gold in Delhi style.

As jewellery is small and often minutely detailed it is all too easy to take a literally myopic view of it. Of course, every motif, every structural detail must be scrupulously examined and correlated, but while doing this it is all too easy to lose sight of the general form of the piece, its outline and topography. It should be looked at, front and back with equal care, and then held at arms length to appraise the general layout and contours.

According to personality and length of pocket the collector's quest begins to take a definite direction after a while. A woman will most likely buy things that look well on her; everyone perforce buys what they can afford, or perhaps a little more than they can afford. Some will buy mourning jewellery not only because it is still relatively cheap, but because it reflects so strongly the character of its age, for the good collector is also a historian—he cannot help himself. Some, if they can afford it, will collect the work of one craftsman—Giuliano perhaps; others whose lack of spending money is compensated for by a certain originality will seek out jewels by Childs and Childs, or Watherston and Brogden, less famous, less easy to recognize, but fine in their own way. A fascinating collection could be made of jewels in a particular material—cast iron, cut steel, hair, or bog oak. This kind of specialization has its advantages. Few laymen, from lack of time or experience, can hope to match the dealer's all round knowledge. What they can do, however, is to specialize, to narrow their terms of reference to a smaller field and then learn it inside out. In this way it is possible sometimes to spot something that others have missed.

The usual sources of supply for the collector are of course shops. Some antique shops make a speciality of selling jewellery, but even the average suburban high street jewellers have a few pieces tucked away among the wrist watches and the rolled gold. Some quite spectacular finds have been made in places as unlikely as this. One should visit the antique markets of course, but even the ordinary Saturday morning markets have a barrow or so of bric-à-brac. They might not yield a purchase for weeks, but sooner or later you will strike lucky. Jumbles and white elephant stalls too sometimes yield the odd find, although here the usual position is reversed and it is up to the buyer to see that a good cause is not coming second best out of the transaction.

The auction sale is perhaps the most exciting way of acquiring anything short of stealing it. Sales have the kind of excitement that is not generated anywhere else, a kind of spontaneous combustion. One can get carried away. The best way to keep a level head is to examine the goods and make all your decisions well before the sale—make up your mind which lots you really want and how much you want to pay for them. Even if you think that a coveted lot will make more money than you have to spare, examine it carefully and mark it in your catalogue all the same—you might be lucky. Sometimes—especially in the larger city auction rooms—some of the lots comprise as many as twenty or thirty pieces of which only one or two are of interest to you. There are two ways of setting about their acquisition: you can buy the whole lot, take out the pieces you want and then put the remainder back in a later auction sale. It could be, however, that having taken out what you want the cream of the lot has been skimmed, leaving the unsaleable residue which, having once got rid of it, the auctioneer will be very reluctant to take back again. It is prudent to ask him beforehand whether he would be prepared to do this for you. The other alternative is to let the lot go and to note who buys it. After the sale you can then approach him and ask if he would be prepared to sell you the pieces you want. Most dealers will be willing to turn the pieces over on the spot for a reasonable profit. One should remember that to say to a complete stranger 'I'll give you seven quid for it' is to invite the retort 'Oh no you bloody well won't'. If you cannot meet his asking price, ask courteously if he can accept less—it does not help to get people's backs up.

It is an error to assume that if you buy an article from a shop you will be able to sell it immediately for the same price. Although this is a truism it is surprising the number of people who ignore the simple fact that the dealer is making a profit and that the buyer is bound to lose a percentage of the purchase price. After a few years, of course, the piece will have advanced in value enough to take up the slack.

Some pieces of jewellery increase in value more quickly than others. In general, the more desirable the jewel the more rapid the increase: fine quality will show a higher proportionate increase than medium quality. One must not forget, too, that in jewellery 'quality' refers not only to the workmanship but also to the materials, the standard of the gold and the colour and purity of the stones. While most people are not after a capital gain, everyone likes to feel that they have got their money's worth.

After a while the buyer runs through a sort of catechism with himself as he turns the jewel over in his hand, asking himself questions about every detail as they catch his eye. Is the cutting of the stones contemporary with the workmanship of the setting? If they are later the conclusion is obvious. Are they indeed the sort of stones which you would expect to see in a piece of that kind? Is the scrap of material that lines the hair or miniature compartment of silk or man-made fibre? Does the case smell of glue? If it does it may have been made recently. When the finger tips are run lightly over the settings of the stones do they catch in the skin? If they do the piece has not been smoothed by use and may only recently have been made. Remember also that many a jewel has spent the last hundred years in a bank vault to emerge in perfect condition, even though the case that contains it has almost mouldered away. Singly none of these points prove anything, but collectively several of them make a body of circumstantial evidence. One day you will be offered a piece that gives all the right answers and yet you feel, for some reason that you cannot explain, that all is not right with it. Leave it alone—it means that your eye has picked out nuances of proportion or colour too subtle for the brain to register. Only time and practice will develop this kind of instinct, and after a while you will come to rely on it.

Every collector makes errors and there is nothing like a mistake for clearing the eye and sharpening the wits. After all, strops, as these dud purchases are called in the trade, can usually be sold off even if it means taking a loss. Besides there is always the glorious bargain which wipes out the memory of the most humiliating gaffe—everybody has those too.

Appendix: Gold and Silver Marks

Systems of marking gold and silver are often very complicated. The following is a guide to the marks most commonly seen on jewellery, although the list has of necessity been greatly abridged and simplified.

AUSTRIA/HUNGARY

(1)   Gold ·750 standard 1866–1922

(2)   Gold ·580 standard 1866–1922

(3)   Silver ·800 standard 1866–1922

(4)   Silver ·750 standard 1866–1922

(5)   Import mark 1891–1901

FINLAND

(6)   Since 1810 on both gold and silver. Finnish work may also show the town mark (e.g. a rowing boat for Helsinki), date letter and standard.

FRANCE

(7)   This and similar marks were used on gold jewels in France and French occupied countries between 1798 and 1819

(8)   This and similar marks were used on silver jewels between 1798 and 1819 in France and the occupied countries

(9)   Silver, Paris 1809–1819

(10)   Gold, Paris 1819–1838

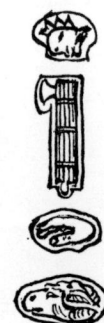

(11)   Gold, Paris 1838–

(12)   Gold, Provincial after 1838

(13)   Gold, occasionally seen on light gem set or enamelled work

(14, 15) Silver after 1838

(16)   Export after 1879

(17)   Import after 1893

GERMANY

(18)   Gold 1884, Silver 1884, Crown and Crescent

HOLLAND

(19)   Gold 1853–

(20)   Gold 1859–1893; between 1893 and 1906 the dolphin was
        enclosed in a triangle

(21)   Importation 1814 to 1831

(22)   Gold articles weighing between two and five grams

ITALY

(23)   Rome—marks traditionally depict crossed key and papal crown

(24)   Modena 1818–1872

(25, 26) Parma 1818–1872

PORTUGAL

(27)   Lisbon 1887–1938

(28)   Lisbon 1886–1938. Approximate guarantee

(29)   Filigree work 1886–1938

RUSSIA

(30)   Gold since 1861. The number 56 indicated the standard in zolotniks. Pure gold would be at 96 zolotniks

(31)   St. Petersburg assay mark (anchor kedge and trident)

SWITZERLAND

(32)   Gold ·750 standard

(33)   Gold ·585 standard

Bibliography

D'ALLEMAGNE, H.R. *Les Accessoires du Costume et du Mobilier Depuis le XII jusqu'au Milieu du XIX Siècle*, Paris, 1928

BILLING, ARCHIBALD, *The Science of Gems, Jewels, Coins and Medals*, London, 1875

CLIFFORD SMITH, H., *Jewellery*, London, 1908

EVANS, JOAN, *A History of Jewellery 1100–1870*, London 1953 (new edition, 1970)

FLOWER, MARGARET, *Victorian Jewellery*, London, 1951

HOLME, CHARLES, ed., *Modern Design in Jewellery and Fans*, London, 1902

HUGHES, GRAHAM, *Modern Jewellery*, London, 1964

LEWIS, M.D.S., *Antique Paste Jewellery*, London, 1970

Die Pforzheimer Schmuck und Uhrenindustrie, Erich Maschke, Pforzheim

Les Poinçons de Garantie Internationaux Pour l'Argent, Tardy, Paris

TOUZET, ANDRÉ, *Emplois Industriel de Métaux Précieux*, Paris, 1910

TWINING, LORD, *History of the Crown Jewels of Europe*, London, 1960

VEVER, HENRI, *La Bijouterie Française au XIXe Siècle*, Paris, 1908

WILSON, H., *Silverwork and Jewellery*, London, 1966 (reprinted 1971)

Index

Adelaide, Queen, 36
Ador, Jean Jaques, 64
agates, 23, 48, 54, 55, 56, 64, 88
aiguillettes, 48
Albert, Prince, 39
Alexandra, Queen, 71
Alfred jewel, 95
Algeria, influence on designs, 44
Allen, Kate, 76
aluminium bronze, 57
aluminium jewellery, 71, 77
amazonite, 77
amethyst: Arts and Crafts movement, 77; Brazilian, 28; Celtic crosses with, 95; Fabergé eggs with, 74; heat-treatment, 29; in machine-made jewellery, 40; seals, 31, 32; Siberian, 33; star motifs with, 53
amphora pendants and earrings, 53, 58; fig. 4, plate 29
Amsterdam, diamond cutting, 65
animal motifs: in seals, 31; crystal intaglios, 55; tiepins, 58, 70
aquamarines, 28, 40
Arcot diamonds, 27
art deco, 82
art nouveau, 77–83; plates 41, 52, 53
Art Workers Guild, 75
Arts and Crafts Exhibition Society, 75
Arts and Crafts movement, 75–7, 82, 83
Ashbee, C. R., 75; plate 49b
assay marks, 29, 105–6
Assyrian designs, 94
Asturias, peasant jewellery, 86
Aucoc, Louis, 78
Aumale, duchesse d', 46
Australia, malachite from, 51
Austria, Renaissance style jewellery, 90–1
Autran, Jean François, 64

Bacciochi, Elisa, 20
bagues hieroglyphiques, 37
Bahia, diamonds, 48
Bapst, Eberhard, 28; plate 7
bar brooches, 67, 73; plate 47a

basket-weave patterns, 54
Bassi, 54
Beaconsfield, Lord, plate 18b
bee motifs, 60, 68
Beechey, Sir William, plate 18a
beetles: maybug, 58; South American, 60
belcher rings, 42
Belgium, peasant jewellery, 100–1
Benoîton, 57
Bensons, 65
Berlin iron, 24–5, 86; plate 5
Bernhardt, Sarah, 78
Berry, duc de, 31
birds, brooches, 35
Birmingham, 39–42, 63, 77
Bismarck, 61
Blanchet, 25
bloodstone, 55
blue john, 47
Bobrovka garnets, 69
bog oak jewellery, 47
Bohemia, garnet cutting, 65
Bolzani, 57
Bon, 52
Bonelli, Angelo, 20
Boquet, 25
Boucheron, 77, 80, 81, 94; fig. 7, plate 53b
boxes, decorative, 56
bracelets: Assyrian designs, 94; cannetille, 29; cast iron, 25; adapted from ferronnières, 33; diamond, 50, 51; Empress Josephine and, 23–4; expanding, 50; French Restoration, 29; garnet, 55; gothic style, 88; granite, 47; half hoop, 71, plates 45a, 45b; horn, 79; in the 1890s, 71; Indian influence, 66; jarretière, 50, plate 27b; manchettes, 50, plate 27c; mourning, 86; paired, 39; serpent designs, 43–4; silver, 61; skein of gold chain, 21–3; with miniatures, 39, 50; with pendants, 50
Braga, 102
Brazil: diamonds from, 26, 48, 68; semi-precious stones, 28
Brazilian beetles, 60
Breadalbane, Marquis of, 95

Briançon, 78

Bridge, John, 27; plate 20

Briet, 80

Brogden, John, plate 64b

brooches: aiguillettes, 48; Assyrian designs, 94; bar, 67, 73, plate 47a; bird motifs, 35; cameo, 46, 54; coloured glass, 31; crescent, 67; diamond, 28, 61, 68; dragonfly, 68, plate 40a; Etruscan style, 92; garnets, 55; gothic style, 88; Greek style, 94; horseshoe, 60; in the 1860s, 53, 61; in the 1870s, 61; influence of arab design, 44–5; insect, 68; Irish designs, 95, fig. 8; lizard, 69; machine-made jewellery, 35; Maltese cross, 26; mourning, 84–6, plate 54; optical effects, 53; peasant jewellery, 99; puzzle motifs, 37; Renaissance style, 90; revolving, 85–6; Scotch pebble inlaid, 55; seed-pearl, 46; staghorn, 47; tortoiseshell, 56

Brooke, Rupert, 98

brust spange, 100

buckles, 34, 39

Burma rubies, 69

Burra Burra, malachite, 51

butterfly brooches, 68

buttons, 51, 100

Byron, Lord, plate 1e

Byzantine style, 97, 100

cadenas bracelets, 50

cairngorms, 34, 95

cameos: 19–23; agate, 92; cast-iron jewellery, 25; coral, 58; cutter's tools, 21, fig. 1; imitation cameos, 21; mourning jewellery, 85, 86; opal, 70; Renaissance style, 90; sardonyx, plate E; settings, 21–3; shell, 46, 104, plate 23c; stone, 54; with enamelled surrounds, 45, plate E

cannetille work, 28–30

Caracci, Annibale, Plate D

carbuncles, 29, 45, 53

Carnac, Mrs., 30

cast-iron jewellery, 24–5, 86; plate 5

Castellani, Alessandro, 91n

Castellani, Augusto, 91n

Castellani, Fortunato Pio, 75, 91, 105; plates 62, 64a

Catalonia, peasant jewellery, 101

cats' eyes, 70, 77

Cavour, 58

Cellini, Benvenuto, 80, 89

Celtic designs, 76, 95; plate 65b

Ceschka, Otto, 82

chains: Benoiton, 57; Leontines, 57, plate 33a; longchains, 36, 68, 88, plate 19; machine-made, 57; of the 1830s, 36–7; of the 1890s,

71; Renaissance style, 90; silver, 61; tortoise-shell, 56

chalcedony, 36, 77

champlevé enamelling, 35, 44, 94; plate D

Charlemagne, 88

Charles Frederic, Margrave, 64

châtelaines, 61

Child and Child, 107; plate 64c

Chinese style, 97

chokers, peasant jewellery, 99; plate 68

Christesen, 97; fig. 9

chrysoberyls, 28

chrysolites, 45

chrysoprases, 29, 77

citrine, 29, 31, 32

Civilotti, 58; plate Fa

Clarence, Duke of, 39, 87

classical style, 53, 91–4

Clementine, Princess, 50

Clerkenwell, 40

cloisonné work, 95

cluster rings, 23

coiffure lamballé, 46

collars: English, 26; French, 26; of 1830s, 33–4; serpent design, 43–4

collecting, 103–9

collet-settings, 25, 26

combs: cannetille, 30; horn, 79; tortoise-shell, 56

Comstock lode, 61

Connemara marble, 47

Cooke, Mr., 55, 82

copper jewellery, 77

coral jewellery, 46, 53, 57, 58–60, 99; plate 34

Cordier, 25

cornelian, 31, 36, 56

coronals, laurel leaf, 24

Coulon, 71

Cox Savory, T., 36

craftsmen, schism between designers and, 18

Creevey, Thomas, 30

creole earrings, 19, 56

crescent brooches, 67

Crimean war, 51

crocidolite, 70

croix-à-la-jeanette, 44, 100, plate 16c

crown-jewels, French, 19

crowns: 92; bridal, 99

crystal, 31, 32, 95

crystal intaglio, 54–5; plate 31f

cufflinks, 55, 73

cut steel jewellery, 25, 32–3

Cuttack filigree, 66

'Cymric', 77; plate 50a

Dalmatia, peasant jewellery, 100

David, 19
dealers, 107–8
de Beers, 68
Delhi, 30
Denmark, peasant jewellery, 100
Derbyshire, spar jewellery, 47
Descomps, Joe, 81
designers, schism between craftsmen and, 18
Deslions, Anna, 52
Destape, M., 78
diamond dust, for the hair, 57
diamonds and diamond jewellery: bracelets, 50,
    51; Brazilian, 26, 48, 68; brooches, 28, 61, 68;
    cascading drops, 48; cutting, 68–9; English
    filigree work, 30; flower motifs, 61; French
    Restoration, 28; hair ornaments, 57; Maltese
    crosses, 36; naturalism in designs, 28; neck-
    laces, 71; of the 1860s, 61; Russian necklaces,
    33; serpent designs, 43; setting, 25–6; South
    African, 68; stars, 53, 67
Dickens, Charles, 84
die stamping, 40
Disraeli, Benjamin, 37
Dixon and Sons, 39
Dodge, Nehemiah, 63
Doenhof, Countess, 24
dog collars, 71, 100
doublets, 21, 91
dragonfly brooches, 68; plate 40a
Drogheda, 95
Duval, Felix, 63

earrings: creole, 19, 56; influence of arab
    design, 45; late 18th century, 19; novelty, 53;
    of the 1830s, 34, 36; of the 1860s, 52–3;
    peasant, 100, 101, 102; *poissarde* design, 19;
    seed-pearl, 46; sporting motifs, 60; tortoise-
    shell, 56
Easter eggs, 74
ebonite, 86
Edleston, John, plate 1e
Egypt, influence on designs, 24, 94; plate 65
electrogilding, 40
Ellis and Son, 47
emeralds: cameos, 54; doublets, 91; English
    filigree work, 30; Russian necklaces, 33; in
    Spanish jewellery, 48
Emmanuel Brothers, 55, 58
enamelled work: champlevé, 34–5; Easter eggs,
    74; Giuliano's use of, 89; Holbeinesque, 90;
    large areas, 45; mourning jewellery, 84, 85;
    peasant jewellery, 101; plique-à-jour, 79–80;
    repairs, 103; revival in 1890s, 76; serpent
    bracelets, 43–4; star designs, 54; Swiss, 34;
    tiepins, 73

esclavage, 63
Etruscan style, 91–4; plates 61a, 62
Eugenie, Empress, 50, 69
expanding bracelets, 50
Extremadura, peasant jewellery, 102
eyeglasses, 44

Fabergé, Peter Carl, 74, 105; plate 48
Fahrner, 82
faking gems, 20
Falize, Lucien, 90; plate 64d
Fannière, Auguste, 90; plate 58
Fannière, Joseph, 90; plate 58
fawney droppers, 42–3
ferronnières, 33, 104
filigree work, 28–30, 66, 101
Fisher, 76
flatness, in late eighteenth century jewels, 19
flower motifs: brooches, 31; diamond jewellery,
    28, 61; necklaces, 34; tiaras, 45–6
fly motifs, 60, 68, 70
fob seals, 31
foiling, precious stones, 25, 29
Foncier, 19
Fontenay, Eugène, 58, 80, 94; fig. 4
Fosse, 57
fossil jewellery, 47; plate 23d
Fouquet, Georges, 81; plate 52d
Fox, George, 27
Franco-Prussian war, 58
Frankfurt-am-Main, 24
Frédéric, Charles, plate 7
Freiburg, 65
French jet, 86
French Revolution, 17–18
Freshwater pearls, 95–6
Frichot, 25
Friesland, peasant jewellery, 99
frog motifs, 69
Froment-Meurice, 58, 88

Gablonz, 65
Galicia, jet from, 102
Garibaldi, 58
garnets: carbuncles, 29, 45, 53; demantoid, 69;
    doublets, 91; from Freiburg, 65; machine-
    made jewellery, 40; mid-century use, 45;
    rosettes, 55; in Russian jewellery, 33, 34
Gass, S. D., 48, 50
Gautrait, Lucien, 81; plate 53a
Geneva, enamelling, 34
Germany: mechanization, 64; peasant jewel-
    lery, 100
gipsy setting, 73

girdles, peasant jewellery, 100
Girometti, Giuseppe, 21
Gismondi, 58
Giuliano, Carlo, 89–90, 92, 105, 107; plates 56, 57, 60
Glasgow School, 76–7, 82
glass intaglios, 55
Gmund, 64
Golconda diamonds, 26
gold: coloured, 31, 45, 53, plate 28; marks, 105–6, 110–12; nuggets, 70; rolled, 64; test for, 32
Gondomar, 102
Gorham, Jabez, 63
gothic style, 88
Grandhomme, 90
granite jewellery, 47
granulation, 91
Grasset, Eugène, 81
Great Exhibition 1851, 47–8, 54
Greek style, 53, 90, 91–4; plates 59c, 60, 61b, 63
Green, Richard A., 94
Grisi, gift from Czar to, 45
Guild and School of Handicraft, 75
guilloché, 45

hair, horse, 47; plate 19
hair compartments, in jewellery, 37; *see also* lockets
hair jewellery, 85; plate 55
hair ornaments, 30, 33, 51, 53, 56–7, 79
hair pins, peasant, 100
half-hoop bracelets, 71; plates 45a, 45b
half-hoop rings, 23, 54, 73
half-pearls, 67
hallmarks, 105–6
Hanau, 64
Hancock and Burbrook, 65
Hancock and Co., 55, 58
Hardman, 88
Haweis, Mrs., 66, 75
head-dresses, peasant, 98–9; plates 66, 67
heart designs, 74
Heligoland, 100
helmets, Frisian, plates 66, 67
Hirzell, Herman, 82
Hogg, Mrs., plate 18a
Holbeinesque pendants, 90; plates Fc, Gb
Holland, peasant jewellery, 98; plate 68
Holmstrom, August, plate 48a
Home Arts and Industries Association, 75
horn, 79
horsehair jewellery, 47; plate 19
Hugo, Victor, 60

humming-bird jewels, 60
Hungary, peasant jewellery, 101
Hunt and Roskell, 51, 58, 94

Ibiza, peasant jewellery, 101
Imperatrice, 57
India: diamonds from, 26; filigree work, 30; jewellery, 66–7; reproduction jewellery, 107
inscriptions, 37
insect motifs, 60, 68; plate 44c
intaglio: crystal, 54–5, plate 31f; glass, 55
Irish designs, 95
iron jewellery, 24–5, 86; plate 5
Isler, Luigi, 54
Italy: champlevé enamelling, 35; influence in 1860s, 58; peasant jewellery, 101, plates, 70, 71; reproduction jewellery, 106
ivory, 47

Jade, from Peking, 58
Jaipur, 67
Japanese design, 78, 97
jarretière bracelets, 50; plate 27b
jaspers, 55
jet, 57, 86, 102
Jeuffroy, Romain Vincent, 19
Johnson, Edward, 95
Josephine, Empress, 19, 23–4
Jugendstil, 82, 83

Kashmir sapphires, 69
Katwijk, peasant jewellery, 99
Killin, 95
knife wires, 71
Knight, Payne, 20–1

'Laboratory of Flowers', 57
labradorite, 70, 104
'Ladies Watch Protector', 39
Laesoe, 100
Lalique, René, 78–80, 89, 105; plates 51, 52
Lambert and Co., 55
lapis lazuli, 56, 77
lava, jewellery, 60; plate 35
Lefèbre, 65
Lefournier, 80
Lejeune, 57
Lemonnier, G., 48; fig. 3
Leonardo da Vinci, 33
Leontines, 57; plate 33a
Levy Prins, Messrs., 47
Liberty's, 77
Lightning Ridge, opals from, 70
Lion, Auguste, 57; plate 33b
Littledale, 91

lizard brooches, 69

lockets: basket-weave patterned, 54; early 19th century, 26; Etruscan style, 92; Indian influences, 66; machine-made, 35; mourning jewellery, 86; Pringle's, fig. 5; silver, 61; tortoise-shell, 56

London and Ryder, 61

London Exhibition 1862, 54, 58, 60–1, 92

Londonderry, Lady, 30

longchains, 36, 68, 88; plate 19

Louis XV, King of France, 20

Louis XVII, King of France, 20; plate 7

Louise, Queen of Prussia, 24

lucky charms, 74

machine-made jewellery, 35, 39–40, 63–5, 66

Mackintosh, Charles Rennie, 77

McLeish, Annie, 76

Maclise, Daniel, 37; plate 18b

McNair, Herbert, 77

Madras, 30, 66, 88

Malabar, 67

malachite, 51, 56, 77

Maltese crosses, 26, 35–6; plates 14a, 14b, 14c

manchette bracelets, 50; plate 27c

marble jewellery, 47, 56

Marchant, 21

Marcus, 77; plate 50b

Maria Feodorovna, Dowager Empress, 74

Marie Antoinette, 19, 65; style of, 28

Marie Louise, 20, 24

marine forms, 60, 76

marks: gold and silver, 29, 105–6, 110–12; jewellery, 105

Masriera, Luis de, 82

Massin, Oliver, 61, 75, 80

Matsys, Quentin, 75

Mayhew, Henry, 42

Mazzini, Giuseppe, 58

medallions, 81–2

medieval style, 76, 88

Melillo, Giacinto, 92, 94; plates 62c, 63

memorial brooches, 84–6; plates 54a, 54b

middle ages, style of, 76, 88

Middle East, influence on designs, 44

Millais, 73

miniatures, 48–51, 85, 90

Mississippi freshwater pearls, 70; plate 52d

'Mizpah' inscriptions, 63

moonstones, 70, 77

Morawe, 82

mother-of-pearl, 46, 55

mourning jewellery, 84–7; plate 54

Mucha, Alphonse, 78, 81

mythological subjects, cameos, 46

naked figure motifs, 80, 82

Napoleon, 19, 24–5

Nassuck diamond, 27

necklaces: cameo, 21; cannetille, 29; cast iron, 24–5; diamond, 71; diamond chain, 28; Egyptian style, 95; enamelled, 35; French Restoration, 28, 29; gothic style, 88; knife wires, 71; of the 1830s, 33–4; of the 1860s, 53; Renaissance style, 89; Russian emerald and diamond, 33

nephrite, 70

Neri, Paolo, 54

New Zealand, nephrite from, 70

Newgate tokens, 43

niello work, 43

Nienhuis, Lambert, 82

Nitot, 19

Norman peasant jewels, 100

North Africa, influence on designs, 44

Norway, peasant jewellery, 99; plate 69

'novelty' earrings, 53

Oberstein, Idar, 54, 64–5

Obry, Hubert, 31–2

Olivia of Cumberland, Princess, 30

onyx, 54, 55, 60, 86

opal, 43, 70, 71, 77

operculum, 77

palmettes, 67

pampille style, 45

Paris, setting fashion trends, 25, 26

Paris Exhibition 1867, 87, 94

Paris Exhibition 1900, 81, 83

paste jewellery, 52, 104

peacock motif, 75

pearls: Benoiton, 57; dog collars, 71; in doublets, 91; freshwater, 70, 77, 95; half-pearls, 67; Scottish, 95; set in turquoises, 55

peasant jewellery, 91, 98–102; plates 66–72

pendants: celtic designs, 95; Etruscan style, 92; Holbeinesque, 90, plates Fc, Gb; Maltese cross, 26, 35–6; mourning, 84–5; of the 1860s, 53; peasant jewellery, 100, 101; Renaissance style, 89, 90

Pentland pebble, 55

peridots, 50, 69, 70, 77

Pforzheim, 64

Phillips, Robert, 60, 74, 92–4

Piani dei Greci, peasant jewellery, 101

Piesse and Lubin, 57

Piggot diamond, 27

Pilsen, 100

pins: hair, 51; stock, 32, plate 13; tiepins, 58, 70, 73, plate 46

Pistrucci, Benedetto, 20–1
Pistrucci, Elena, 54
Pius VI, Pope, 19
plant motifs, 76, 82
plique-à-jour enamel, 79–80
poissarde earrings, 19
Portugal: chrysoberyls, 29; filigree jewellery, 29; peasant jewellery, 102, plate 72
Pringle, R., 60, 68, 85; figs. 5, 6
Provent, 25
Providence, New Jersey, 63–4
Prussia, cast-iron jewellery, 24
Prutscher, 82
Pugin, A. W. N., 88
puzzle motifs, brooches, 37

quartz, 31

Raffles, Moll, 18
Ramsden, Omar, 77
Raphael, 34
Regent diamond, 19
Reimers, Lorenz, plate 69
reloj, 102
Renaissance style, 88, 89–91
repoussé work, 30–1
reproduction jewellery, 106–7
Rettie and Sons, 47
Richard, 25
Riffaut, 80
Rigeaud, 65
rings: cast-iron, 24; cat's eye, 70; cluster, 23; collecting, 103–4; filigree work, 30; fin de siècle, 73, fig. 6; French Restoration, 28, 30; French Revolution, 18; hair, 85; half-hoop designs, 23, 54, 73; linked hearts, 74; mourning, 84–5, plate 54; peasant, 100
Risorgimento, 58
rivières, 25, 34, 71
rolled gold, 64
Roman mosaics, 21, 94; plates C, 62b, 65a
Roman settings, 21, 73
Roman style, 91–4; plate 61a
rose-cut diamonds, 68–9
rose motifs, 88
Rouel, 57
rubies, 30, 67, 68, 69
Rundell, George, 27
Rundell and Bridge, 18, 27, 28, 43
Rushton, H., & Co., 85n
Russia: Easter eggs, 74; malachite from, 51; necklaces, 33; silver snuffboxes, 48

St. Cuthbert's cross, 95

Salamanca, peasant jewellery, 101
Salzburg, 91, 100
Samuels, E. L., 56
sapphires: bracelets, 50; filigree work with, 30; insect brooches, 68; Kashmir, 69; pansy motifs, 74; seals, 31, 32
sardonyx, 54
Savary, 52
scallop shells, 61–2
scarabs, 92, 94; plate 62d
Scheveningen, peasant jewellery, 99
Schey, Mme., 25
Scotch pebble, 55, 95; plates 31e, 65b
Scottish designs, 95
Scythian style, 97
seals, 31–2; plate 12
seed-pearl jewellery, 46–7; plate 25
semains, 37
serpent design, 43–4, 53; plates 21, 29
serpentine, Cornish, 50
settings: cameo, 21–3; collet, 25–6; French Restoration jewellery, 29; gipsy, 73; open-work claw, 69; Roman, 21, 73; star-set, 73
Sezession, 82, 83
shell cameos, 46, 104; plate 23c
Siam, rubies from, 67, 68
Siberia: amethysts from, 33; emeralds from, 33
Sicily, peasant jewellery, 101
silver, marks, 110–12
silver jewellery, 61, 77
Simpson, Edgar, 76
Sligo, Marchioness of, 27
Smookler, Gerald, 42
snake chains, 43–4, 53; plates 21, 29
snuffboxes, 48
sølje, 99; plate 69
South African diamonds, 68
South West Africa, crocidolite, 70
souvenir jewellery, 48, 60
Spain: emerald jewellery, 48; peasant jewellery, 101–2
Spanish combs, 23
spider motifs, 68, 70
spinels, 33
sporting motifs, 31, 60, 73
staghorn, brooches, 47
stampings, 40
star motifs, 53–4, 65, 67, 73
steel, cut, 25, 32–3
Steele, Edwin, plate 44a
stock pins, 32; plate 13
stomachers, peasant, 101
Storr and Mortimer, 38
swag shops, 42
Sweden, peasant jewellery, 100

Switzerland: enamelling, 34–5; ivory jewellery, 47

symbolic elements, 37

Talleyrand, 18
Tallien, Mme., 18
Tara brooch, 95
Taylor, George Watson, 28
Thesmar, Fernand, 80
Thomson and Profage, 60
tiaras: cannetille, 30; coral, 58; gothic style, 88; Hellenistic Greek style, 24; Imperial Russian, 71, plate 43; mid-century, 45–6
tiepins, 58, 70, 73; plate 46
tiger claws, 66
topaz, 28, 29, 31, 32, 34
tortoise motifs, 69
tortoise-shell, 56; plates 30a, 32b
tourmalines, 28
turquoises: Arts and Crafts use of, 77; chains, 71; chrysoberyls used with, 29; in circular brooches, 53; dog collars, 71; half-pearls used with, 67; in the 1830s, 31; longchains, 36; serpent designs, 43; target clusters, 55

Unger, Elsa, 82
Unger, Moritz, 95–6
United States: machine-made jewellery, 63–4; silver, 61; tortoise-shell work, 56

Varenne, M., 78
Velde, Henri van der, 82
Verkmeister, Rudolph, 24
Vever, Ernest, 80–1
Vever, Henri, 17, 81
Vever, Paul, 81
Victoria, Queen of England, 38–9, 43, 50, 55, 66
Vienna Sezession, 82, 83
Viking style, 96–7; fig. 9
vitola, 102
Voss, 99

Warwick and Sons, 58
watch chains, 57
Waterhouse, 95; fig. 8
Watherston and Brogden, 57, 107
Wellesley, Marquis of, 18
Wellington, Duke of, 24; plate 5
West, 95
Whitby, jet from, 86
Wicklow gold, 95
Wigstrom, Henrik, plates 48b, 48c
Wilde, Oscar, 69–70
William IV, King of England, plate 20
Wilson, Henry, 76, 77, 105; plates 49a, 49c
Wolfers, P. H., 82

Yugoslavia, peasant jewellery, 100

zircon, 29

1789  1820

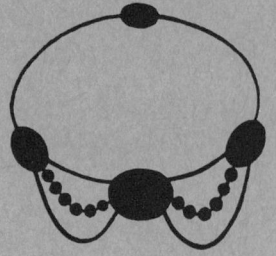

1820  1840

1840  1860

1860  1875

1875  1900

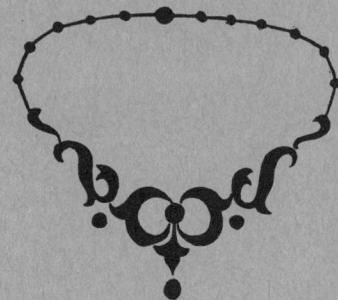